The Jewel in the King's Crown

The Story of the King James Bible

The Jewel in the King's Crown

The Story of the King James Bible

David Allen

2010
Stoke-on-Trent

Berith Publications
an imprint of

Tentmaker Publications
121 Hartshill Road
Stoke-on-Trent
Staffs.
ST4 7LU
www.tentmaker.org.uk
www.tentmakerpublications.com

ISBN No. 978-1-901670-45-5

British Library Cataloguing Data
A catalogue record for this book is available from the British Library.

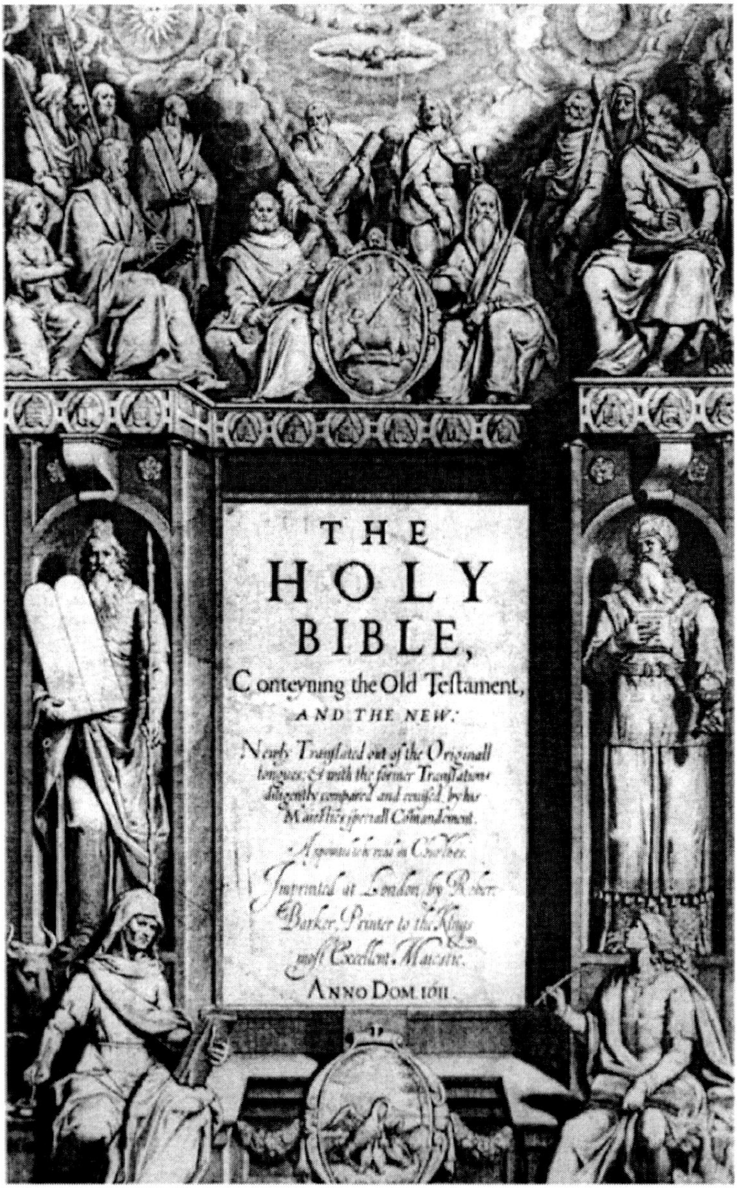

Title page of King James Bible of 1611

Burntisland Parish Church, where at the General Assembly of the Church of Scotland, King James VI first declared his desire to have a 'new Bible'.

For my wife
and children,
Matthew, Rachel, and James.

Contents

Illustrations

Note on Dates

DURING this period two calendars were in use. The Julian, or Old Style, used in England, was ten days behind the Gregorian, or New Style, used in most continental countries. Moreover, on the Continent a year began on 1 January, but for most purposes in England a year began on 25 March.

In order to rectify the error of ten days which had crept into the Julian calendar, Pope Gregory XIII, by the bull *Inter gravissimas*, ordained that 4 October 1582 should be followed by 15 October, the intervening days being dropped. The alteration was adopted at the exact time in Italy, Spain, Portugal, Brabant, Flanders, and most Roman Catholic countries followed suit shortly afterwards. Protestant countries, however, with the exception of Holland, Zeeland, and Denmark, held to the 'old style'. The change was not made in England until 1752.

In this book dates are given according to the Old Style so far as the day and month are concerned, but the year is taken to begin on 1 January.

Preface

THE Authorised Version of the Holy Bible, also known as the King James Bible, has been described as the "noblest monument of English prose". Some would contend that it is the finest literary achievement in the English language, a religious and literary classic. Some men praise it for its pure English and forceful style, others for its beauty and majesty, and still others for its masterful translation. It is all of that and much more. But even more important, we must see the Authorised Version as the Bible that God has providentially given to His English-speaking Church. It is the Word of God, that is, a faithful translation of the inspired originals,

> ...the very meanest translation of the Bible in English, set forth by men of our profession ... is the Word of God. As the King's Speech which he uttered in Parliament, being translated into French, Dutch, Italian, and Latin, is still the King's Speech.[1]

Following the defeat of the French at the Battle of Agincourt in the fifteenth century, English began to emerge as the national language. The Universities of Oxford and Cambridge, however, continued to use Latin as the language of academia. Erasmus lectured at both universities in his favourite Latin tongue. The Church, for her part, had moved away from Latin to the vernacular by the mid sixteenth century, and with that move there arose the need for an English Bible.

Luther's translation of the German Bible in the 1520s inadvertently sowed the seeds for an accurate and reliable English Bible in the hearts of the English Reformers. The King James Bible was the polished jewel which emerged from the chrysalis of the sixteenth century English translations. It gave to the English people a national Bible. Linguistically, it consolidated English at the forefront of living European languages. Without question, the printing of the King James Bible in 1611 marked an epoch-breaking landmark in the history of the English language. It shaped the English language for three hundred and fifty years. The Authorised Version formed the basis of Milton's *Paradise Lost*, Bunyan's *Pilgrim's Progress*, and Handel's glorious *Messiah*. This Bible expanded the horizons of our culture, and without its incalculable influence the English-speaking world would have been irredeemably impoverished.

This Bible united monarch and subjects, church and laity, and was the cornerstone of every aspect of English culture. The translators created a scriptural rhetoric that was as plain and dignified as Tyndale's and as rich and resonant as any book in the English language. There is a rich linguistic musicality to the whole, which was lacking in previous translations. The text was to be read in churches, and therefore was first tested on the ears of the translators. The result is a 'feeling for syllable and rhythm', invigorating every word and fixing itself upon the memory.

Contrary to modern opinion, it was not written in Jacobean English, and certainly not in Shakespearean English. It was written in a form of English that no one had ever spoken. In some respects, its language was archaic even in 1611. It was English shaped by the Hebrew and Greek originals that they were translating. It was a translation in what can only be called 'Biblical English'. The translators were constrained by the form of the original. No straining here for the language of the ploughboy, or the mythical 'man in the street'! They constructed a form of English which was determined by the Hebrew and Greek originals, but that would nevertheless be understood by the ploughboy. Neither Tyndale before them, nor the King James translators, translated into the language of the ploughboy.

The English language had passed through many and great changes, and had at last reached the very height of its purity and strength. The Authorised Version has ever since been the grand English classic. It is the noblest monument of the power of English speech. It is the pattern and standard of excellence. It is the most full and refreshing of all the "wells of English undefiled". It has given a fixed character to our language.

H.L. Mencken wrote:

> It is the most beautiful of all the translations of the Bible; indeed, it is probably the most beautiful piece of writing in all the literature of the world... Many learned but misguided men have sought to produce translations that should be mathematically accurate, and

> in the plain speech of everyday. But the Authorised Version has never yielded to any of them, for it is palpably and overwhelmingly better than they are... Its English is extraordinarily simple, pure, eloquent, and lovely. It is a mine of lordly and incomparable poetry, at once the most stirring and the most touching ever heard of.[2]

During the eighteenth and nineteenth centuries, missionary work carried the influence of the King James Bible to Africa and Australasia, so that wherever Christianity was established it was nourished and nurtured by this incomparable translation. This Bible became the guiding text of Puritan America, and by the end of the seventeenth century it had become treasured by Americans as much as by the British as one of their national texts.

The great Jacobean Bible is still greatly cherished, long after versions which were intended to supplant it have perished. The King James Bible is still far from being a spent force, whether in private or in public. Why is this? What is unique about the King James Bible? These are questions that we will address in the pages which follow, but consider the words of Psalm 8:3-5 as they appear in the Authorised Version:

> *When I consider thy heavens, the work of thy fingers, the moon and the stars which thou hast ordained;*
> *What is man, that thou art mindful of him? And the son of man, that thou visitest him?*
> *For thou hast made him a little lower than the angels, and hast crowned him with glory and honour.*

In this exquisite passage there is an absolute simplicity of vocabulary, but it is matched by a majestic and stately rhythm. The language is both majestic and sublime, and yet, at the same time it is so ordinary, so down to earth. There is here, an irreproachable authority mingled with a rich musicality in every word. The King James translators throughout their epic work use phrases that are richer, deeper, more vigorous, and capable of enshrining complex thought, than anything produced in the twentieth and early twenty-first centuries.

> The churches and biblical scholarship have, by and large, abandoned the frame of mind which created this translation... The belief in the historical and authentic truth of the scriptures, particularly the Gospels, has been largely abandoned, even by

> the religious... It is impossible now to experience in an English church the enveloping amalgam of tradition, intelligence, beauty, clarity of purpose, intensity of conviction and plangent*, heart-gripping godliness which is the experience of page after page of the King James Bible. Nothing in our culture can match its breadth, depth and universality... Unlike the churches themselves, the words of this Bible remain alive, a way of speaking, and a form of the language which is still a vehicle of meaning in circumstances when little else can be.[3]

Well does the Translators' Preface speak of God's sacred Word as "that inestimable treasure which excelleth all the riches of the earth".

It at once formed and fixed our language. It continues to bring home the knowledge of God's revealed truth to countless thousands of minds than ever received it through the original tongues.

The average reader of the King James Bible may enjoy the delightful assurance, that, if he study it in faith and prayer, and give himself up to its teachings, he shall not be confounded nor misled as to any matter essential to his salvation and his spiritual good. This majestic translation will safely guide him into all things needful for faith and practice, as would the original Scriptures, if he could read them, or if they could speak to him as they spoke to the Hebrew in Jerusalem, or to the Greek in Corinth.

The English reader enjoys, by the good providence of God, a translation so exact, so plain, and trustworthy, that he may follow it with implicit confidence as *"a light to his feet and a lamp to his path"*.

As we approach the four hundredth anniversary of its publication, we shall seek to trace the complex history of its publication, whilst looking at some of the personalities involved, and make some digressions into the socio-political climate of the late Tudor and early Jacobean period.

I would like to thank all those who have encouraged and assisted me in this project and especially Phil and Joy Roberts for their time and care in correcting the manuscript and preparing it for publication.

---

* Resounding loudly, esp. with a plaintive sound, as a bell.

Introduction

THE King James Version, used of God in such a mighty way for four hundred years, had its beginnings in a most unexpected and surprising way, even in the midst of disappointment. Fourteen representatives of the Church of England, including four Puritans, had gathered together at Hampton Court for an ecclesiastical conference in January 1604. The conference was called by King James I in an effort to ameliorate growing friction between the Puritan and the High Church, or Ritualistic, wings of the church. On Saturday, January 14, 1604, King James assembled his lords, bishops, and other of the clergy in the Privy Chamber in the Clock Tower of Hampton Court to discuss three principal matters:

First: concerning the Book of Common Prayer, and Divine Service used in the Church.
Second: excommunication in the Ecclesiastical Courts.
Third: the providing of fit and able Ministers for Ireland.

James I (1603–1625), King of England, was also James VI of Scotland. He was the first king to rule the whole of Britain. He was the only son of Mary Queen of Scots and Henry, Lord Darnley. Through both his parents he was the great-grandson of Margaret Tudor, sister to Henry VIII of England, and he was thus heir to the English throne should Elizabeth, the Queen of England, have no children. Born at Edinburgh Castle on the 19 June 1566, his early life had been difficult. After his father had been murdered, his mother had married the murderer and he saw her for the last time before he was one year old. His childhood was a weird blend of flattery and Presbyterian sermons, self-indulgence and the terror of being kidnapped. He was a precocious child, apt at languages, with a retentive memory. From the age of twelve he exercised some authority in government, but by 1583, at the age of seventeen, he was no longer content to be the pawn in the hands of the ruling aristocracy. By 1586 James had established a government of moderates who moved towards a firm relationship with England and a strong control over Protestant affairs. He was a nervous king, constantly in fear of assassination and this made him cautious in his foreign affairs. By 1596 he had reached agreement with Elizabeth of England whereby he became her successor, and James would do nothing to endanger that prospect. He remained silent when his own mother was tried and executed in February 1587, and then remained neutral during England's war with Spain and the invasion of the Spanish Armada in July 1588.

He became increasingly nervous of the power of the Protestants, especially once Presbyterianism was introduced by Act of Parliament in 1592. These Reformers regarded themselves as beholden to God, not to the king. The king was as much a vassal of God as were they. This meant that James VI effectively had no authority over the Church, a matter of which Andrew Melville was prone to remind the King. James disliked the Geneva Bible of the Presbyterians because of the footnotes, which he felt encouraged disloyalty to the King, and he produced his own book, *Basilikon Doron*, which espoused the divine right of kings. This was a direct challenge to Melville's Presbyterianism. Melville believed that James could not abolish the General Assembly, but nevertheless, it was James who had statutory control over the holding of any Assembly. He could thus control when the Assembly could meet and who was on it. He called such an Assembly of the Church of Scotland at Burntisland in 1601, and it was at that Assembly, that he first suggested there be a new translation of the Bible.

After 1596 James was in complete control of his kingdom. He had married Anne of Denmark in 1589, and had a son and heir, Henry, born in February 1594, and a daughter, Elizabeth, born in August 1596, and another son, Charles, born in November 1600. No other king was so confident in his kingdom. Then, on 26 March 1603, a messenger arrived at Holyrood to inform the King that Queen Elizabeth had died two days before. Two days later another messenger arrived to say that the English Privy Council had decreed James was her successor. On 5 April James left Scotland for England.

James arrived at Westminster in April 1603 and was crowned King James I of England on 25 July 1603 at Westminster Abbey. He had grand schemes to unite England and Scotland and establish a Great Britain. Unfortunately these plans failed. Although the Scottish Parliament, which had been left under the control of James's second cousin Louis Stuart, passed an Act of Union in 1607, the English Parliament would have nothing to do with it, so that England and Scotland remained two distinct kingdoms, but ruled by one king. James rapidly found that governing England was not like Scotland. James was pompous, full of self-importance, and paranoid about his safety. The English could not understand this foreigner with his Scottish accent. In addition, his appearance was unattractive; he was short of stature and walked with a rolling gait. He had large bulbous eyes, and apparently had trouble swallowing, so that he frequently drooled. This affliction also affected his speech, which was, at times, slurred. Meanwhile James took a while to become accustomed to the English Parliament and way of life. In fact, he and his Parliament usually disagreed so strongly, that he regularly dissolved it in order to find other ways to meet his needs, especially for money. James disliked having to acquire the approval of Parliament to raise money for foreign activities.

King James, the sovereign, made voluble pretensions to wisdom and goodness. Pontificating about all manner of current themes from poetry to kingship, his uncouth manner and dress earned him contempt. Having learned early in youth to escape immediate danger by evasion and deceit, he continued such methods in England. Resorting to mean and illegal ways of raising money without Council or Parliament, he lost the support of his people. Head of an avowedly Protestant country in great danger from Catholic Powers, he constantly flirted with them, even to the point of executing Raleigh in the hope of making powerful friends abroad, replacing those alienated at home. His last years saw the loss of the Crowns of Bohemia and the Palatinate from his daughter Elizabeth and her husband. He sent his favourite Buckingham to dangle Prince Charles at the Spanish Court for a bride; and when this suit was rejected, the two young men cast off their foolish old father, declared war on Spain, with a toleration for Catholics at home, and arranged a treaty of marriage between Charles and Henrietta Maria of France. This once ingenious and clever monarch became gradually more incompetent. Premature senility had dulled his powers, and it was not without good reason that he earned the reputation as "the wisest fool in Christendom", a phrase coined some years earlier by Henry IV of France.

Recent research has shown that the King suffered from porphyria, a disease which weakens and incapacitates. The symptoms of abdominal pain, excessive nervousness, and mental disturbance were all apparent during the last decade of his reign. The King suffered from attacks of colic, vomiting and diarrhoea, which were preceded by moods of depression, as well as weakness and spasm of the limbs, and a fast and irregular pulse. He also had the ultra-sensitive skin of the sufferer from porphyria, making him thin and fragile, itching and sweating easily, and subject to bruising. His mental disturbance could be interpreted as premature senility. Agitated by constant mistrust of everyone and tyrannised by perpetual fear of his life, on 5 March 1625 the King fell sick. The poor King, weakened by the unpleasant demands of dysentery, lay speechless and died on 27 March 1625, in his fifty-ninth year. The details of his autopsy provide an apt summary of the man: all the vitals were sound, as also was his head, which was very full of brains, but his blood was wonderfully tainted with melancholy. John Donne preached over his corpse at Denmark House. The funeral was held in Westminster Abbey and his body placed in the tomb of Henry VII. Thus the first Stuart was laid to rest with the first of the Tudors.

> And so James came to the end of his days, perhaps not with all the honours painted by Rubens on the ceiling of the Banquet House in Whitehall (where he and his queen had often stumbled about in conjugal drunkenness at masques and charades, and from the window of which his son would walk to his death), yet not with the utter rejection his folly deserved. In spite of the harsh obituaries of the historians on his contribution to the Civil War, the greatest glory of his reign is in the magnificent Bible, "The Authorised Version" of Scripture which he gave us.[1]

The Puritans had many objections concerning the English Church as it was then established. They were expecting that their new king,

James I, would give further impetus to the reformation of the Church. They had met him on his way to London and presented him with the Millenary Petition signed by a thousand ministers. The Hampton Court Conference was to "hear and determine things pretended to be amiss in the Church". The Puritans were in the minority, and King James supported the cause of the bishops who were opposed to further reformation. In the midst of the debate on the catechism, a matter which fell under the first heading, Dr John Reynolds, the president of Corpus Christi College, suddenly petitioned the King,

> ...that there might be a new translation of the Bible, because those which were allowed in the reigns of Henry VIII and Edward VI were corrupt and not answerable to the truth of the original.

This motion was not pre-planned, but rather, spontaneous and incidental in order to keep the Puritans from losing all ground at the conference. This motion pleased the King,

> Whereupon his Highnesse wished, that some especial pains should be taken in that behalf for one uniform translation, professing that he could never, yet, see a Bible well translated in English; but the worst of all, his Majestie thought the Geneva to be.[2]

> The very historical truth is that upon the importunate petition of the Puritans, at his Majesty's coming to the Crown, the conference at Hampton Court having been appointed for hearing their complaints; when by force of reason they were put from all other grounds, they had recourse at the last, to this shift, that they could not with good conscience subscribe to the Communion Book, since it maintained the Bible as it were translated, which was as they said, a most corrupt translation.[3]

The Puritans did object to the *Great Bible* and the *Bishops' Bible*, which were quoted in the Prayer Book, but they did not feel that much of a need for a new translation. They were content with their *Geneva Bible* and its strong Calvinistic comments. The motion for a new translation was incidental to them. On the other hand, the bishops were not entirely in favour of a new translation either. Bishop Bancroft of London expressed his opposition this way, "If every man's humour should be followed, there would be no end of translating."

So neither party in the Church of England was zealous for a new translation.

It was the King's zeal and enthusiasm for the project that caused the work to be undertaken and that saw the work through to the end, and became the driving force behind this grand undertaking,

> ... your Majesty did never desist, to urge and to excite those to whom it was commended, that the work might be hastened, and that the business might be expedited in so decent a manner, as a matter of such importance might justly require.[4]

The Authorised Version of the Bible is not a 'Puritan Bible', nor an 'Anglican Bible', and not even a 'King James' Bible'. It is a Bible brought into being by the wondrous working of Divine providence, the result of the almighty work of God. Even the translators acknowledge that it was God who had put the zeal for a new translation into the heart of the King:

> Let us rather bless God from the ground of our heart, for working this religious care in him, to have the translation of the Bible maturely considered of and examined.[5]

God took the incidental and spontaneous remarks of a Puritan, the zeal of the King for his throne and, in the midst of opposition from the bishops, gave to His Church a Bible that has been her blessing and strength for four hundred years.

CHAPTER I

The History of the English Bible

No translation of the whole Bible had been made before the days of Wyclif. Partial translations had been made in Anglo-Saxon times by:

Caedmon, in the seventh century, who produced a rhyming version of events in Old Testament history.

Aldheim, Bishop of Sherborne, and the monk ***Guthlac***, in the eighth century, who produced Anglo-Saxon versions of the Psalms.

The venerable ***Bede***, who completed a translation of the Gospel of John.

Alfred the Great, who, "at the head of his laws," set in Anglo-Saxon the Ten Commandments, with such of the Mosaic injunctions in the three following chapters of Exodus as were most to his purpose.

To the ninth century must be attributed the Anglo-Saxon version of the Gospels, published by Archbishop Parker in 1571.

Towards the end of the tenth century the monk ***Aelfric*** had the extraordinary merit of translating the Pentateuch, the books of Joshua and Judges; those of Esther, Job, and Judith; also the two books of Maccabees, with a part of the first and second book of Kings.

The Norman Conquest brought to an end the attempts to produce the Scriptures in Anglo-Saxon. The Normans brought with them a French translation of the whole Bible. But French was only understood by upper classes; Anglo-Saxon lived on amongst the middle and lower classes.

The first attempt after the Conquest to place any portion of the Scriptures before the English people in their own language was the ***Ormulum***, a rhyming paraphrase on the Gospels and the Acts of the Apostles made about the beginning of the thirteenth century.

Later in the thirteenth century appeared a poem reciting the principal events in Genesis and Exodus, and a translation, in verse, of the whole of the Psalter.

The earliest version in English prose of any entire book of Scripture was a translation of the Psalter into Latin and English, made about the time when Edward III ascended the throne in 1327, by ***William de Schorham***, Vicar of Chart-Sutton, near Leeds in Kent.

This was followed immediately by another version, the work of ***Richard de Rolle***, chantry priest of Hampole, near Doncaster, who died in 1349.

So that, down to the year 1360, the Psalter appears to be the only book which had been entirely rendered into English.

Within less than twenty-five years of that date, a prose version of the whole Bible, including the apocryphal as well as the canonical books, had been completed, and was in circulation among the people. For this invaluable gift, England is indebted to **John Wyclif**. He did not translate it all, but he took the major part in the labour of preparing it. The accomplishment of the work must be attributed mainly to his zeal, encouragement, and direction. Indeed, Knighton, a chronicler of the day, writes somewhat scathingly,

> This Master John Wyclif has translated into English the gospel which Christ gave to his clergy and doctors of the Church, to be by them communicated to the weaker sort, and the laity according to their need, and has thus made it more accessible to the laity, and to women who are able to read, than it was to the well-educated and intelligent clergy.[1]

And again, Archbishop Arundel, in a letter to Pope John XXII, asking him to condemn the heresy of Wiclif and his followers, after severe vituperation, writes, "he has completed his malice by devising a translation of the Scriptures into the mother tongue."[2]

JOHN WYCLIF was born in 1320 at Wycliff-on-Tees, Richmondshire, in Yorkshire, and died at Lutterworth on the 31 December 1384. His life was closely connected with Oxford where he was, successively, Fellow of Merton, Master of Balliol, and Warden of Canterbury Hall. In 1372 he was presented by the King to the rectory of Lutterworth.

It was from Lutterworth that he directed his 'poor preachers' or 'Lollards' to appeal to Holy Scripture in all their exhortations and instructions. In fact, he considered it of divine, and therefore of absolute, authority in all matters of faith and practice. He had gradually come to this conclusion. In his *Trialogus* he writes,

> We do not sincerely believe in the Lord Jesus Christ or we should abide by the authority of His word, especially that of the evangelists... Inasmuch as it is the will of the Holy Spirit that our attention should not be dispersed over a large number of objects, but concerned on one sufficient source of instruction, it is his pleasure that the books of the old and new law should be read and studied, and that men should not be taken up with other books, which, true as they may be, and containing Scripture truth as they may, by implication, are not to be confided in without caution or limitation.[3]

And again,

> ...it is impossible that any word or any deed of the Christian should be of equal authority with Holy Scripture."[4]

When, therefore, the Pope asserts that his decrees in matters of faith have the same authority as the Gospel, he is, in Wyclif's opinion, guilty of blasphemy, because he arrogates to himself the attributes and prerogatives of Deity. Because of his view of the authority and sufficiency of Scripture, he earned the name 'the Evangelical or Gospel Doctor'. He had an amazing knowledge of Scripture. He took the different parts of Scripture in close connexion, making Scripture its own interpreter, comparing spiritual things with spiritual. He dug deep into the vast mine of Scriptural truth, being fully assured that, if he laboured prayerfully in this work, its treasures would be more unfolded to his astonished and delighted view.

The deep veneration that he felt for Holy Scripture, and the supreme importance which he attached to it, led him naturally to the conclusion that the people ought to be allowed to read it in their own tongue. He expressed that view in his *Wicket*,

> Those who call it heresy to speak of Holy Scriptures in English must be prepared to condemn the Holy Ghost, who gave it in

> tongues to the Apostles of Christ, to speak the word of God in all languages that were ordained under heaven.[5]

And again, in the *Mirror for Temporal Lords*,

> Those heretics are not to be heard who fancy that secular men ought not to know the law of God; but that it is enough for them to know what priests and prelates tell them by word of mouth; for Scripture is the faith of the Church, and the more it is known in an orthodox sense the better. Therefore, as secular men ought to know the faith, so it is to be taught them in whatever language is best known to them.[6]

The Bible, uncorrupted by the false glosses of a Church that claims for itself an exclusive right to interpret the Scriptures, was to be the moral lever by which his country was to be raised from her present state of degradation. This was a sublime conception for the age in which he lived. Difficulties, apparently insurmountable, stood in the way of the design, which embraced not only the literal translation of the Bible but also its circulation among all ranks and orders of his fellow countrymen. Many would have shrunk back terrified by the prospect of formidable opposition and persecution. Bishops and priests, and many of the laity, might have been expected to band together in a dark confederacy against them. He, therefore, stood in a position of comparative isolation.

The translators are wrapped in obscurity. We scarcely find in Wyclif's writings any references to the progress of his work. The fact was, that he and those who aided him were afraid that, if they blazed abroad the matter, the powerful hand of authority would prevent them from continuing the translation and would inflict severe persecution upon them. The consequence is that we are ignorant of the different stages of a work that prepared the way for the Reformation and affected the spiritual destinies of millions.

The Bible was completed by the end of the year 1382. In all probability it was Wyclif who translated the New Testament, and Nicholas of Hereford the Old Testament. When Nicholas was forced to flee in 1382, it was revised in a free style by John Purvey, Wyclif's faithful assistant at Lutterworth, the 'Librarian of the Lollards'. In addition to Nicholas of Hereford, and Purvey, Wyclif was aided by other disciples, former Oxford scholars in and out of hiding. It was an exact literal translation of the Latin Vulgate, and therefore in many places the meaning was obscure. Nevertheless, though itself a translation of a translation, it marked a memorable event in the history of English literature,

> enriching its language, and aiding to give it consistency, although its limited circulation, the rudimentary character of its prose, and its derivation from an incorrect Latin version, prevented it from exercising that marked influence upon our speech.[7]

Altogether there are extant a total of two hundred and thirty manuscripts of the two Wyclif Bibles. Of these, one hundred and fifty consist of the Purvey revision. Most of the copies of these Bibles were penned after 1409 when English Scriptures were forbidden to lay readers.

So great was the eagerness to possess the Bible that those who could not procure the volume of the book would give a load of hay for a few chapters. They would hide the forbidden treasure under the floors of their houses and expose their lives to danger rather than surrender the book; they would sit up all night, their doors being shut for fear of surprise, reading or hearing others read the Word of God; they would bury themselves in the woods, and there converse with it in silence and solitude; they would, while tending their flocks in the field, still steal an hour for drinking in the good tidings of grace and salvation.

Wyclif's Bible marks an epoch in the development of the English language. Thus, while Chaucer was labouring to fix the English tongue among the higher classes, Wyclif established it yet more permanently in language at once simple and beautiful for his fellow countrymen. It was the great work that hastened on the Reformation in England.

At once, the hierarchy and clergy of the Roman Church were filled with terror and indignation. They knew their power was gone if all might, without intervention of the priesthood, consult the sacred oracles. Hence the fury of the persecutor awoke against the followers of Wyclif. Archbishop Arundel and Convocation issued the following stringent prohibition in 1408,

> That no unauthorised person should hereafter translate any portion of Holy Scripture into English, ... and that no such book ... should be read, either in whole or part, publicly or privately,

> that was composed in the time of John Wyclif, or since, under the penalty of the greater excommunication, till the said translation be approved by the Bishop of the diocese.[8]

Wyclif had fully counted the cost, and weighed the consequences of his actions. He knew that his life would be endangered. He says, for instance, in *Trialogus*,

> We have no need to go among the heathen in order to die a martyr's death. We have only to preach persistently the law of Christ in the hearing of Caesar's prelates, and instantly we shall have a flourishing martyrdom, if we hold out in faith and patience.[9]

Through the efforts of Wyclif's 'poor preachers' and others, the Scriptures were circulated and their pages opened to the delighted view of many thousands of fellow countrymen. These 'poor priests' or 'Lollards' lived in poverty and preached the Gospel to the people. They carried the torch of the English Bible from the fourteenth to the sixteenth century. Through their incessant labours, the people were led to see that the Church of Rome had corrupted the faith once delivered unto the saints, and they cast off the superstitions of their forefathers.

Wyclif spent his last days at Lutterworth in much weakness. His indefatigable energy—a distinguishing feature of his character—had gradually worn out the material tabernacle of his body. His personal character was unimpeachable, for even his enemies have not uttered a syllable against his personal character.

At the close of his life he virtually had to be carried into his pulpit. Many of his friends had, like Demas, forsaken him. He stood alone with the sword of persecution suspended by a thread hanging over him; but still with voice and pen he laboured incessantly to effect a reform in the Church. He had denounced unflinchingly the arrogance of the priests and their corruptions of the truth of God's Word.

On December 28 he suffered a stroke in his church at Lutterworth whilst conducting the service of the Lord's Supper and was carried to his house, where he breathed his last on December 31, 1384. Wyclif is one of the greatest men that our country has ever produced. He had a burning love for Christ and an ardent desire for the salvation of souls. He truly was 'The Morning Star of the Reformation'.

At the Council of Constance the Church of Rome determined to wreak her impotent fury upon his bones. Accordingly, in 1415, a decree was passed branding Wyclif as a heretic and directing that his body and bones should be taken from the ground and thrown away from their burial in the Church. That decree was carried out in 1428, some forty four years after his death.

As we stand in Lutterworth Church we wander back to that distant age. Around the grave in the chancel, we see Chicheley, Archbishop of Canterbury, Bishop Fleming of Lincoln, once a devoted follower of Wyclif, and other dignitaries and clergy, all anxious to display their enmity to one who had denounced the corruptions of their Church. The church is crowded with the officials and townspeople, who are attracted by the novelty of the spectacle. The sound of the pickaxe falls on the ear. Slowly rising through the opening thus made is seen the coffin of the great heretic. Placed on the shoulders of men it is carried through the door in the chancel (which is still standing), down that winding road to the River Swift, which glides along tranquilly at the foot of the hill. A fire is kindled on the bridge and the bones of Wyclif are taken out of the coffin and are flung into it. There they are reduced to ashes that are then cast into the river.

Many in that crowd would doubtless behold with tears the indignities there offered to the remains of one to whom they had listened in their youth as he spoke to them of the love of the Saviour, or warned them to prepare for death, judgment, and eternity. He was the one who had often visited them in their homes, and spoken to them in the time of sickness and sorrow, pouring the oil and wine of heavenly consolation into the wounded spirit.

> The brook did convey the ashes into Avon; Avon into Severn; Severn into the narrow seas; they into the main ocean; and thus the ashes of Wyclif are the emblem of his doctrine, which now is dispersed all the world over.

Wyclif's Memorial in Lutterworth carries the following inscription:

Sacred to the Memory of John Wyclif
Earliest Champion of Ecclesiastical
Reformation in England.
He was born in Yorkshire.

In the year 1375 he was presented to
The rectory of Lutterworth:
Where he died on the 31 of December 1384.

At Oxford he acquired not only the
Renown of a consummate schoolman,
But the far more glorious title of
The Evangelical Doctor.

His whole life was one perpetual
Struggle against the corruptions
And encroachments of the Papal
Court, and the impostures of
Its devoted auxiliaries,
The Mendicant Fraternities.

His labours in the cause of Scriptural
Truth were crowned by one immortal
Achievement, the translation of the
Bible into the English tongue.

This mighty work drew on him,
Indeed, the bitter hatred of all who
Were making merchandise of the
Popular credulity and ignorance:
But he found an abundant reward in
The blessings of his countrymen of
Every rank and age, to whom he
Unfolded the words of eternal life.

His mortal remains were interred
Near this spot; but they were not
Allowed to rest in peace.
After the lapse of many years, his
Bones were dragged from the grave,
And consigned to the flames:
And his ashes were cast into the
Waters of the adjoining stream.

The first printed English edition of the New Testament from the Greek was that of **WILLIAM TYNDALE**, one of England's first Protestant martyrs. His parents had, in all probability, fled from the North Yorkshire Dales (Tynedale) during the War of the Roses and adopted the name of Hychyns. Tyndale describes himself in the opening lines of his *Obedience to the Christian Man*, as: "William Hychins unto the Reader." The name of Hychins was afterward abandoned and the family resumed their old and rightful one of Tyndale.

It was on the 6 October 1536 that William Tyndale, having spent a very uncomfortable year in Vilvorde Castle, near Antwerp, Belgium, was escorted to his place of execution. There they tied him to the stake and strangled him to death; then in that public place, they burned his body. If you love the Authorised (King James) Version, well, under God, humanly speaking, 90% (and some would argue 92%) of this wonderful and majestic translation of the New Testament, comes from the pen of William Tyndale. He was a great and mighty Bible translator, who said,

> For I call God to record against the day we shall appear before our Lord Jesus to give a reckoning of our doings, that I never altered one syllable of God's Word against my conscience, nor would this day if all that is in the earth, whether it be pleasure, honour or riches might be given me.[10]

Tyndale had been with Luther and Melanchthon, and it was Tyndale who replied to a Catholic priest,

> I defy the pope and all his laws... If God spare my life, ere many years I will cause a boy that driveth the plough to know more of the Scriptures than thou dost.[11]

Tyndale, like Calvin and Luther, had been brought up in the Roman Catholic system, brought up in a country in which the Church was at its lowest ebb of spiritual vitality—and the County of Gloucestershire where Tyndale lived was a hive of Popery! The clergy and people were shrouded in a mist of superstition. The Bible was an unknown book, but there developed within Tyndale a burning and compulsive burden to translate the Bible into our mother tongue—and that against the prohibition imposed by the Convocation of Canterbury. He entered

Magdalen Hall, Oxford, in 1505, but even there the study of Scripture was discouraged. We find Tyndale writing,

> They have ordained that no man shall look on the Scripture until he be noselled* in heathen learning eight or nine years, and armed with false principles with which he is clean shut out of the understanding of the Scripture.[12]

The ten years he spent in Oxford before his graduation in 1515 were years of transition from medieval Romanism to the doctrines of the Reformation. Tyndale grew and increased in the knowledge of the Scriptures, so much so that he began to expound the Scriptures to the Fellows of Magdalen Hall. Everything was brought to the touchstone of Holy Scripture, and it was this attitude to the authority, sufficiency, and supremacy of the inspired Word, which characterised the strength and vigour of his intellect. Foxe tells us that his mind was singularly addicted to the knowledge of the Scriptures.

Leaving Oxford, he moved to Cambridge, where Erasmus had taught from 1511-1514, and where the influence of the learned Dutchman was still powerful at Queen's College. Tyndale came under this influence and, according to Foxe, he was "further ripened in the knowledge of God".[13]

He left Cambridge in the year 1521. That was a glorious year! It was the year Martin Luther was summoned to Worms and stood before the Diet making that wonderful stand against the might of Rome,

> Since then your serene majesty and your lordships seek a simple answer, I will give it in this manner, neither horned nor toothed: Unless I am convinced by the testimony of the Scriptures or by clear reason (for I do not trust either in the pope or in councils alone, since it is well known that they have often erred and contradicted themselves), I am bound by the Scriptures I have quoted, and my conscience is captive to the Word of God. I cannot and I will not retract anything, since it is neither safe nor right to go against conscience. I cannot do otherwise, here I stand, may God help me. Amen.[14]

---

* Led, taught or fostered.

The cry was heard throughout Europe, "Here I stand, I am captive to the Word of God." In that same year, William Tyndale left Cambridge and God led him to Little Sodbury Manor. It was the Manor House of Sir John Walsh, and William Tyndale was asked to be the chaplain to Sir John Walsh's children. Gloucestershire was the stronghold of the Roman Church, having six mitred abbeys within its borders, and possessing the most famous relic in Christendom, 'The Blood of Hailes.' This, preserved in a phial in the Abbey of Hailes, near Winchcombe, was said to be the blood of Christ, the very sight of which was guaranteed to ensure the salvation of the beholder!

John Foxe, in his *Book of Martyrs*, says that Sir John Walsh,

> "kept a good orderly house, and there resorted unto him sundry abbots, deans, archdeacons, with divers other doctors, and there together with Master Tyndale sitting at the table, did many times enter into communication, and talk of learned men such as Luther and Erasmus, and questions upon the Scriptures."

Tyndale never hesitated to express his own opinions, which often differed from those of his master's guests, and, in order to refute their errors, he would confront them with the appropriate "open and manifest Scripture". Tyndale was a young man, fresh out of college, chaplain of the house! Sitting around the table were all sorts of dignitaries! Tyndale had many a conversation with these men.

Let me quote you part of such a conversation from 1521. A priest, seated across the table, turned to William Tyndale and said,

> "Your Scriptures only serve to make heretics." Tyndale very graciously turned to the priest and said, "On the contrary, the source of heresy is pride. Now the Word of God strips a man of everything, and leaves him as bare as Job." Then the priest turned to William Tyndale and said this, "The Word of God! Why even we don't understand it. How then can the common people understand it?" Tyndale replied, "You know who taught the eagles to spy out their prey. Well, that same God teaches His hungry children to spy out their Father in His Word. Christ's elect spy out their Lord and trace out the paths of His feet and follow Him."[15]

On another occasion a high ranking priest turned on him rather angrily and suggested that the pope's word was more important than

God's Word! In the same year that Luther stood before the Diet of Worms and uttered those glorious words, Tyndale responded to that ignorant priest thus,

> I defy the pope and all his laws... If God spare my life, ere many years I will cause a boy that driveth the plough to know more of the Scriptures than thou dost.[16]

This was an echo of Erasmus, who had written,

> I would desire that all men should read the Gospel and Paul's epistles; and I would to God that they were translated into the tongues of all men. So that they might not only be read, and known of the Scots and Irishmen, but also by Turks and Saracens... I would to God the ploughman would sing a text of the Scripture at his ploughbeam, and that the weaver at his loom with this would drive away the tediousness of time. I would the wayfaring man with this pastime would expel the weariness of his journey.[17]

Thereafter, the priests raged and railed against Tyndale and brought a charge of heresy against him, and he was brought before the Chancellor. Tyndale recalled, "He threatened me grievously, and reviled me and rated me as though I had been a dog."[18] Tyndale was now a man of one Book. He gave his life because of his love for the Word of God and because of his love for the Lord Jesus Christ. He was a scholar, but a scholar with a warm and sanctified heart, with a concern for the ordinary people. He once said,

> "I have perceived by experience how that it was impossible to establish the lay-people in any truth, except the Scriptures were plainly laid before their eyes in their mother-tongue."[19]

That was Tyndale's great desire and all consuming passion in life. It soon became evident to Tyndale that Little Sodbury would no longer serve as a safe retreat for one who gave such utterance to his life-long ambition and, therefore, in July 1523, he left the Manor House at Little Sodbury for London, hoping in vain to find encouragement for the great task before him from the Bishop of London, Cuthbert Tunstall! Tyndale recalls, "My Lord answered me, his house was full; he had more than he could well find."[20] He became the guest of a godly merchant, Humphrey Monmouth, in whose home he began to translate the Word of God into English. There, in Monmouth's library, he read the works of Luther. Humphrey Monmouth had a wharf underneath the present Cannon Street Station, and had barges that God was going to use later on. Tyndale stayed a short time in the home of Humphrey Monmouth, but eventually he said to Monmouth,

> It's no good. My being in your house is putting your life in jeopardy... I understood at last, not only that there was no room in my Lord of London's palace to translate the New Testament, but also that there was no place to do it in all England.[21]

There's only one thing he could do, and so, in May 1524, he left the country he loved and never saw it again. He went to Europe, settling in Hamburg, and began the work of translating the Scripture from Erasmus's Greek translation of 1522. Having completed the translation of the New Testament, Tyndale found his way to Cologne towards the end of 1525 where he entered into an arrangement with one of that town's infamous printers, Peter Quentell, to print his New Testament. It was there that Cochlaeus (Johann Dobneck), one of the bitterest opponents of the Reformation, sought to frustrate the work of Tyndale. One day he overheard the printers boasting confidently over their wine, that England would soon be Lutheran. Dobneck plied them with more wine and learned that there were in the press three thousand copies of the Lutheran New Testament translated in English. This latter day Judas then revealed the plot to a nobleman of Cologne, Hermann Rinck—a man well-known to King Henry VIII and to the Emperor Charles V—who obtained an interdict to stop the work. News of the Senate's action reached the ears of Tyndale, who immediately, in company with Roye, rushed to the printers and seized the precious manuscripts, fleeing in September 1525 by ship up the Rhine to Worms.

Worms was a Lutheran stronghold. Here the work recommenced at the press of Peter Schoeffer and, by the end of 1525, some six thousand copies of the Testaments printed at Worms were ready for distribution.

The New Testaments came in to England, smuggled through the customs in bales of cloth, in sacks of flour, in barrels and cases of every kind, up the Thames to Humphrey Monmouth's wharf. Tyndale made the Bible speak for God straight to the hearts of the common people. It was widely circulated to the joy and comfort of many who had long walked in darkness.

> The peculiar genius … which breathes through it, the mingled tenderness and majesty, the Saxon simplicity, the preternatural grandeur, unequalled, unapproached in the attempted improvements of modern scholars, all are here, and bear the impress of the mind of one man – William Tyndale.[22]

Considered as a literary undertaking, Tyndale's work marks an epoch in the literary history of the English speaking world. As a master of English prose, Tyndale stands unrivalled as he expressed the glorious truths of the Bible in the clearest manner, and thus exercised a permanent influence on the literary taste of the English people. That is what made the appeal immediate and widespread in Tyndale's day, and that is what must keep it fresh and searching while the English tongue is spoken among men. Loane comments,

> His own style was often rugged, but his sense of cadence was superb. He was simple and homely, and yet he was majestic and sonorous. His flair for the right word never seemed to fail him, and his text is rich in the kind of phrase, which haunts the mind with a lasting sense of beauty. He could use an obvious word without seeming commonplace; he could coin an eloquent phrase without seeming obtrusive. Some of the most familiar quotations in the Authorised Version come direct from Tyndale, and so many of its finest chapters bear the impress of his style and diction.[23]

He was skilled in seven languages: Hebrew, Greek, Latin, Italian, Spanish, English, and French, and whichever he spoke, Buschius said, "you would think it was his native language."[24]

Tyndale aimed to be homely and graphic in style, hence he gave us *shewe breed* from Luther's *shaubrot* in Hebrews 9. He was not above expanding a phrase into a *captain of soldiers of Italy*, in Acts 10, nor of causing Peter to declare that Christ should never wash his feet *while the world standeth,* John 13. He was all for familiar touches: *We sailed away after the Ester holidayes*, Acts 20. The chief priests and the Pharisees went to Pilate on *the next day that followed good fridaye*, Matthew 27. *I will tarry*, says Paul, *at Ephesus until witsontyde,* 1 Corinthians 16. John was *in the Spirit on a sondaye*, Revelation 1. The people of Derbe and Lystra brought oxen and garlands into *the churchporch*, Acts 14. Joseph *went into his own shire town to be taxed*, Luke 2. Christ warned his disciples, *when ye pray, babble not much, as the Gentiles do,* Matthew 6. At the feeding of the five thousand the disciples *gathered up of the gobbetts that remained twelve baskets full*, Matthew 14.

As a pioneer in English translation Tyndale's task was a lonely one. He said,

> "I had no man to counterfeit, neither was helped with English by any that had interpreted the same, or such like, in Scripture before time."

He was aware of faults, saying,

> "I count it as a thing not having its full shape, as begun rather than finished."

His scrupulous desire to render the original with the homeliest clarity may be seen in the many small revisions he made in 1534, the year before his arrest. In 1526 Jesus' accusers went not into the Judgment Hall so that *they might eat the Pasche*. In 1534 this was changed to *eat the paschal lamb,* John 18. At first the Ethiopian official in Acts 8 was simply a *gelded man,* and in 1534 he rose to *chamberlain* (A.V. *eunuch*). In Matthew 26, *unleavened bread* was changed to *sweetbread* (A.V. reverted to the former). At first Paul was arrested by an *under captain,* later by a *centurion* in Acts 22 (A.V. retained this). In Matthew 6, for example, the earlier edition has, *Each day's trouble is sufficient for the same self day.* In 1534 the sense is stronger, *The day present hath ever enough of his own trouble.* In certain instances Tyndale uses words which offended people like Sir Thomas More: *congregation* instead of *church; repentance* instead of *penance; favour* instead of *grace*; and *love* for *charity.*

Throughout Tyndale's 1534 revision there is revealed a vitality and continuity in its paragraphs, without verse divisions, that is thrilling. Full of vigour, racy, forceful, graphic and direct, it has a wonderful simplicity and correctness which seems to excel all its successors.

Cardinal Wolsey took steps to suppress the seditious book! A search was made and all copies of Tyndale's New Testament were ordered to be given up. At the same time the Bishop of Rochester (Fisher) was charged to preach at St Paul's Cross on the 1 February 1526, denouncing the books as replete with dangerous heresies. At the conclusion of the sermon, at which Wolsey was present, surrounded by a great company of mitred abbots, friars and bishops, great baskets of Tyndale's heretical New Testament were brought out and burned. In October of the same year at Oxford, Tunstall, the Bishop of London, was the preacher when Tyndale's New Testament was denounced and publicly burnt. Cardinal Campeggio, on the 21 November 1526, later wrote to Wolsey praising him for his diligence in protecting the Christian Church from the mistranslation of the Holy Bible in the common tongue by the followers of Luther's abominable sect.

These public denunciations and burnings served only to increase demand for Tyndale's New Testament. Wolsey had determined to buy up all of the copies of the 'pestilent' New Testament. Bishop Tunstall commissioned a London merchant, named Packington, to buy up all the copies he could find in the city of Antwerp and return them to England to be burnt at St Paul's Cross.

Packington came to Tyndale, and said,

> "William, I know thou art a poor man, and hast a heap of New Testaments and books by thee, for the which thou hast both endangered thy friends and beggared thyself; and I have now gotten thee a merchant which with ready money shall despatch thee of all that thou hast, if you think it so profitable for yourself." "Who is the merchant?" said Tyndale. "The Bishop of London," said Packington. "Oh, that is because he will burn them," said Tyndale. "Yea, marry*," quoth Packington. "I am the gladder," said Tyndale, "for these two benefits shall come thereof: I shall get money to bring myself out of debt, and the whole world will cry out against the burning of God's Word, and the overplus of the money that shall remain to me shall make me more studious to correct the said New Testament, and so newly imprint the same once again, and I trust the second will much better like you than ever did the first." And so, forward went the bargain; the Bishop had the books; Packington had the thanks; and Tyndale had the money.[25]

* True.

Justly famed as Tyndale's New Testament was and is, very few people acknowledge Tyndale's scholarship and contribution to the English Old Testament. Hebrew was not taught at either Oxford or Cambridge until 1524, the year after Tyndale had left England for his life's work. His knowledge of Hebrew, no doubt, was gleaned from the many Jews who lived in the old German towns. Hebrew studies were popular in Germany, especially Worms, where Tyndale's first Testaments were completed. There one of the largest and oldest Jewish communities survived. It was there that Buschius, a humanist scholar, observed that Tyndale spoke seven languages, including Hebrew, so well that each "seemed to be his native tongue".

The Hebrew Old Testament was already in print. Hebrew grammars were extant: Pellican's since 1503, Reuchlin's complete dictionary since 1506, and Sebastian Munster's Hebrew text since 1525. Immediately after the printing of his New Testament, Luther issued his translation of the Pentateuch in 1523, followed by the Historical Books in 1524, plus a separate edition of Jonah in 1526—a series of steps which Tyndale sought to emulate. Tyndale argued in his tract *Obedience* that Greek translated into English better than Latin, but Hebrew did so much better still. He argued that:

> Greek agreeth more with English than Latin, and the Hebrew tongue agreeth a thousand times more with English than Latin. In a thousand places thou needest only translate into English word for word, while in Latin thou must seek a compass if it is to have the same grace and sweetness as it hath in the Hebrew. It may a thousand times be better translated into English.[26]

In 1529, Tyndale, having completed his translation of Deuteronomy and desiring to get it printed, took ship to Hamburg, but was shipwrecked on the coast of Holland and lost everything. Finding another ship, he eventually arrived at Hamburg and rewrote his translation. By 1530 he had started upon the Old Testament from the Hebrew. He had done the whole of the Pentateuch, that is, Genesis to Deuteronomy. As soon as the script of the Pentateuch was finished Tyndale returned to Antwerp so that Hoochstraten could print it. This he did under the pseudonym of Hans Lufft and dated it 17 January 1530. With a prologue to each book and a general introduction, the work amounted to seven hundred and fifty pages. There was no general title page as each book had its own so that they could be sold separately or together. In Exodus there were eleven full page illustrations of Aaron and the furniture of the Tabernacle, said to have been paid for by the money which Bishop Tunstall spent for Testaments to burn them! Numerous marginal notes were packed with useful information about Hebrew words, names, customs and grammar, but were more anti-papal than those in the New Testament. In Leviticus 21, for example, where priests were forbidden to *make any baldness* on their heads, the margin reads, *Therefore, our prelates got the example of their bald pates from heathen priests* ! It was not, however, because of its marginal annotations, but for the music of its text, its accuracy and its independence, that this version of the Pentateuch has survived four centuries and is still, like Tyndale's New Testament, predominantly in the King James Bible.

By 1531 he had translated the whole of Jonah, which was printed at Antwerp by Martin de Keyser. The book was very popular among those on the side of reform, with its rebellious prophet, a victorious message, and a repentant people. Luther had issued it separately, and now Tyndale did likewise. Using only seven pages for the Bible's text he devoted thirty-eight to the prologue! In it he likened clerics who hindered the Scriptures to the Philistines who stopped up Abraham's wells, and went on to warn readers of the fate which reduced England to "half a wilderness" for refusing Wyclif's call to repentance. After its first edition, Tyndale's *Jonah* disappeared (except for the prologue, which was reissued in some editions of Matthew's Bible), until 1861, when a copy was found which is now in the British Library.

By 1534, he had revised Genesis; and in the following year, the year of his arrest, he produced a publication entitled, *The New Testament, yet once again corrected by William Tyndale.* When *Jonah* was printed in 1531 he still had five more years of exile in which to use his pen for reform. The extent of his work is described concisely in *Hall's Chronicles of 1548.* After listing the parts in print, the rest were recorded as, "Judges, the books of Kings ... to Nehemiah (that is the whole of the books from Joshua to Nehemiah, eleven in all), the prophet Jonah, and no more of Holy Scripture." Tyndale's unprinted portion almost doubled the amount in print. It also means that both parts of his total contribution between 1525 and his arrest in May 1535 amounted to 47% of the whole Bible. Nor was this unprinted part lost. The manuscripts were rescued by John Rogers and incorporated into Matthew's Bible.

The character of the man matched his work. He chiselled the Hebrew and Greek text in English granite while others carved it in wood. Steadfast as a rock, yet tender as a woman, he utterly refused royal invitations to return home and use his pen in service of the Crown, but exercised it most eloquently to encourage John Frith to face the flames of martyrdom.

Bitter opposition rapidly ensued, and Tyndale took up his pen to answer his critics: Cardinal Wolsey, whom he named 'Thomas Wolfsee' and 'Caiaphas the Cardinal', [27] and Thomas More that 'Proctor of Purgatory'. The bishops were, in Tyndale's words, 'blind buzzards and shameless hypocrites.'[28]

Demaus rightly says that the one word that fits the life and work of Tyndale is the word heroic.

> His was the first voice raised in accents clear enough and loud enough to reach the ear and touch the heart of his people; his was, in fact, one of those great lives which form a kind of landmark in our national history... No mere scholar would have lived as he lived, toiled as he toiled, daring Churchmen and Statesmen, braving peril and exile, for the sake of God's Good News in England. The one grand aim of his life was to give to England a version of the Scriptures in the language of the people, and for that high purpose, he had been quite content to bear the pains of privation and run the risk of martyrdom.[29]

From 1531 onwards, Tyndale's security was in jeopardy and he quit the Low Countries. For many months he wandered up and down the Rhine like a fugitive, hoping in that way to baffle the ingenuity of his hostile pursuers. Eventually he settled at Antwerp, and there he returned with all his energy to his great work of translation. The work of revision and translation occupied Tyndale's attention to the last.

While engaged in his daily routine of translation and correction, he was caught in a spider's web of guile and treachery by Henry Phillips. The Low Countries had become a dangerous place. The inquisition was armed with unrestricted authority to seize all suspected persons and try, confiscate, and execute, without any right of appeal. While resident in Antwerp he was the guest of an influential citizen named Thomas Poyntz, a warm and true friend, who was able to offer protection to Tyndale by reason of the privilege which exempted citizens and their guests from being arrested in their houses. Inside Poyntz's house Tyndale was safe.

In May 1535, plans were laid to lure Tyndale away from his safe refuge. Phillips had wormed his way into the confidence and affections of Tyndale, pretending to be a convert to the Protestant cause. Tyndale was invited out to dinner and, as he left the shelter of his friend's roof, he was seized by two officers stationed either side of the narrow entrance to the house. He was arrested and taken to Vilvoorde Castle in Belgium, where he spent his final year. In that cell he wrote his final letter, discovered just over a hundred years ago. It gives us a real understanding of how these Reformers behaved. It also gives us a clue as to Tyndale's manner of life and his faith, when he knew that death was around the corner. It gives us a view of what it was like to be in a cell, awaiting death:

> I believe, right worshipful, that you are not unaware of what may have been determined concerning me. Wherefore, I beg your lordship, and that by the Lord Jesus, that if I am to remain here through the winter, you will request the Commissary to have the kindness to send me from the goods of mine which he has, a warmer cap, for I suffer greatly from the cold in the head and am afflicted with a perpetual catarrh which is much increased in this cell; a warmer coat also, for this which I have is very thin; a piece of cloth too, to patch my leggings. My overcoat is worn out, my shirts are also worn out. He has a woollen shirt, if he will be good enough to send it. I have also with him leggings of a thicker cloth to put on above; he has also warmer nightcaps. And I ask to be allowed to have a lamp in the evening, it is indeed wearisome sitting alone in the dark. But most of all I beg and beseech your Clemency to be urgent with the Commissary that he will kindly permit me to have a Hebrew Bible, Hebrew Grammar and Hebrew Dictionary that I may pass the time in that study.[30]

How beautifully reminiscent of the mighty Apostle Paul, *Do thy diligence to come shortly unto me... The cloke that I left at Troas with Carpus, when thou comest, bring* with thee*, and the books,* but *especially the parchments.* (2 Timothy 4.9,13)

There was neither glass nor shutters for the windows of Tyndale's cell, and the rain and the snow came in. There was no central heating, no fire in the corner of the room and, no doubt, over his feet there ran a rat or two. His coat was thin and he had a perpetual catarrh; he was cold. But uppermost in his mind were the words of Paul, *This one thing I do.* Here was a man who was freezing, yet *This one thing I do.* There is work to be done to the end. In that cell whilst awaiting death he translated from the Hebrew the book of Joshua through to the book of 2 Chronicles. That's the measure of the man. Foxe tells us,

> that ... he converted his keeper, the keeper's daughter, and others of his household; also the rest that were with Tyndale conversant in the castle reported of him that if he were not a good Christian man, they could not tell whom to trust.[31]

At the end of July 1536, Tyndale was condemned as a heretic, degraded from the priesthood, and handed over to the secular power for punishment. On 6 October 1536, he was brought forth to the place of execution, was there tied to the stake with an iron chain around his waist and with a piece of hemp in a noose round his neck; a pile of straw and faggots were placed round his feet. It was then he lifted up his voice, crying thus at the stake: "LORD, OPEN THE KING OF ENGLAND'S EYES." The rope was wrenched tight from behind and then the faggots were lit with a torch to blaze around his strangled body. A martyr's crown made a fitting end to a life such as his had been.

Meanwhile, back in England, an extraordinary development had taken place. Henry VIII had fathered a daughter, Elizabeth, by Anne Boleyn, broken with the Pope, divorced his wife Catherine of Aragon, and made himself head of the English Church. Under Cranmer, Convocation itself had petitioned for an English Bible. In the same year that Tyndale was martyred, King Henry VIII issued the royal warrant for placing one Bible in every parish church throughout the land. Tyndale's prayer was answered.

The first complete English Bible was that produced in 1535 by MILES COVERDALE. Born in 1488, a few years before Tyndale, he was brought up an Augustinian friar and ordained a priest at Norwich in 1524.

He studied philosophy and theology at Cambridge in the Augustine priory under Robert Barnes, who was the means of his conversion to the Reformed faith. He "drank in good learning with a burning thirst, and was a young man of friendly, upright nature, with a very gentle spirit". When the Church was reformed he was one of the first to make a pure confession of Christ. He gave himself wholly to the propagating of Christ's true Gospel (See Appendix 1).

Six years after his conversion, Coverdale helped Barnes to prepare his defence against angry charges brought by Wolsey. A year later, in 1527, he was briefed by Thomas Cromwell about future plans for Bible translation. In 1528 he left Cambridge, abandoned the cowl, adopted the dress of a secular priest, and preached Lollard views in Suffolk until he was forced to flee to Hamburg in 1529. There he helped Tyndale with the Pentateuch. This was printed at Antwerp where Coverdale seems to have served as press corrector for M. De Keyser until 1534, when he again joined up with Tyndale on biblical work.

The year 1535, when Coverdale was 47, was among the happiest and busiest of his long life. Approached by Cromwell, he was set to work to produce by the turn of the year an English Bible based upon secondary sources. Not for him the slow and painstaking task of grappling with Greek and Hebrew, but rather the gathering of ripe fruit from other scholars. He was fluent in German, and had to hand two marvellous German Bibles, Luther's work and the Zurich Bible. The latter was handsomely printed by Christopher Froschover with prefaces, pictures and notes all set neatly in type, a model for the appearance of his own Bible. He also had two Latin Bibles at his elbow, the old Vulgate and the new version of Pagninus. Above everything was the massive contribution, ready for use, which Tyndale had printed piecemeal over the previous decade, and which now found its rightful place in the Bible of his friend.

By the middle of August much of the work was done, including the dedication to the King. Leaves were parcelled up and delivered to James Nicolson, a printer of Flemish origin established in St Thomas's Hospital in Southwark, by Vicar Constantine, a colporteur. Nicolson forwarded them to Cromwell with a plea that they might be shown to the King with a request for a royal privilege. This privilege was delayed for two years. Cranmer only wanted an English Bible if it was translated from Greek and Hebrew. The original title page declared that this Bible was "faithfully translated out of Douche (German) and Latin into English MDXXXV". This smelt too much of Luther for the bishops! The King asked the bishops if they found errors therein? "Many," they replied, "but not heresies." "Then in God's name, let it go forth among our people," said the King. This it did, but without the offending words "Douche and Latin" on the title page.

The original dedication was addressed to the King as "Defender of the faith" (a title given to him by the Pope for writing against Luther), and as "Supreme Head of the Church of England". It expressed a desire that "the prosperous age which God gave unto Abraham and Sara his wife, be given unto you with your dearest wife Queen Anne". In the summer of 1535, following a series of miscarriages after the birth of Elizabeth, Anne was once more with child. She paid a visit to Sir John Walsh at Little Sodbury Manor (Tyndale's former host and home), quite unconscious of that foremost English translator languishing in a Belgian dungeon. Sadly, this godly queen suffered another miscarriage, which both angered and disappointed Henry, so that he had her beheaded on the trumped up charge of adultery. On the following day he married Jayne Seymour!

Coverdale wrote in the dedication,

> I ... thought it my duty, when I had translated this Bible, to dedicate it unto your Highness, humbly submitting my poor translation unto the spirit of truth in your Grace, having God to my witness that I have not altered one word but have purely and faithfully translated it out of five sundry interpreters.

It was Coverdale's greatest achievement. Eloquent, lucid, musical, vigorous yet restrained, pungent but refined, lively and dignified; it still reads well. Much of it was incorporated into future translations.

Each book is prefaced by a brief summary of its chapters. Marginal notes are confined to cross references, and contentious interpretations are omitted. The three sections of the Poetical Books, the Prophets, and the Apocrypha, were all translated by Coverdale from the Zurich Bible. The following are examples of Coverdale's unique style: the first comes from 2 Samuel 16 where King David was cursed by the foul-mouthed Shimei shouting *"Get thee forth, get thee forth, thou bloodyhound!"* The Book of Job is perhaps most characteristic of Coverdale's work. Listen to that glorious affirmation of Job, *O that my words were written. O that they were put in a book. Would God they were graven with an iron pen in lead or in stone. For I am sure that my Redeemer liveth, and that I shall rise out of the earth in the latter day, that I should be clothed again with this skin, and see God in my flesh. Yea, I myself shall behold him, not with other, but with these same eyes.* Then at the end of the Book of Job, Coverdale names the three daughters of Job as *Day, Poverty,* and *All plenteousness!* Other English Bibles retained the names in the Hebrew, although the Genevan margin offered a more correct interpretation, *Beautiful as the day, Pleasant as Spices,* and *Horn of Beauty.* Another example of Coverdale's unique style is from Ecclesiastes 11, where he says, *Send thy victuals over the waters,* which was much more picturesque than the Bishops' *Lay thy bread on wet faces.*

In Isaiah, Coverdale describes the Lord, *sitting on a high and glorious seat and his train filled the palace, from above flakred the seraphims.* All other versions have *stood* but not *flakred,* which suggests the Seraphim hovered like flakes of snow. In chapter 12 we read, *With joy shall ye draw water out of the wells of the Saviour.* Then in chapter 40, Coverdale writes, *Unto them that have the Lord before their eyes shall strength be increased, eagles wings shall grow upon them. When they run they shall not fall, and when they go they shall not be weary.* In Isaiah 18, the Lord is presented as thinking over His purpose on a hot day in summer. He says, *I laid me down and pondered the matter in my house at noonday, and there fell a misling shower, like a dew, as it happened in the harvest.* Here, *misling* describes something between a mist and drizzle, a picture of a damp heat-haze over corn fields.

In Jeremiah chapter 8, we read, *There is no more treacle in Gilead,* which has given rise to the nickname for Coverdale's Bible as 'The Treacle Bible'. These few illustrations give but a brief glimpse of Coverdale's homely style. The ripe fruits of Coverdale's labours can still be read in the *Church of England Prayer Book,* where the Psalms consist of Coverdale's version as preserved in the 'Great Bible'. Five editions of Coverdale's Bible were issued. The first and best was printed abroad in 1535. The second and third, a folio and a quarto, were printed by Nicolson during 1537. The fourth was printed by Froschover at Zurich in 1550, and the fifth and last by Richard Jugge in 1553.

JOHN ROGERS, who produced the 'Matthew's Bible', had embraced the doctrines of the Reformation. Rogers was born about 1500 at Deritend in the parish of Aston, near Birmingham. He was educated at Pembroke Hall, Cambridge, and graduated with an MA in 1526, before being appointed Rector of Holy Trinity in London. He held this curacy until he became chaplain to the Merchant Adventurers at Antwerp in 1534. According to Foxe he was still a papist at this time, but he chanced to fall in with Tyndale and Coverdale and

> ...cast off the heavy yoke of popery, perceiving it to be impure and filthy idolatry and joined himself with them two (Tyndale and Coverdale) in that painful and most profitable labour of translating the Bible into the English tongue.[32]

Coverdale having begun his own translation of the Bible early in 1535, and following Tyndale's arrest in May of the same year, it was left to Rogers to complete Tyndale's task. His work was a compendium of Tyndale's Pentateuch of 1531; the Historical Books, Joshua to Nehemiah, from manuscripts left in his possession by Tyndale; and Tyndale's revised New Testament text of 1535; in all amounting to six hundred leaves out of eleven hundred for the whole Bible. For the rest he adapted Coverdale's version, editing and conforming it nearer to the Hebrew, which he knew and Coverdale did not. He also corrected the numbering of the Psalms according to the original, and translated *Hallelujah* as *Praise the Everlasting*, following the Reformed French Bible of Calvin's kinsman, Olivetan. Rogers included the 'Prayer of Manasses', which Coverdale, following Zurich usage, had omitted. Moreover, he borrowed from Olivetan a helpful concordance explaining Hebrew sayings, together with an attack on the authority of the Apocrypha. Uniquely, he portrays the Song of Songs as a drama with different speakers such as 'Christ', the 'Synagogue', the 'Church', and the 'Spouse'. He also includes Tyndale's annotations and prologues, especially the one on 'justification by faith', based on Luther's preface to Romans. He also copied prologues and annotations from Olivetan's French Bible.

In the following passage from 1 Kings 3, on Solomon's wise judgment between two harlots, we see the more musical style of Coverdale as against the more accurate text of Rogers based on Tyndale.

Then said the woman whose son lived unto the King (for her motherly heart was kindled with pity over her son), O my lord give her the child alive and kill it not. But the other said let it be neither mine nor thine, but let it be parted.

Coverdale

Then spake the woman whose the living child was unto the King (for her bowels yearned over her son) and said, I beseech thee my lord, give her the living child and in no wise slay it. And the other said it shall be neither mine nor thine, but divide it.

Matthew's

The first edition of Matthew's Bible was a splendid folio with two hundred illustrations, prefaced by two full page woodcuts by Lucas Cranach, one a symbolic title page and the other of Adam and Eve. Both these were used in Luther's Bible of 1533.

This Bible was printed by Andrew Crom at Antwerp, but while it was at the press Richard Grafton and Edward Whitchurch, Merchant Adventurers and members of the wealthy Grocers' Company, bought the whole first edition, fifteen hundred copies, for £500.

A copy of Matthew's Bible was delivered to Archbishop Cranmer in August 1537. He was delighted to receive it and forwarded it to Thomas Cromwell saying it was

> "...a new translation of a new print, better than any heretofore made. And forasmuch as the book is dedicated unto the King's Grace, and great pains and labour taken in setting forth the same, I pray you exhibit it unto the King's Highness and obtain a licence that the same may be sold and read, until such time as we Bishops shall set forth a better translation, which I think will not be till a day after Domesday".[33]

The licence was immediately granted, and Matthew's Bible was printed with the words, "set forth with the Kings most gracious licence," printed in red at the foot of the title page.

However, Matthew's Bible did not meet with universal approval. Foxe tells us that many of the clergy were greatly perturbed by its publication, chiefly because of the Prologues and the Table of Commonplaces touching the marriage of priests and the Mass. This resentment was eventually reflected in a royal proclamation saying

> ...because of printed books from abroad and published with privilege but containing annotations by which dissensions have been set up concerning the sacraments &c, therefore no printer shall publish any books of Scripture till they are examined by the King, or by one of the Privy Council, or a Bishop.

But all of these rules had been followed by Grafton and Whitchurch. Then another proclamation was issued in 1538 that

> ...one book of the Bible of the largest volume in English be set up in some convenient place in every church, where parishioners may most commodiously resort to the same and read it; the charges to be borne between the parson and the parishioners. God save the King.

This injunction not only meant that the two Bibles already in print were quite inadequate to meet the need of the ten thousand parishes, but forced Cromwell to be involved with the third English Bible of the sixteenth century.

THE GREAT BIBLE of 1539 was conceived in those words, "of the largest volume." The printers were to be Richard Grafton and Edward Whitchurch, with Miles Coverdale overseeing the project. By and large, Coverdale used Tyndale's translation of the New Testament and those Old Testament passages that he had completed before his martyrdom. In other words, Coverdale was using Matthew's Bible as a basis and making that despised Bible the foundation text of our English Bible! He did make more use of Erasmus' Greek text, particularly in Revelation, and Pagninus in the Old Testament.

In the 1539 edition, Coverdale had made forty changes from his 1535 text of Isaiah 53, and then in 1540 made a further twenty alterations:

Coverdale Bible 1535 *He shall be the most simple and despised of all, which yet hath good experience of sorrows and infirmities.*	***Cromwell Bible, April 1539*** *He is despised and abhorred of men, he is such a man as hath good experience of sorrows and infirmities.*	***Cranmer Bible, April 1540*** *He is despised and abhorred of men, he is such a man as is full of sorrow and hath good experience of infirmities.*

The work began in June 1538. The title page stated that this Bible was "truly translated after the verity of the Hebrew and Greek texts, by the diligent study of divers excellent learned men, expert in the foresaid tongues". But the 'excellent men' numbered but two, Coverdale and Grafton. There was no printer in England capable of such an undertaking and therefore Whitchurch approached Francis Regnault, a Parisian printer.

As the pages were set up the type proofs were sent to Thomas Cromwell. Four small signs appeared here and there in the margins. *A pointing hand* was to indicate explanations of the text; *a clover leaf* for differences in the originals; *a feather* for what was not in the original; and *a cross* for all cross references. However, all such helps were forbidden by hostile clergy, and when the Bible came out, even the little signs gave offence.

Opposition to the Great Bible project mounted. British Papists lodged their protests with the University of Paris, which controlled all printing. The London Booksellers' Company cancelled all orders for Service Books produced by Regnault. Then there was the royal proclamation forbidding English Bibles printed abroad. But the greatest blow of all was the Inquisition, which began on 13 December. Regnault was arrested, the two Englishmen (Grafton and Whitchurch) fled for their lives, and 2,000 unbound Bibles were seized by the University of Paris and burnt. Whitchurch was given £400 by Cromwell to return to Paris and obtain the blocks from the printer, which he did, and brought them back to London where the Bible was eventually printed.

There were seven early editions of the Great Bible. The first appeared in April 1539 and was called 'Cromwell's Bible'. Three more were printed in April, June, and November 1540, and were called 'Cranmer's Bible', because they were prefaced by his Prologue, followed by three more in May, November, and December 1541, which brought to fruition the purpose of the injunction of 1538 for a Bible in every parish church. The first edition of Cromwell's Bible sold for 10s 4d (52p) each, and held a royal patent issued in November 1539,

> ...for the Bible to be printed by the oversight of the Lord Cromwell, Keeper of our Privy Seal, in our name, special care and charge, that no manner of persons print any Bible in the English tongue during the next five years ensuing, but only such as shall be admitted by the said Lord Cromwell.

The chief fault of the Great Bible was that it was still not a direct translation from the Hebrew and the Greek. It was at best a patchwork quilt, a compendium of previous translations, including the Vulgate. Pressure was mounted by the bishops to restore the Latin Vulgate to first place. Therefore, with the King's permission in 1542, Convocation decided to revise the Great Bible according to the Latin Vulgate. Bishop Gardiner submitted a list of ninety Latin words, which for their majesty were to be retained unaltered. Cranmer, shortly before his execution, was able to persuade the King to transfer the revision to the two universities, where the whole matter was discreetly forgotten.

By the time Coverdale's final revisions were published, he was in exile. He had recently married Elizabeth McAlpyne, and according to the *Six Articles,* priests who married were to be hanged! Thus he returned to the continent, only returning in June 1548 when he was appointed chaplain to Edward VI.

Twenty years were to pass between the Great Bible of 1540 and the GENEVA BIBLE of 1560. In those twenty years there had been five monarchs and four changes in the national religion.

First, there was Henry VIII who reigned for a further six years and continued to sit on the fence between Rome and Reform. He was succeeded by the boy Edward VI, under whose reign rapid reform took place. Some fourteen complete Bibles and twenty four New Testaments were issued in his brief reign. These included two editions of Coverdale's Bible, three of Matthew's, four of the Great Bible, and no less than seventeen of Tyndale's New Testament. In 1549 Coverdale preached a Lenten sermon at St Paul's Cross, entitled 'Pulling down the Mass' (Appendix 1). Continental reformers were given Chairs at the Universities: Peter Martyr at Oxford and Martin Bucer at Cambridge. The first Prayer Book of 1549 was published, followed by another in 1552, and by the 42 (now 39) Articles, thus supplying the Church of England with a liturgy and a creed.

Henry VIII had settled the succession by Act of Parliament, naming his three heirs, Edward, Mary and Elizabeth, in that order. The prospect of Mary ascending the throne was terrifying for the cause of Reform. Desperate measures were taken to alter the succession, and following the death of Edward VI, Lady Jane Grey was proclaimed

Queen. Her reign lasted nine days! Within three weeks, Mary Tudor was Queen and Lady Jane had been decapitated in the Tower.

Instantly, under Mary Tudor, there was a reversion to Popery and the persecution of the English Reformers. All the Reformed legislation was swept away in one Act. Mary was intent on marrying Philip II of Spain, the rising champion of the Roman cause. If Mary had a son by this 'Spanish Match', England would once more become a vassal pawn in a papal Europe. Mary was determined to lead her people away from the 'darkness of Protestantism', into the 'light of Rome'. Her zeal for this cause knew no bounds.

The leaders of the Reform, men such as Latimer, Hooper, Ridley, Cranmer, and Rogers, would soon die a martyr's death. First to suffer was John Rogers, editor of the Matthew's Bible, who was burnt at Smithfield on February 4, leaving behind a wife and eleven children. By the time of Mary's death in November 1558, some three hundred martyrs had endured a terrible death by fire. One third were clergy; and of two hundred lay victims, sixty were women.

Coverdale, because married to a member of the Danish Royal family with whom Mary needed to retain commercial links, was allowed to escape to the continent. Countless others, who had not been arrested, fled to the continent. William Whittingham, a close friend of Calvin, was among those who went abroad. He established a Reformed congregation at Frankfort which invited John Knox to serve as their minister.

The same year that saw the martyr fires kindled in England witnessed Calvin's triumph in Geneva. The English refugees in Geneva shared "in this most perfect school of Christ". The English exiles were quick to avail themselves of the printing facilities in Geneva. Their first publication was the *Geneva Service Book*, which had been translated from Calvin's French liturgy. It was a comprehensive prayer book with over five hundred pages, and contained confessions of faith and prayers for use in public worship; orders of ordination, baptism and the Lord's Supper; prayers for the sick; a catechism and examination for children; a metrical psalter with several versions of Psalm 51; and prayers to be used at home. John Crespin printed it on 10 February 1556. Knox took it back to Scotland where it became the charter of Scottish Presbyterianism.

Their next publication was the *Geneva Psalms* of 1557. This was a small psalter, and was produced for those awaiting martyrdom back in England. The title page had a palm branch (emblem of martyrdom), on a skull (symbol of death), over a scorpion to illustrate the Apostle's words, *O death, where is thy sting?* The marginal notes contain many encouragements for those under persecution. The text of this psalter was based upon Coverdale.

The year 1557 was the worst year of Marian persecution, but it was in that year that the most important English work was produced by the Genevan exiles. A fresh version of the New Testament was printed by Conrad Badius. It was undoubtedly the work of William Whittingham, and much influenced by Calvin, whose *Epistle declaring that Christ is the end of the Law* forms the preface. The basic text was that of Tyndale printed by Jugge in 1552, which had been revised in accordance with Robert Estienne's Greek Testament of 1550 and Calvin's latest revisions of the French Testament. It was also influenced by the Spanish Testament of 1556 and Calvin's Commentaries. It marked the first English Testament to be set in Roman type, and was the first to be divided into verses. Words which were added to make the sense of the passage were for the first time set in italics.

Meanwhile, back in England, Queen Mary had suffered another false pregnancy and was abandoned by her Spanish consort Philip II. Her health began to deteriorate rapidly and, thankfully, Mary Tudor had less than a year to live. Nevertheless, the fires continued to burn, sometimes twenty souls being burnt at a time.

In Geneva, Christopher Goodman preached a sermon entitled, 'How Superior Powers may be Disobeyed and Resisted.' This was published in January 1558 with the names of the author, William Whittingham, and the publisher, John Crespin, attached. This sermon was to have important ramifications in the production of the King James Bible. The sentiments of Goodman found their way into the Genevan footnotes in the Old Testament and caused James I to despise these 'republican sentiments'.

The exiles had been thoroughly revising the text of the English Bible when news of Mary Tudor's death reached them. In the previous year they had revised the Psalter and had included eleven new psalms, nine of which were composed by William Whittingham.

Among the editions was Psalm 124 based on the words by Beza. How the exiles must have sung this psalm with great joy!

Had not the Lord been on our side,
may Israel now say;
Had not the Lord been on our side,
when men rose up to slay;
They had us swallow'd quick, when as
their wrath 'gainst us did flame:
Water had cover'd us, our soul
Had sunk beneath the stream.

Then had the waters, swelling high,
over our soul made way.
Bless'd be the Lord, who to their teeth
us gave not for a prey.
Our soul's escaped, as a bird
out of the fowler's snare;
The snare asunder broken is,
and we escaped are.

Our sure and all-sufficient help
is in JEHOVAH'S name;
His name who did the heav'n create,
and who the earth did frame.

Mary Tudor was succeeded by her sister, Queen Elizabeth, in 1558. During Elizabeth's reign two versions were made:

The first was the **GENEVA BIBLE** produced in the Reformation city of Calvin and Beza in 1560. Its translators were all exiles who had fled England and Scotland because of persecution on account of their Reformed doctrines during the reign of Mary. Initially many settled at Frankfort, but eventually they formed the English Church in Geneva from 1555-1559. The chief editors of the Geneva Bible were William Whittington, Anthony Gilby, Christopher Goodman and William Cole, assisted by William Kethe (of the 'Glorious One Hundredth' fame), Thomas Wood and Miles Coverdale. The Protestantism of these "deare brethren", as Whittingham called them, could not be questioned. Gilby's letters of admonition flowed back to England with such exhortations as "To my loving Brethren that is troubled about the Popish Apparel, two short and comfortable Epistles". Work had commenced at the end of 1557 and the first edition was produced in April 1560. On 2 December 1558 we find John Bodley, the wealthy merchant who paid for the Bible, together with William Williams, negotiating with the widow of Jean Girard, one of Calvin's chief printers, for the use of the latter's workshop.

According to Whittingham, they had been engaged "for the space of two years or more night and day". The rest of the English congregation in Geneva had departed for home early in 1559, leaving a little company of a dozen men, eight wives, and six children, twenty-six in all, to linger on in the city of Calvin. At length Whittingham and Williams were the last to depart. They did so with a glowing testimonial from the city council professing

> '...great content and pleasure as from people who served God, and rejoicing in the Lord who is the holy cause of their return to the country which He has graciously revisited.' Signed this 30 day of May 1560, J.F. Bernard, Secretary.

Thus the English colony in Geneva came to an end. They had been small in numbers and were only residents for a few short years, yet that little company of exiles has had such a profound effect. It led to the establishing of Presbyterianism in Scotland, Puritanism in England, and it changed the destiny of the British Isles and North America.

The Genevan scholars resolved that their version should be issued in a cheap and handy form, and that it should be adorned with such marginal notes as the common man required for the understanding of Scripture.

The margins of this Bible were remarkable for what the editors called 'Brief Annotations'. These ran to three hundred thousand words, equivalent to one third of the length of the whole Bible itself! They abound in excellent aids to understanding the text. The division of the text into verses, in itself a major change, provided an excellent opportunity for increasing the use of cross-references to some six and a half thousand. Another excellent aid was the use of *italics* for words not in the original but added to make the sense clearer. As well as these textual aids, three other helps appeared in the margins: two thousand alternative readings, seven hundred and twenty-five literal renderings, and twenty-one variant readings in the New Testament taken from other Greek manuscripts cited by Estienne in his great Latin Bible.

There was also an attempt to achieve a uniformity of spelling, particularly in the spelling of proper names. In most cases the changes made passed into the King James Bible: *Agar* was changed to *Hagar; Esdras* to *Ezra; Esai* to *Isaiah.* Equal concern was shown for the names of animals and birds, also for weights, measures and place names. Moreover, there were thirty-one illustrations, twenty-five of which were printed from the same blocks used in the French Bible. They comprised three sets, ten in Exodus of the furniture of the tabernacle; eight in 1 Kings of Solomon's temple and palaces; five in Ezekiel of his temple and his vision of God. Added to all these was a cut of Israel at the Red Sea. Also there were four maps: a sketch of the garden of Eden, a drawing of Noah's ark, and the tabernacle surrounded by the tents of Israel.

The first edition has a unique woodcut illustration of Israel at the Red Sea that seems to be peculiar to the Geneva Bible. It appears on the title pages of both the Old and New Testaments, and is also inserted at Exodus 14.

It carries the following inscription,

> In this figure four chief points are to be considered: first, the Church in the world is ever subject to the Cross and to be afflicted after one form or another. The second, that the ministers of God following their vocation shall be evil spoken of and murmured against, even of them that pretend the cause and religion that they do. The third, that God delivereth not his Church incontinently out of dangers, but to exercise their faith and patience continueth their troubles, yea and often times augmenteth them as the Israelites were now in less hope of their lives than when they were in Egypt. The fourth point is, that when the dangers are most great, then God's help is most ready to succour: for the Israelites had on either side the huge rocks and mountains, before them the sea, behind them the most cruel enemies, so that there was no way left to escape to man's judgment.[34]

Here were the Genevan exiles, driven to Geneva with Mary behind them, opposed on either side. These godly and heroic exiles felt hemmed in and shut up to their task by divine providence. In the preface of the Geneva, or Breeches, Bible there is an echo of Tyndale:

> And this we may say with good conscience protest, that we have in every point and word, according to the measure of that knowledge which it pleased Almighty God to give us, faithfully rendered the text, and in all hard places most sincerely expounded the same. For God is our witness that we have by all means endeavoured to set forth the purity of the word and right sense of the Holy Ghost for the edifying of the brethren in faith and charity.[35]

The Geneva text showed a scholarly expertise throughout. While Luther, especially Coverdale, and even Tyndale to some extent, were all concerned to make attractive translations, Genevan scholarship asked only what the original meant. The heavy dependence of the King James Bible upon the Geneva Bible demonstrates its superior excellence by providing the King James's men with more material than any other single source, including such well known phrases as these: *Except a man be born again,* John 3.3; *smote them hip and thigh,* Judges 15; *Remember now thy Creator in the days of thy youth,* Ecclesiastes 12.1; *Solomon in all his glory,* Matthew 6.29; *My beloved Son in whom I am well pleased,* Matthew 3.17; *A little leaven leaveneth the whole lump,* 1 Corinthians 5.6; *A cloud of witnesses,* Hebrews 12.1; *The ministry of reconciliation,* 2 Corinthians 5.18.

The first edition was a quarto, meticulously set in Roman type. It was in fact an exact copy of a Genevan French Bible of the same date, printed by Anton Rebul, and which contained the latest fruits of Calvin's revision and exegesis. With the exception of Lamentations and the Prayer of Manasses, each book had a preface or 'argument', which owed much to Calvin and the French Bible. There were also chapter headings, and the verses were numbered. This Bible was remarkable for its lively page headings, also adapted from the French. These were full of interest, social, doctrinal, and poetic, well-designed to catch a casual eye. Another feature was the placing of accents over the main syllable of proper names, as was done in the 1559 Psalms, a useful help which was abandoned after the second edition.

The Geneva Bible at once became popular, being portable and moderate in price. It became the people's Bible, and for upwards of fifty years it was the version in demand. Between 1560 and 1640 not less than one hundred and fifty editions were printed. It was the Bible of Knox and Melville. It was read in all places of worship in Scotland between 1560 and 1610. The first edition of the Bible printed in Scotland was the Genevan Bible, printed by Thomas Bassandyne and Edward Arbuthnet in Edinburgh between the years 1576 and 1579.

The popularity of the Geneva Bible caused widespread consternation to the authorities of the Ritualistic wing of the Church of England. They were alarmed that an unauthorised version of the Scriptures was preferred to the one that had been ordered to be read in the churches—and the Genevan was extolled by scholars and divines!

With regard to The Great Bible, John Bodley was

> ...granted privilege and licence for seven years to imprint the English Bible with annotations, faithfully translated and finished in this present year 1560 and dedicated to us, provided that the Bible to be imprinted may be so ordered in the edition thereof as may seem expedient to the Bishops of Canterbury and London. In witness thereof, the Queen, at Westminster 8 January 1561.

But such a publication was delayed for sixteen years. The Bishop of Ely, Dr Cox, chose this moment to remind the Queen's secretary,

William Cecil, of the old plan of the bishops of the realm to make a national Bible. He wrote saying,

> A thing there is worthy to be considered, the translating of the Bible to be committed to mete men and to be viewed over and amended, I called upon it in both my masters' times [Henry VIII and Edward VI] sed frustra. Yet, God be praised, we have men able to do it thoroughly. 19 January 1561.

Under the Elizabethan Settlement of 1559 the Great Bible was officially sanctioned. Yet, after one edition of that version, printed by John Cawood in 1561, and five editions of Tyndale's Testament by Richard Jugge in the same year, followed by another Great Bible by Richard Harrison, Scripture printing lapsed for several years.

Thus, the church authorities felt it was expedient to provide the English people with a new version, which might supplant in the affections of the people the popular, and in their estimation insidious, 'Genevan Version.'

The second version to be produced in Elizabeth's reign was the **Bishops' Bible**. In 1564, the Archbishop of Canterbury, Matthew Parker, resolved that the Church have its own version of the Scriptures, and after four years the new version was published.

Parker had been born at Norwich in 1504, and was educated at Corpus Christi College, Cambridge, where he obtained a Fellowship at the age of twenty-three. He was a friend of 'Little' Bilney, whom he comforted in his last hours before martyrdom at Norwich. As Master of Corpus Christi he welcomed Martin Bucer to Cambridge, and later preached his funeral sermon. Upon the accession of Mary he resigned his post and went into hiding in his native East Anglia. When Elizabeth succeeded Mary in 1558 she called upon him to accept the archbishopric, which he did reluctantly. He had acquired a library of 6,700 rare books and manuscripts from those scattered at the dissolution of the monasteries, many of which may still be seen in his former college. He also maintained a medieval type scriptorium at Lambeth Palace, employing transcribers, illuminators, engravers, printers and bookbinders. Chief among the printers were Richard Grafton, John Daye, and Richard Jugge.

In the midst of such treasures and expertise, the idea of producing an official successor to the Great Bible, revised by his bishops as suggested in Cranmer's time, appealed greatly to Archbishop Parker.

Most of those who took part in the revision were members of the Episcopal bench and so the title 'The Bishops' Bible' was given to it. It was a remarkable effort by sixteen high-ranking clerics, half of whom had been former exiles. Like the King James Bible it is the work of a committee but, unlike the King James' translators, each translator of the Bishops' version worked independently.

Archbishop Parker prepared a few instructions to guide his Episcopal brethren:

First, they were to follow the common English translation (Great Bible) and "to recede from it but where it varieth manifestly from the Hebrew and Greek original."

Secondly, they were to use "such sections and divisions in the texts as doth Pagninus in his translation, and ignore the Protestant contribution to biblical scholarship by Estienne, Beza and Calvin."

Thirdly, "for the verity of the Hebrew, follow the said Pagninus, and Munster especially, and generally others learned in the tongues." [This provided the bishops with a loophole to the second rule.]

Fourthly, "mark such chapters and places as contain genealogies, or other places not edifying, with some note, so that the reader may eschew them in public reading." [This instruction was ignored by the bishops!]

Fifthly, "all such words as sound in the Old Translation (Great Bible) to lightness or obscenity to be expressed with more convenient terms and phrases." [The bishops did the very opposite of this injunction. Coverdale, editor of the Great Bible, was very prone to soften homely expressions. In eight passages where urine is mentioned (1 Samuel 25.22,24; 1 Kings 14.10; 16.11; 21.21; 2 Kings 9.8; 18.27; Isaiah 36.12), he used 'stale' twice and 'water' in the other six. The Genevan editors bluntly used 'piss' in every case, an example which the bishops followed in all but one.]

Sixthly, "the printer to bestow his thickest paper in the New Testament because it will be the most used."

Putting in round figures, the Bishops' Bible had four hundred folios or eight hundred pages. The largest contribution, of one hundred and fifty pages, was the Archbishop's portion. He translated Genesis and Exodus; Matthew and Mark; and Paul's epistles from 2 Corinthians to Hebrews.

The other contributors were:

Edwin Sandys, Bishop of Worcester and Marian exile, who translated Kings and Chronicles (98 pages);

Andrew Pierson, Prebendary of Canterbury, who revised Leviticus, Numbers, Job and Proverbs (92 pages);

John Parkhurst, Bishop of Norwich and another Marian exile, translated Ecclesiasticus, Susanna, Baruch and Maccabees (86 pages);

Richard Davies, Bishop of St David's, and Marian exile, who revised Joshua to 2 Samuel (86 pages);

Robert Horne, Bishop of Winchester and Marian exile, translated Isaiah to Lamentations (84 pages);

William Barlow, Bishop of Chichester and Marian exile, revised Esdras, Judith, Tobias and Wisdom (84 pages);

Thomas Bentham, Bishop of Lichfield and Marian exile, translated Ezekiel and Daniel (50 pages);

Edmund Scambler, Bishop of Peterborough, revised the Gospels of Luke and John (46 pages);

Edmund Grindal, Bishop of London and exiled in Strasburgh, revised the 12 Minor Prophets (36 pages);

Nicholas Bullingham, Bishop of Lincoln, revised 1 Peter to Revelation (32 pages);

Richard Cox, Bishop of Ely and exiled in Frankfurt, revised Acts and Romans (26 pages);

William Alley, Bishop of Exeter, revised the Book of Deuteronomy (26 pages);

Gabriel Goodman, Dean of Westminster, revised 1 Corinthians (10 pages);

Andrew Perne, Dean of Ely, who revised Ecclesiastes and Song of Songs (10 pages);

TB, whose identity is unclear, revised the Psalms (47 pages). [Parker lists no translator in connection with the Psalms. These were first assigned to Guest, the Bishop of Rochester,

> but when he declared his intention of bringing his translation in exact conformity with the New Testament, Parker withdrew the task from him and gave it to someone else. The name was never included, but some editions have the initials TB at the end of the Psalms.]

Everything was done to make it attractive. It was issued in magnificent style, profusely illustrated with woodcuts, and embellished with copperplate portraits of Queen Elizabeth. On the title page of some editions it is stated "Cum gratia et privilegio". This was not, however, the authority of the Crown, but of the Church. In 1571 an order was issued by the Convocation of Canterbury that

> ...every archbishop and bishop should have in his house a copy of the holy Bible of the largest volume, as lately published at London, and that it should be placed in the hall of large dining-rooms, that it might be useful to their servants or to strangers.

Despite this, the Bishops' Bible never became popular with either laity or clergy, nor did it command the respect of scholars. It was no more than a Latinised revision of The Great Bible.

So far, we have traced the development of the English Bible through the sixteenth century. There were six Protestant translations of the Scripture: Tyndale's, Coverdale's, Matthew's, The Great Bible, Geneva, and Bishops'. In addition, because the strength of the English Reformation was the English Bible, the Roman Catholic Church were forced 'against their will' to produce their own version of the Scriptures, the Douai-Rheims.

Tyndale's supreme merit lay in his cleaving to the syntax of the original text. The Geneva Bible, with its verse divisions and extensive notes of explanation and application, revealed an intense desire to interpret the text. For that reason it quickly became the people's Bible. The Bishops' was so backward looking and so uneven, that its principal merit was that it made the King James Bible necessary!

JOHN WYCLIF
The Dorset Portrait

Lutterworth Parish Church

Page from Wyclif's New Testament

Portrait of that godly man, William Tyndale

Little Sodbury Manor

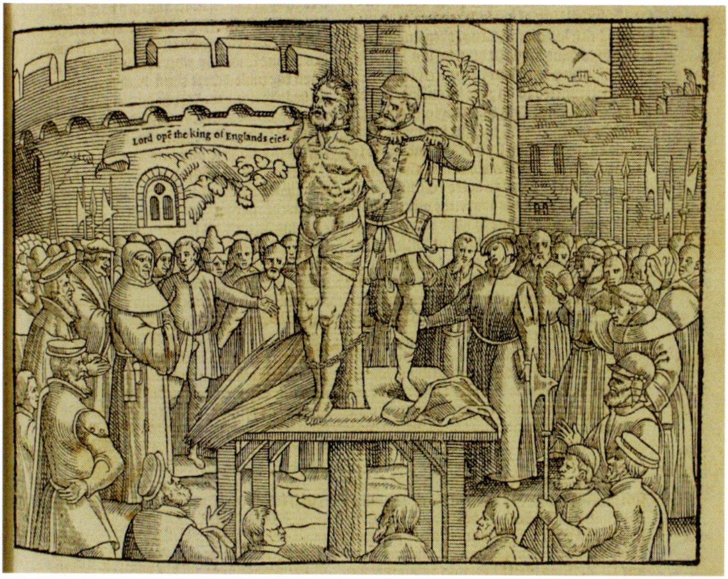

Martyrdom of William Tyndale at Vilvorde Castle, Belgium, 6 October 1536

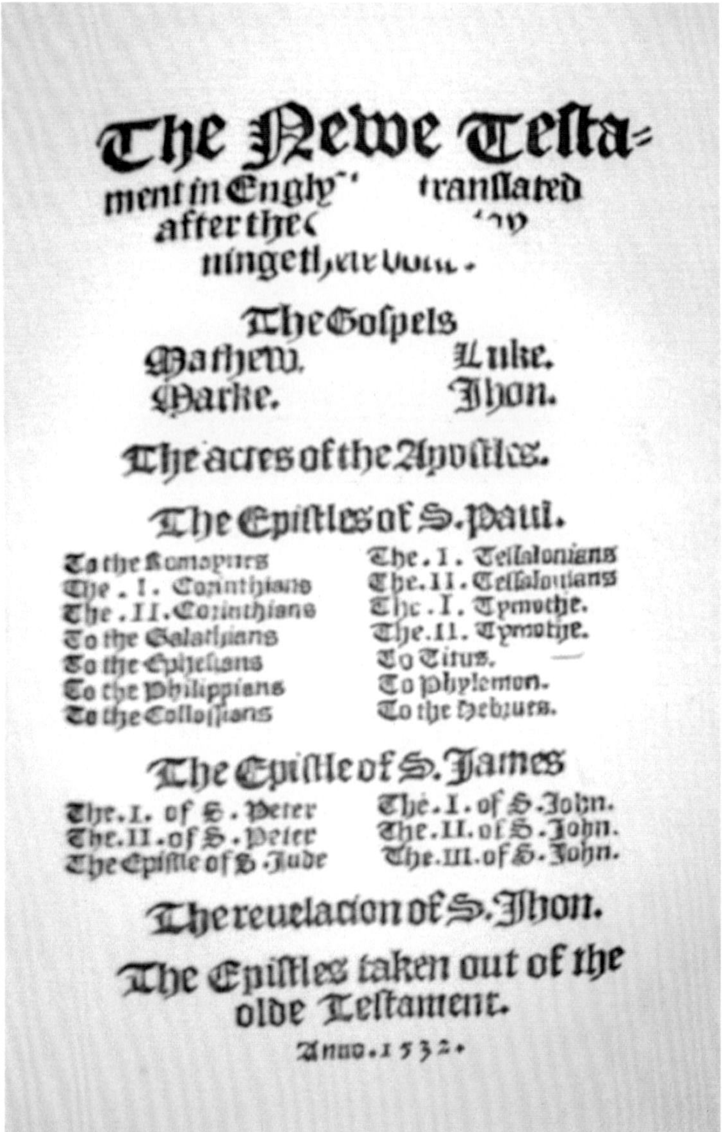

The Newe Testa=
ment in Engly[illegible] translated
after the[illegible]
[illegible]

The Gospels
Mathew. Luke.
Marke. Ihon.

The actes of the Apostles.

The Epistles of S. Paul.

To the Romayns — The. I. Tessalonians
The. I. Corinthians — The. II. Tessalonians
The. II. Corinthians — The. I. Tymothe.
To the Galathians — The. II. Tymothe.
To the Ephesians — To Titus.
To the Philippians — To Phylemon.
To the Collossians — To the Hebrues.

The Epistle of S. James

The. I. of S. Peter — The. I. of S. John.
The. II. of S. Peter — The. II. of S. John.
The Epistle of S. Jude — The. III. of S. John.

The reuelacion of S. Ihon.

The Epistles taken out of the olde Testament.

Anno. 1532.

Title Page of Tyndale's 1532 New Testament

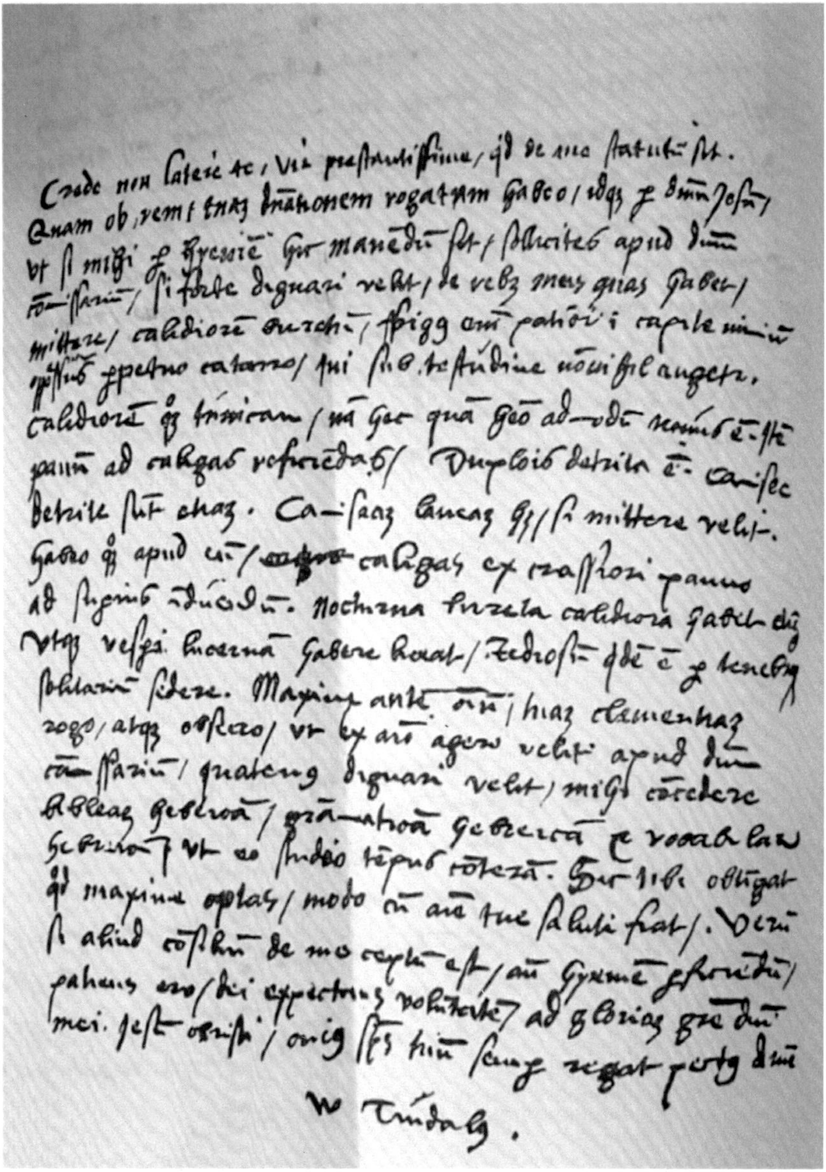

Tyndale's handwriting

Fo. cxcix.

The Epistle off the Apostle Paul/to the Romaynes.

The fyrst Chapter.

Paul the servaunte off Jesus Christ/called vnto the office off an apostle/putt a parte to preache the gospell of God/which he promysed afore by his prophetts/in the holy scriptures that make mension of his sonne/the which was begotten of the seede of David/as pertaynynge to the flesshe: and declared to be the sonne of God with power of the holy goost/that sanctifieth/sence the tyme that Jesus Christ oure lorde rose agayne from deeth/by whom we have receaved grace and apostleshippe/that all gentiles shulde obeye to the fayth which is in his name/of the which nombre are ye also/which are Jesus Christes by vocacion.

To all you of Rome beloved of God/and sainctes by callynge. Grace be with you and peace from God oure father/and from the lorde Jesus Christ.

Fyrst verely I thanke my god thorow Jesus Christ for you all/because youre faith is publisshed through out all the worlde. For god is my

Aa

Page from Tyndale's New Testament

Title Page of Tyndale's 1526 New Testament

Miles Coverdale

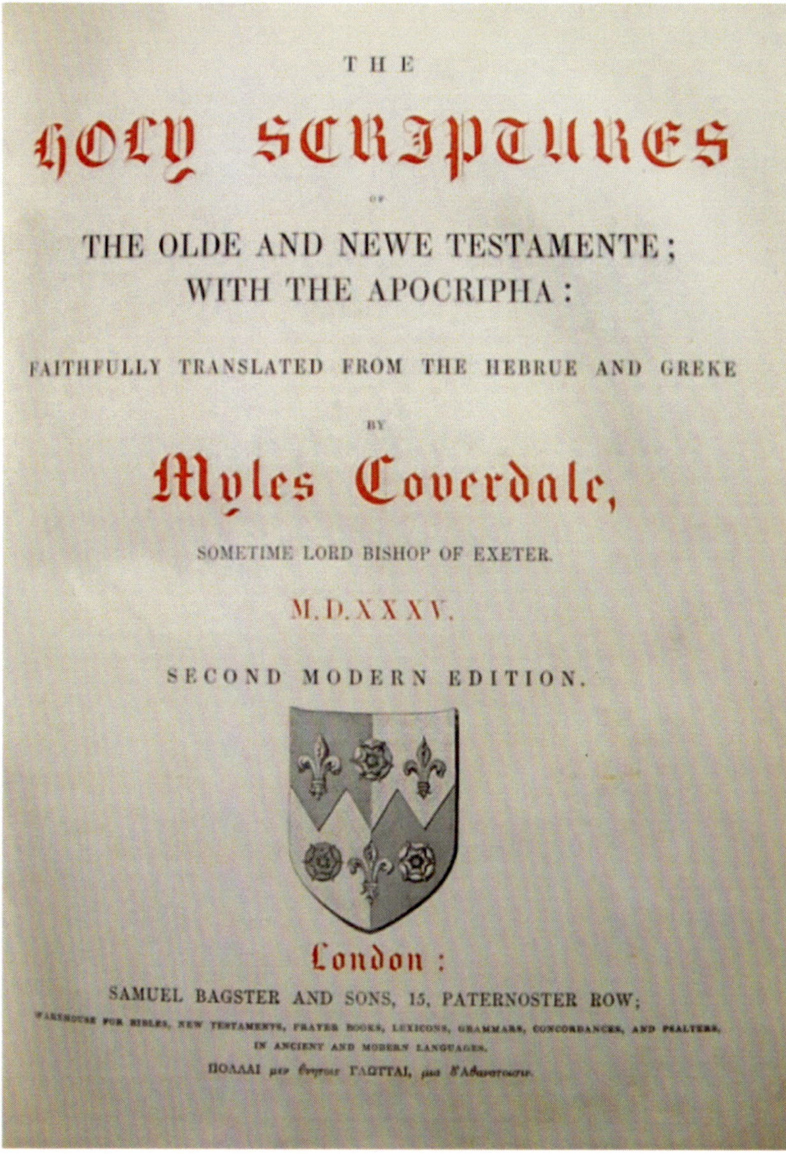

THE

HOLY SCRIPTURES

OF

THE OLDE AND NEWE TESTAMENTE;
WITH THE APOCRIPHA:

FAITHFULLY TRANSLATED FROM THE HEBRUE AND GREKE

BY

Myles Coverdale,

SOMETIME LORD BISHOP OF EXETER.

M.D.XXXV.

SECOND MODERN EDITION.

London:

SAMUEL BAGSTER AND SONS, 15, PATERNOSTER ROW;

WAREHOUSE FOR BIBLES, NEW TESTAMENTS, PRAYER BOOKS, LEXICONS, GRAMMARS, CONCORDANCES, AND PSALTERS,
IN ANCIENT AND MODERN LANGUAGES.

ΠΟΛΛΑΙ μεν θνητοις ΓΛΩΤΤΑΙ, μια δ'Αθανατοισιν.

Title Page of Coverdale's Bible 1535

The Byble /
which is all the holy Scrip-
ture: In whych are contayned the
Olde and Newe Testament truly
and purely translated into En-
glysh by Thomas
Matthew.

Esaye. j.
Hearcken to ye heauens and
thou earth geaue eare: for the
Lorde speaketh

M, D, XXXVII,

Set forth with the Kinges most gracyous lycēce.

Title Page of Matthew's Bible with woodcuts by Lucas Cranac

CHAPTER 2

Queen James the First – God's Silly Vassal

God gives not Kings the style of Gods in vain,
For on his throne his Sceptre do they sway:
And as their subjects ought them to obey,
So Kings should fear and serve their God again.

James I in his *Basilikon Doron*

THE last years of the reign of Queen Elizabeth were years of increasing loneliness for her. She had outlived her generation. One by one the great men who had served her passed away. The death of Lord Burghley in 1598 moved Elizabeth profoundly: the loss of such a servant, counsellor and friend was irremediable. In the Indian summer of her life she tried to revive something of the feverish activity that had characterised her youth. As one historian remarks:

> The further Elizabeth descended into the vale of years, the stronger were her efforts to make ostentation of a youthful gaiety of spirits and an unfailing alacrity in the pursuit of pleasure ... To remark to her the progress of time, was to wound her in the tenderest part; and not even from her ghostly counsellors would she endure a topic so offensive as the mention of her age."[1]

Her spirits further lapsed into an extraordinary depression that nothing seemed able to shake. For a while she refused to go to bed, lying upon cushions without eating, as though nature could somehow be defeated by her iron will. But the struggle could not be long maintained.

Sir Robert Sidney, writing to Sir John Harington in the summer of 1600, commented upon the rapidly ageing queen:

> I do see the Queen often ... She doth wax weaker since the late troubles, and Burghley's death often draws tears from her goodly cheeks; she walketh out but little, meditates much alone; and sometimes writes in private to her best friends ... At going upstairs she called for a staff, and was much wearied in walking about the house.[2]

At the end of January 1603, she removed from Westminster to Richmond, partly to escape the foulness of the weather in the capital and partly to rest her failing body. Meanwhile, many of her nobility were in clandestine talks with the King of Scots, James VI, seeking to win his favour. Camden writes,

> It is incredible with what flying speed Puritans, Papists, and ambitious persons of all sorts, flatterers and others, every one of them forward for their own hopes, posted day and night by sea and land into Scotland, to adore the rising sun and gain his favour.[3]

News of their actions reached the Queen and increased her melancholy, as she felt "creeping age at her gate". By March a heavy dullness of spirit descended upon her and she would sit for long periods in silence, her mind given wholly to meditation, impatient of conversation except with the Archbishop of Canterbury. She refused all medicine, and could not be persuaded to lie down in her bed, "because she had a persuasion that if she once lay down she would never rise."

Lord Cecil approached her with regard to the succession. She replied, "I have said that my throne was the throne of kings, and I would not that any base should succeed me." When Cecil asked what these words meant, it is reported that she said, "I will that a king succeed me, and who but my kinsman, the King of Scots."

She died on 24 March 1603. Whether true or apocryphal we cannot tell, but words attributed to her in her final hours certainly sum up her sad final and lonely years, "All my kingdom for an inch of time!" Yet in her pomp, this 'iron lady' in August 1588 rode through Tilbury camp wearing steel armour "like some Amazonian empress", in order to give her troops a rousing speech:

> Let tyrants fear. I have always behaved myself that, under God, I have placed my chiefest strength and goodwill in the loyal hearts

> and goodwill of my subjects; and therefore I am come amongst you, as you see, at this time, not for my recreation and disport, but being resolved in the midst and heat of the battle to live or die amongst you all; to lay down for God, my kingdom and for my people, my honour and my blood, even in the dust. I know I have but the body of a weak and feeble woman: but I have the heart and stomach of a king—and a king of England too—and think it foul scorn that Parma or Spain or any Prince of Europe should dare to invade the borders of my realm.[4]

When comparing her reign with that of James Stuart, she was more a king than a queen, and he more of a queen than a king! She truly had the heart and stomach of a king, whereas James had the heart and stomach of a woman! Whilst Elizabeth was struggling to breathe her last few fleeting breaths, courtiers headed by Sir Robert Carey rode post haste for Edinburgh with the news of her death. James VI of Scotland would shortly enter into his heritage and, as the first of the Stuarts, would reign over the united kingdoms of England and Scotland. A new reign and a new age had begun!

Following the death of her first husband, Francis II, King of France, Mary had married her cousin, Henry Stuart, Lord Darnley. Darnley was the son of Margaret Douglas, the niece of Henry VIII, so that he had a close claim to the English throne. He was even an English subject—hence the Anglicised spelling of his family name. In 1565, Elizabeth permitted him to travel up to Scotland to visit his father. By July he had married his cousin, Mary Queen of Scots, thus uniting two claims to the throne. It was a disastrous and dangerous liaison, because it meant that both husband and wife had claims and pretensions to the English throne. Darnley was also his wife's heir to the Scottish crown! Mary's finest quality was her tremendous courage, and she is known to have expressed the wish that she were a man! She refused to grant her husband the Crown Matrimonial, the right to succeed her if she predeceased him.

Her disillusion with her husband grew. He was a man with poor intellect and no political judgment. After a few brief months he took to frequenting brothels in Edinburgh and Stirling and drowning his morose spirit in drunkenness, believing the accusations of Douglas, the Earl of Angus, that his wife Mary had an Italian lover. Rumour was rife in Holyrood that Mary was conducting an affair with her secretary, David Riccio, and that she was pregnant with his child! Though their suspicions were almost certainly unfounded, the Queen indiscreetly spent long and late hours closeted together with Riccio in Holyrood House. Riccio had "free access to her bedchamber at all hours and she used him with greater familiarity than was fit".[5]

During her brief infatuation for Darnley, with Mary herself six months pregnant, Darnley ordered the savage butchery of Riccio at Holyrood in March 1566. Mary was forced to watch her secretary's gruesome death. Melville wrote:

> The King (Darnley) was before gone up to the Queen and was leaning on her chair, when Patrick Lord Ruthven entered with a helmet on his head. The Queen said: "What strange sight is this, my Lord, I sie in you? Are you madd?" Ruthven said, "We have been too long madd." The wretched Riccio tried to conceal himself behind the Queen, crying for mercy, but he was dragged to an outer hall by a Border laird named Andrew Ker of Fawdonside, where George Douglas brutally plunged the King's dagger into his body. Lord Herries, however, wrote that Lord Morton was the first to strike, "and he was slain with three and fifty wounds." When Riccio was already dead, the cowardly Darnley plunged his dagger into the dead man. For the pregnant Queen it must have been a terrible experience to see these men in sombre light with their naked swords, thus maybe creating in the infant stirring in her womb his invincible aversion to any form of violence.[6]

Mary suspected that her husband had intended to assassinate her and her unborn child (which he now believed was Riccio's), so that he could ascend to the Scottish throne and also, eventually, that of England. Andrew Kerr of Fawdonside had held a pistol to Mary's head throughout this terrible butchery!

James Stuart, the son of Mary Queen of Scots, was born in the late morning of 19 June 1566 in Edinburgh Castle. By all accounts it was a difficult birth. The room was furnished with a fireplace, panelled walls and the coat-of-arms of the House of Stuart and, on the ceiling, the crowned monograms. In the early afternoon she was visited by her husband. The Queen turned to him,

> My Lord, here I protest to God, and as I shall answer to Him at the great day of judgment, this is your sone and no other man's sone, and I am desirous that all here, both ladies and others, bear witness, for he is so much your sone that I feare it will be worse for him.[7]

James, their only child, was born into an atmosphere of marital strife, murder, plot and counterplot, in which rumours of his own illegitimacy were to plague him. The birth of James, a male heir, strengthened his mother's place in the English succession. He was 'christened' by the Archbishop of St Andrews at the hour of vespers on the second Lord's Day of December 1566 in the Chapel Royal with the full rites of the Roman Catholic Church. Lord Darnley did not attend the 'christening', nor the festivities which followed, confirming in the minds of many that he did not believe Mary and was convinced that Riccio was the father of James!

Claims of James' illegitimacy plagued his life and he was frequently reduced to tears when his enemies tormented him with the rumour. But such claims can be dismissed when one compares the portrait of Lord Darnley with James. The facial features of the boy James clearly reveal a paternal relationship with Darnley. From his father he inherited his thick, light-brown hair, and those sad, heavy-lidded eyes, which were in turn passed on to his son Charles I. From his mother he inherited the long nose and small mouth, and an impediment in which it always seemed that his tongue was too large for his mouth. He was broad-shouldered, of middle height, and had bowing legs (as a result of suffering rickets in childhood), which made his steps uneven and erratic.

Mary's deep-seated hatred of her husband intensified, and by the autumn of 1566 she was in an adulterous affair with Lord Bothwell. Bothwell was a cunning, ambitious, and conniving man who exploited Mary's infatuation for his own ends. Eight months after the birth of James, his father Lord Darnley was assassinated. On the night of the 9 February 1567, the house in which Darnley was recovering from syphilis was blown up by gunpowder and he himself was strangled. Many Scottish nobles, and Mary herself, had a motive for his death. One of the chief suspects was Bothwell, whom Mary married within weeks of the death of Darnley, even though Bothwell was still married to the Earl of Huntley's sister, Lady Jane Gordon! They were forcibly separated after a few months' marriage, and never met again. Bothwell fled to Denmark, where eleven years later he died chained to a pillar and insane.

Mary, twenty-four years of age, was incarcerated by the Scottish nobles on the small island of Lochleven and was forced to sign an Act of Abdication on July 24, 1567, in favour of her son, whom she would never see again. Thus, the thirteen month old baby became King James VI of Scotland and was crowned on the 29 July 1567 in the church outside the gates of Stirling Castle. John Knox preached a coronation sermon while two great lords stoutly maintained that he would uphold the Protestant faith. The Earl of Moray, the illegitimate son of James' grandfather, King James the Fifth, his uncle, was made Regent of the kingdom.

James, an infant of thirteen months began to reign over his Scottish subjects. Thus the powerful nobles of Scotland, and in particular his uncle, were in control of affairs until James came of age. James was to experience little peace or security, for he was nurtured throughout his bleak and pathetic infancy in a wasps' nest of intrigue and plot. Unlike his parents, he was a Scot, born and nurtured for thirty-six years in that land of granite.

His uncle, the Earl of Moray, was assassinated in 1570. James, therefore, at the tender age of four had lost his father and uncle; and his mother, whom he never saw after he was thirteen months old, was languishing in an English prison. The regency passed to the Earl of Lennox, James's paternal grandfather, who also was killed in September 1571, thus completing a triumvirate of tragic deaths. Thus, as a five year old boy, James saw the bloodstained body of his dying grandfather, the Regent, being carried past him at Stirling Castle. James's father, grandfather, and uncle all dead, and James not yet five years old!

The Earl of Mar became Regent until he died through natural causes in 1573, but not before he had terrified the boy king. Thereafter the ruthless and brutal Earl of Morton assumed the power of regency. The little king had known nothing of a family life; he had never tasted affection, nor the embrace of a mother's tender caress. His first seven years were devoid of affection and emotional stability. His surrogate mother, Lady Mar, was harsh and strict, with the result being that James lived in perpetual fear of her.

His education was in the hands of two scholars of outstanding eminence: George Buchanan, humanist and historian, then aged about sixty, and Peter Young, to whom James became greatly attached. Buchanan was a brilliant scholar and poet, but an inveterate enemy of Mary, and there is clear evidence that he exacted his vengeance upon James, repeatedly telling the young boy that his mother was an adulteress, a whore, and a murderess. He was a harsh and brutal man with a cruel temper, who not only made James a great scholar, but deepened the boy king's fragile emotional wounds. In contrast, Peter Young stimulated James' early interest in theology, particularly in Calvinistic learning, for Young had studied at Geneva under Theodore Beza. Nevertheless, it was under Buchanan's tutorship that James acquired his formidable learning.

Each morning, before breakfast, the young James would study New Testament Greek, followed by either Isocrates or Plutarch; then, after breakfast, he would study Latin; followed after dinner, by composition, arithmetic and cosmography. By the age of eight he was able to translate the Bible from Latin into French and then into English. James, at an early age, possessed a retentive memory and could recite whole verses and even pages from a book from memory. At the age of fifteen he wrote poetry, the following being an extract from his poem on the Battle of Lepanto and the triumph of 'Christian Europe' over the Turks:

My pen for pity cannot write,
My hair for horror stands
To think how many Christians there
Were killed by pagan hands.
O Lord, throughout this labyrinth
Make me the way to view
And let thy holy three-fold spirit
Be my conducting clew.[8]

James was never allowed to have a childhood. He was a little 'old man', whose childhood would come in later life! Those who would criticise King James I would do well to ask themselves how they would have responded to such a violent and love-starved upbringing.

Little wonder he was described as being timorous of character. Amazingly, the young king developed a dry sense of humour, and an ability to form his own judgments without necessarily sharing them immediately.

Scotland had been a decided Protestant country since 1560 and James was schooled in the Calvinistic Scottish Protestant Church of John Knox. He was to remain an 'intellectual Calvinist' all his life, though early on he rejected Presbyterianism. Throughout his life he delighted in theological debate and, as we shall see later, he was more than a match for his bishops at the Hampton Court Conference. His intellectual powers set him apart from all other British sovereigns. He judged wisely, had a most retentive memory, understood matters clearly, asked keen and penetrating questions, and gave sound replies.

From this loveless if educative background, James was unable to resist love and affection when it was offered him. From his mother he had inherited an emotional and passionate nature. His mother all her life had a painful need for adulation, and both she and her son James were highly susceptible to flattery. His emotional nature made him long to be loved and to love in return. He was a lonely boy, for he once described himself alone without father or mother, brother or sister. James's formative years were characterised by a lack of love, the violent death of his three closest male relatives, and the incarceration of his mother; yet they instilled within James a true pacific spirit and a desire to be loved. The young king, at an early period of his reign, fell under the influence of two worthless and profligate courtiers. The very first person to show any affection to the loveless James was Esmé Stuart Seigneur d'Aubigny, a French connection of the Stuarts. It is a sad sign of our degenerate age that many have suggested that the relationship which developed between them was of a homosexual nature. Modern historians likewise imagine, on the basis of probabilities, that he had such relationships with Robert Carr and Sir George Villiers. That same degeneracy would seek to rewrite history, and portray the 'Virgin Queen' committing fornication with her 'playboy', Sir Walter Raleigh!

Esmé Stuart arrived on the scene at a crucial moment in the king's adolescence when James was but thirteen years of age. The thirty year old Esmé arrived from France in September 1579 and showed great affection toward his much younger cousin. He was a secret agent of the Guises, whose motive for coming to Scotland was to gain the friendship of the King of the Scots in order to promote the cause of France and the Papal religion in the kingdom of Scotland. For the first time in his young life, here was a relative showing some deep family affection for him, and there is nothing at all to suggest that their relationship was anything more than brotherly love. James admired him and was taken by the glamour of his French upbringing which kindled within the heart of James the fact of his mother's upbringing—but there is nothing at all to suggest that theirs was a sexual love. Indeed, James gave the following advice to his son:

> I truste I neede not to insist here to persuade you from the filthy vice of adultery; remember onely what solemn promise ye make to God at your marriage ... Have the King (James V) my grandfathers example before your eies, who by his adulterie bred the wracke of his lawful daughter and heire, in begetting the bastard (Lord James Moray), who unnaturally rebelled and procured the ruine of his own soverane and sister. [9]

Esmé Stuart took advantage of this brotherly friendship, and rapidly advanced to become the Duke of Lennox, the only dukedom in Scotland. The Presbyterian ministers of the Kirk of Scotland voiced their disapproval of Lennox, the foreign Papist!

The Popish politicians on the continent foresaw, of course, that James VI would mount the throne of England, and there is reason to think that the mission of the polished but insinuating and unprincipled Lennox had reference to that expectation. The Duke of Guise had sent him to restore the broken link between Scotland and France; to fill James's mind with exalted notions of his own prerogative; to inspire him with a detestation of Presbyterian Protestantism, the great foe of absolute power; and to lead him back to Rome, the great upholder of the Divine right of kings. Accordingly, he did not come alone. He was in due time followed by Jesuits and seminary priests.

Lennox plotted that the Earl of Morton be arrested and tried and ultimately executed for the charge of the murder of Darnley, James' father, in 1581. This opened a hornet's nest of political intrigue, which resulted in the kidnapping of James himself in August 1582, when he was forced to sign a proclamation against Lennox.

The second man under whose spell James fell was Captain James Stuart, a son of Lord Ochiltree, a man of profligate manners, whose unprincipled ambition was rewarded with the title and estates of the unfortunate Earl of Arran. The sum of what these two men taught James was that there was neither power nor glory in a throne unless the monarch was absolute, and that the jurisdiction of the Protestant Church of his country was the great obstacle in the way of his governing according to his own arbitrary will. It therefore behoved him above all things to sweep away the jurisdiction of Presbyterianism. An independent Kirk and an absolute throne could not co-exist in the same realm.

Andrew Melville wrote that "those twin debauchees, Lennox and Arran, had foully misused his tender age". Lennox fled to France, leaving the adolescent James in emotional turmoil, and ill-prepared to assume the full government of Scotland, which he did in June 1583 at the age of seventeen, one month after Lennox died in France. His death left the adolescent king desolate.

In the meanwhile, Queen Mary, languishing in confinement, rekindled her hopes of the Scottish and English crowns. In 1581 she proposed a plan known as the Association in which she outlined a joint rule of Scotland with her son as king. She was willing to allow him the title of King and to rule the country in their joint names. She insisted that her forced abdication be annulled and that all important decisions in the kingdom be taken only with her approval! She also wanted James to become a Roman Catholic in order to gain the support of the Catholic powers of Spain and France. It is not surprising, given his loveless life, that he responded without any natural affection. He had last seen her when he was less than thirteen months old, and there was no love in his heart for her. He had never known and experienced a mother's love, and therefore he concluded that "the association desired by his mother should neither be granted nor spoke of herafter". When his mother was tried for treason, James made no attempt to exonerate her and was not prepared to endanger the alliance with England—and hopefully the crown of England. If the choice was between his mother, whom he never knew, and the future crown of England, then the choice was clear. He remained impassive upon hearing the news of his mother's execution on 8 February 1587. James was a shrewd and astute politician who realised he had far more to gain from an alliance with England and friendship with Elizabeth than from a mother he had never known.

Fontenay has given a remarkable character sketch of the King at eighteen:

> For his years he is the most remarkable prince that ever lived. He has three qualities of soul in perfection. He apprehends clearly, judges wisely and has a retentive memory. In his questions he is lively and perceptive and sound in his answers. In any matter which is being debated, be it religion or any other thing, he believes and always maintains what seems to him to be true and just … He is learned in many tongues, sciences and affairs of state, more so I dare say than any others in his realm. In brief, he has a marvellous mind, filled with a virtuous grandeur.[10]

At an early age James possessed many of the qualities that were to make him a successful king of the Scots: immense learning, experience in handling his ministers, cunning and dexterity in surmounting political intrigue, and, above all, a deep belief in the divine right of kings.

Now, James, king in his own right, with no rival claim to his throne, sought a queen. His only experience of women had been the harsh and cruel regime of Lady Mar—no motherly embrace, no sisterly affection. But as King James VI, he needed a queen, who would strengthen his ultimate objective, his claim to the throne of England.

There were two main candidates, Princess Catherine of Bourbon, sister of the King of Navarre, later Henri IV of France, and Anne, younger daughter of Frederick II of Denmark, a country possessing close links with Scotland. Having been given a portrait of young Princess Anne of Denmark, that tall, slim, fair-skinned, golden-haired beauty, James, possessing a strong vein of romance, fancied himself in love. Anne was during the summer of 1589 aged fifteen, a girl of considerable charm and beauty. He therefore embarked on a journey to Norway to meet and to marry her. The marriage took place on November 23 in St Halvard's Church. It was now deep winter. Instead of returning to his native Scotland, James, greatly in love with his young bride, decided to stay on in Scandinavia. They thus spent their honeymoon in her native Denmark. He visited the great Danish scholar Dr Niels Hemmingsen at Roskilde to discuss predestination, and on another occasion gave a speech in Latin to the doctors of theology at the University of Copenhagen that lasted three hours! James and his queen finally returned to Scotland on 1 May 1590. Anne's coronation in the Abbey Church of Holyrood took place on the Lord's Day, 17 May. James was a tender husband, frequently writing verse praising her beauty and high spirits. She bore James seven children, only three of whom survived to adulthood. Sophia, the youngest, was born in 1607, and lies buried in Westminster Abbey. From their correspondence James and Anne reveal a deep bond of marital love and affection. True, she didn't have the intellect of James, but then he never expected intelligence in the 'weaker vessel'. And yes, she had that feminine weakness of the age, her love of dancing, frivolity, and court fooleries. Her idea of pleasure was dancing in a masque written by Ben Johnson, with scenery and costumes designed by Inigo Jones, who also designed a palace which James built for her at Greenwich.

Anne's conversion to Popery from her native Lutheranism, however, was a concern, not only to James's subjects, but to James himself. In Spain, Queen Anne was referred to openly as the "Catholic wife". The Grand Duke of Tuscany was assured by the Queen that she wished to live and die a Roman Catholic. Indeed, at the coronation of King James and Queen Anne on 25 July1603, the Queen declined to take the Protestant communion during the ceremony.

In 1597, and following the North Berwick witchcraft trials, James wrote his own tract entitled, *Demonologie*. For James, the devil was very real, the incarnation of evil, and the witches, mostly old hags, were his instruments. James's hatred of the devil knew no bounds. As a young man of twenty-four he made a study of witchcraft and became quite an expert. Seemingly, a demonic pact, engineered by Francis Bothwell, had been made to overthrow the King.

James in his treatise upon witchcraft explains the purpose of his writing this work:

> The fearfull aboundage at this time in this countrie of these detestable slaves of the Devill, the Witches or enchanters, hath

> moved me to dispatch in post this following treatise of mine, not in any wise to serve for a show of my learning, but only to presse the truth so far as I can, to resolve the doubting harts both that such assaultes of Sathan are most certainly practised, and that the instruments thereof, merits most severely to be punished ... My intention in this labour is only to prove two things ... the one that such diveelish artes have bene and are. The other what exact trial and severe punishment they merite. [11]

Bothwell was arrested and imprisoned, but later escaped to menace the King with the possibility of his sudden and violent death. Given his violent upbringing, James, without a standing army, was ever fearful of his own safety. In 1592 the manic Bothwell surrounded James's palace in Fife with three hundred men, intent upon beating down the gate with a battering ram. Throughout that long and dark night the King sought refuge in the tower, until at last Bothwell called off his men. A year later, Bothwell entered the King's bedchamber at Holyrood with his sword drawn but, with an untypical act of courage, James confronted and disarmed his enemy.

Further attempts were to be made upon the young king's life, most notably the Gowrie Conspiracy of August 1600, when the King was held captive in a locked room in a hostile castle by Earl Gowrie and his brother. The sense of a miraculous deliverance from physical harm was so important to King James that he insisted on its annual remembrance. When he ascended the English throne, he declared a solemn new public thanksgiving on 5 August 1603 to celebrate his deliverance three years earlier.

Sir Henry Wotton, a witty Italianate Englishmen, wrote a perceptive character sketch of the King when he returned to Italy:

> The said King, though born in 1566, does not appear *(non mostra)* to be more than twenty-eight years of age. He is of medium stature and of robust constitution *(di complersione gagliardi)*, his shoulders broad, but the rest of his person from the shoulders downward is rather slender. In his eyes and in his outward appearance there is a certain natural kindness *(bonte)* bordering on modesty. He is partial to literary discourse, particularly of theology and is a great lover of witty conceits *(concetti arguti)*. His speech is learned and even eloquent. He wears his hair short

in imitation of his grandfather James V. About food and clothing he does not care. …

His Court is governed more in the French than in the English fashion. Anyone may enter the King's presence while he is at dinner, and he eats and talks with those about him. Dinner finished, he remains at table for a time before retiring, listening to banter and merry jests, in which he takes great delight.[12]

Antonio Foscarini, a Venetian diplomat, wrote of James in 1619:

> The King is endowed with a strong intellect, a perfect memory and a good disposition. He is familiar in his discourse, and so in the whole Court, especially those who are most about him. He treats all those who serve him with the utmost kindness and familiarity. There are eight or ten people who sleep habitually in his bedchamber, who can enter when they please … The doctors say that constant exercise is his salvation.[13]

Alvise Valeresso, Venetian Ambassador in London in 1622-23 was more critical of James, and wrote of him:

> All good sentiments are clearly dead in the King. He is too blinded in disordered self-love and in his wish for quiet and pleasure, too agitated by constant mistrust of everyone, tyrannised over by perpetual fears for his life, tenacious as against the Parliament and jealous of his son's obedience, all accidents and causes of his almost desperate infirmity of mind.[14]

Anthony Weldon said of James:

> He was of middle stature, more corpulent through his cloathes than in his body, yet fat enough, his cloathes ever being made large and easie, the doublets quilted for stiletto proof, his breeches in plates and full stuffed. …His eye large, ever rowling after any stranger come in his presence … his beard was very thin, his tongue too large for his mouth, which made him drink very uncomely … his skin was as soft as taffeta sarsnet, which fell so, because he never wash't his hands, only rib'd his fingers' ends slightly with the wet-end of a napkin, his legs were very weak, having as was thought some foul play in his youth, or rather before he was born, that he was able to stand at seven years of age, that weakness made him ever leaning on other men's shoulders.[15]

This physical infirmity, which had prevented him from standing on his own two feet until he was seven years of age, and caused him to lean upon his Court favourites throughout his life, has been cited by 'historians' as proof positive of his homosexual tendencies. Of Robert Carr's creation as Viscount Rochester in March 1611, one historian writes,

> There was clearly a sexual element in the relations between the King and his new favourite. James would ... show his dependence by leaning continually on his arm, smooth his flaxen hair... If he behaved in such a manner in public, it is probable that James treated Carr even more intimately in the privacy of his bedchamber.[16]

Sir John Oglander related that King James was "the most cowardly man that ever I knew". He could not endure a soldier or to see men drilled, and to hear of war was death to him. He was a genuine lover of peace. He wore great quilted doublets, pistol-proof, and "he would eye strangers with a continual fearful observation".[17]

The aristocratic rivalries and Catholic/Protestant feuds of the nobles had plagued Scotland throughout the reign of James. But James's harsh, unloving upbringing, beset with violent incident and aristocratic feuds, had made the King a shrewd and sagacious politician. In such a maelstrom of political and religious turbulence he developed his *Via Media* policy, which was to stand him in good stead when he succeeded to the English crown. This tenacity of character—some might call it stubbornness of spirit—was a trait which was to characterise James throughout his life. Once he was committed to a cause he would pursue it with relentless zeal. It was this tenacious spirit that, under the good providence of God, became the driving force behind the Authorised Version of the Bible.

This tenacity was also evidenced in his rebuttal of the Presbyterians. As early as May 1592, Elizabeth was having her own troubles with the Puritans, and she had written to James:

> There is risen both in your realm and mine, a sect of perilous consequence, such as would have no kings but a presbytery and take our place while they enjoy our privilege. Yea, look we well unto them. I pray you stop the mouths or make shorter the

> tongues of such ministers as dare presume to make orisons* in their pulpits for the persecuted in England for the gospel.[18]

James maintained that the king had powers derived directly from God. These views he expounded in his work, *The Trew Law of Free Monarchies,* published anonymously in 1598. In this, the seventh book published by James, he developed the views that had been forming in his agile brain for many years concerning the divine right of kings. His aim was didactic, to teach his subjects their duties to their king. Making use of his experience in Scotland, he stressed how wrong it was to revolt against a ruler. In this work, James declared that even bad kings had rights over the people, in that he had been sent by God to punish the people. James's thesis was that kings existed before parliaments; they were thus the makers of laws, and not the laws the makers of kings.

His *Basilikon Doron,* written in the summer of 1598, commences with a sonnet:

God gives not Kings the stile of Gods in vaine,
For on his throne his sceptre doe they sway;
And as their subjects ought them to obey
So kings should feare and serve their Gods againe.
If then ye would enjoy a happie raigne
Observe the statutes of your heavenlie king,
And from his house make all your laws to spring,
Since his Lieutenant heere ye should reacive
Reward the iust, be stedfast, true and plaine,
Repress the proude, maintaining aye the right
Walk always, as euer in his sight.

James argued that kings were "the breathing images of God", "God's Lieutenants." As King James I of England, what he enjoyed more than anything else was to preside in the Star Chamber, wearing his crown and robe of purple velvet, eager to pronounce judgment, a veritable Solomon! He addressed his people:

> Kings are properly judges, and judgment properly belongs to them from God: for kings sit in the throne of God, and thence all

---

* Prayers or supplications.

> judgment is derived ... I remember Christ saying, "My sheep here my voice," and so I assure myself, my people will most willingly hear the voice of me, their own shepherd and King.[19]

Written in the summer of 1598, when Prince Henry was aged four, he warned his son against the Puritans,

> Take heed therefore, my son, to such Puritans, very pests in the church and commonweal, whom no deserts can oblige ... breathing nothing but sedition and calumnies, aspiring without measure, railing without reason and making their own imaginations the square of their conscience. I protest before the great God that ye shall never find with any Highland or Border thieves greater ingratitude and more lies and vile perjuries than with these fantastic spirits.[20]

Andrew Melville responded by describing James to his face as "God's silly vassal". "And, Sir," said Melville, taking him by his lapels, "when you were in swaddling clothes, Christ Jesus reigned freely in this land in spite of all His enemies." David Black, another Presbyterian Minister, thundered from his pulpit that all kings were devils and came of devils and that Satan was the head of the Court and in the Court.

By now though, King James VI had aspirations for the crown of England. Queen Elizabeth was on the wane, and the question of succession was pressing. James did not have an incontrovertible claim to the English throne. He was the senior descendant of Henry VII of England, given that the line of Henry VIII died out with the death of his remaining child Elizabeth. James had the best hereditary claim, but he was Scottish and, according to the will of Henry VIII, 'foreigners' were to be excluded from the succession. Thus, James' cousin, Arabella Stuart, the only child of Darnley's brother Charles, might be considered to have a better claim, as she was English. However, Arabella had Catholic sympathies, and she was supported in her claim to the throne by the pope! Rome was eager to prevent anyone mounting to the English throne save a prince or princess whose attachment to Roman Catholicism could not be doubted, and on whom sure hopes could be built that he or she would restore the Papacy in England.

Rumour was rife in Roman Catholic circles that James would soon convert to Rome. Many Papists believed that the 'mother's merits', that is, those pretended 'spiritual merits' gained by the 'martyrdom' of Mary Queen of Scots, would shortly be conveyed by God to Mary's son, resulting in his conversion to Roman Catholicism! As early as July 1600, the Spanish Court believed that King James VI of Scotland was on the verge of submitting to the Pope's religious authority. Father Robert Persons thought it was only a matter of time before the Scottish king would be converted to Rome. Throughout the summer of 1601, Henry IV of France, who had himself converted to Rome to secure the throne, declaring to James that "Paris was worth a Mass", was urging James to do the same.

Papal hopes were further strengthened by the conversion to Rome of James's queen, Anne of Denmark, sometime after 1600, but well before March 1603. She was received into the Church of Rome in a secret chamber in the royal palace, and by the summer of 1601 she was writing to Pope Clement VIII assuring him of her fidelity to the Church. Her confessor was the Jesuit, Father Robert Abercromby, who was permitted at court if suitably disguised as a keeper of hawks. The Pope thus had his man at the very heart of court life. Clement VIII had been assured of the devotion of Queen Anne, who would educate her children in the Roman Catholic faith. Further, she received the Pope's absolution and blessing for those occasions when she was called upon to attend 'the rites of heretics'. In July 1602, she informed the Pope that she was urging the conversion of her husband.

But whilst James showed himself tolerant of his wife's defection to Rome, he had in 1600, through his agent in England, nailed his own Protestant colours to the mast:

> ...assure all honest men, on the princely word of a Christian king, that as I have ever without swerving maintained the same religion within my kingdom, so, as soon as it shall please God lawfully to possess me of the crown of that kingdom, I shall not only maintain the profession of the Gospel there, but withal not suffer any other religion to be professed within the bounds of that kingdom.

That strong assurance, doubtless, quieted the fears of the English statesmen, but in the same degree it awakened the fears of Rome.

The Protestant nobility and gentry of England were not prepared to bow the neck to the tyranny of the Church of Rome, and therefore it was Robert Cecil who argued that James was the only worthy candidate, being male and a Protestant, possessed of a strong hereditary claim, and with children of his own to follow him. Above all, he had already been a king for some thirty-five years, and Elizabeth had remarked that none but a king should succeed her.

From the beginning of Elizabeth's decline in 1601, Cecil had secretly corresponded with James, training him in the art of becoming King of England. James wrote to Cecil and opened his mind on matters of religion. He was at pains to show that he was moderate in his opinion:

> My dearest 10. (In correspondence James, Cecil and Northumberland were referred to as numbers, a secret code, James being number 30.) I will never allowe in my conscience that the bloode of any man shall be shedde for diversitie of opinions in religion, but I wolde be sorie that Catholikes should so multiplie as they might be able to practise thaire olde principles upon us … I ame so farre from any intention of persecution, as I proteste to God, I reverence thaire churche as our mother churche … that I did euer holde persecution as one of the infallible notes of a false church.[21]

Thus, James began to look upon England as the "enchanted ground", the "promised land".

The last few weeks of Elizabeth's life were both painful and traumatic. It was January 1603 and the Queen developed a bad cold. She was moved to Richmond, the warmest of her palaces, but she refused all physic. She was losing all will to live. She was sixty-nine years old and plagued with fever. She sat on floor cushions and had to be carried to her bed. Then, at 10.00 a.m. on the last day of the old year, 24 March, the reign of Elizabeth came to an end, and there began a mass stampede north to the land of the Scots. Sir Robert Carey had already posted horses along the old Roman road from London to Edinburgh, to enable him to be the first to break the news to the new monarch. Upon receiving the news, James wrote that he wanted to enter England

> …as the son and righteous heir of England, with all peace and calmness, and without any kind of alteration in state and government as far as I possibly can.

On April 5 he took an affectionate farewell of his pregnant queen, his 'Annie,' in Edinburgh High Street. She was not accompanying him to England, but intended to follow him some weeks later. James made the long journey south, leaving, in his words "the wilderness and barren soil" to arrive at "the land of promise". Whilst on route he received news that his 'Annie' had suffered a miscarriage at Stirling Castle and was gravely ill. He wrote to her:

> My Hairtie, I thank God I carrie that love and respecte unto you quhich [which], by the law of God and nature, I ought to do to my wife and mother of my children, but not for that ye are a King's dauchter, for whither ye waire a King's or a cook's daughter, ye must be all alike to me being once my wife. God is my witness I ever preferred you to all my bairnes, much more than to any subject, but if ye will ever give place to the reports of everie flattering sycophant that will persuade you that when I account well of an honest and wise servant [the Earl of Mar] for his true faithful service to me, that it is to compare or prefer him to you, then will nather ye or I be ever at reste or peace ... I have herin omitted praying God, my hairtie, to preserve you and all the bairnes, and sende me a blithe meeting with you and a couple of thaime [them]. Your own James I.[22]

In later years, King James and his 'Hartie', lived much apart, but James continued to shower his queen with tender affection. One day in June 1613 at Theobalds, Anne, aiming at a deer, killed Jewell, the King's favourite hound. He told his wife not to blame herself, "for he shold love her never the worse," and the next day he sent her a diamond worth £2,000 as "a legacie from his dead dogge". Indeed Chamberlain wrote, "love and kindness increases dayly between them."

On his way south he was bothered by sycophants swarming around him. He was given a tumultuous reception by his new subjects, and James responded as he sprinkled knighthoods like confetti; over three hundred in total were bestowed on those who had prudently taken the golden road north to greet the new monarch. This was the first time that James had travelled to England, and the richness of the country, its great mansions, its parklands, and its quaint villages, impressed him greatly. The journey took him through York, Doncaster, Worksop, the Vale of Belvoir, Newark,

Nottingham, and Hatfield. En route he would spend days in the magnificent houses of the nobility, who indulged the King in his favourite pastime of hunting. At Newark he directed that a pick-pocket be hanged without trial on April 21. He had been caught red-handed, and James, not knowing the common-law of England, acted impulsively and unwisely. He was never to repeat this mistake, for James had a tender conscience and desired to be just and merciful. At Burghley-by-Stamford, James fell from his horse and broke his collarbone, and had to travel to London in his coach suffering considerable pain. At Broxborne, Herfordshire, James issued a writ creating William Herrick of London his principal jeweller. James had a great love for jewels. At the wedding of his daughter in 1613 in the Chapel Royal at Whitehall, Elizabeth was dressed with ropes of pearls. James was covered with jewels said to value £600,000, and Queen Anne wore jewels valued at £400,000.

The summer of 1603 was intensely hot, causing the increase of the dreaded plague in the City of London. Perhaps thirty thousand Londoners died of it. Consequently James, fearful of catching the disease, decided to postpone the coronation of himself and his queen. The coronation of King James and Queen Anne took place at Westminster on 25 July 1603, a day of pouring rain. He was crowned King James I of England, but he adopted, without the consent of Parliament, the title of King of Great Britain. He had entered into his inheritance, as he said, "like a poor man wandering about forty years in a wilderness and barren soil and now arrived at the land of promise."

He was thirty-seven years of age with a broad Scots accent and, though a man of great intellect, having a quick mind and excellent concentration, he could be both uncouth and vulgar. His manners were aggressive and very uncivil. Convivial with friends, he was indifferent and sometimes hostile to the ceremony of court life. He had a profound dislike for all the fripperies of the court. Queen Elizabeth, the virgin queen, was wed unto her people, and had cultivated to perfection the royal artistry of embracing the masses, to whom she was devoted. But with James there was an aloofness which bordered on contempt and even vulgarity. He disliked court ceremony, and even more he detested having to be seen by the people. The Venetian Ambassador made the comment that King James,

> "...did not caress the people nor make them that good cheer the late Queen did, whereby she won their loves: for the English adore their sovereign ... [and] like their King to show pleasure at their devotion ... but this King manifests no taste for them."[23]

James' Court was marked by indecorousness, so much so, that when the King of Denmark visited him in 1606, even the ladies were rolling about in drunken revelry. James indulged himself in those childish games which he had never enjoyed as a child and, when not amusing himself and his queen with these foolish and elaborate masques, he would spend his time in hunting at Robert Cecil's country house of Theobalds where he was fearless in pursuit and reckless of his own safety.

As a man, James was one whom it is easy either to love or despise, but impossible to hate. Though every inch a pedant, he was human. Of cruelty, indeed, he had none. He was truly a lover of peace, *Rex Pacifus.* His instinct to sympathise warmly with anyone who spoke to him, except when annoyed or prejudiced, led to rapid and unconscious vacillations in his conduct. Choosing his favourites for no other merit but their charm as companions, he was too fond of them to deny them anything. He hated the details of administration and loved to live in the abstract heights of a general scheme. Beneath all his carelessness as to the ordering of his Court and in seeing to the execution of his commands, there lay a will stubbornly adherent to a main course of a policy, whether towards Spain, towards the Puritans, or towards Parliament.

His most fatal defect was that he could never tell a good man from a rogue, or a wise man from a fool; still less could he distinguish the great current of opinion and the main tide of political force from the bright, shallow eddies that catch and please a monarch's eye. One who judged thus of persons was not likely to understand the real problems with which his kingcraft had in fact to deal: to penetrate the soul of Puritanism, or to recognise any purpose beyond that of thwarting good government in the turbulent faction of the House of Commons.

His neglect of the affairs of state was to sow the seeds of the Civil War. In the first three years of James's English rule, each of the great problems of the coming century took an irrevocable turn. Against Puritans and against Parliament the King adopted in 1604 a position from which his stubborn character afterwards forbade him to retreat; and by the time his son succeeded him it had become a firmly established principle of royal policy. In the same year, 1604, by making peace with Spain, he prepared the way for his foolish friendship with Catholic powers that soon alienated nationalist feeling from the throne. In the winter of 1605 his attempt to secure the loyalty of Papists, by alternately holding out the olive-branch and the sword, ended in the Gunpowder Plot. This event gave only a momentary resolve in the otherwise ever-vacillating conduct of the Stuart monarchs towards their Catholic subjects. Thus all the main causes that twice combined to drive the Stuarts from the throne were, in three fatal years, set in motion by this most pacific of kings.

The English Parliament would not be browbeaten. James never learnt to understand parliaments, or indeed the country of which he was head. Elizabeth, with feminine charm and masculine energy, had dampened the fires of Puritan independence, but the arrival of a new monarch was the signal for fresh flames to burn up with inextinguishable blaze. James maintained that the king was supreme in government and law, the fount of justice, was divinely right, and could do as he pleased. The attempted interference of Parliament was to him a dangerous novelty. The royal prerogative extended over the Church, foreign policy, and the choice of his own ministers.

Elizabeth had bequeathed a divided church. On the one side were the Puritans with their 'Breeches Bible' who resented the 'rags of popery', and on the other side were the 'High Churchmen' with their 'Bishops' Bible' who, in terms of doctrine, believed what the Puritans believed, but who cherished the ritualism and the ceremonialism and the established ecclesiastical structure. Moreover, the High Churchmen were in the majority and they wanted to impose religious conformity on all. This was the most dangerous and intractable of difficulties which James inherited, but he was equal to the task. In Scotland, James had been tolerant to those who would show toleration. James believed fervently in the *via media,* and he would act as conciliator between the two factions in the Church.

The Puritans had presented him with the Millenary Petition; but the High Churchmen, represented by Archbishop Whitgift, Bancroft, Bishop of London, and the Dean of Westminster, Andrewes, were deeply alarmed by the Puritans' petition, and they lobbied the King, who called the Hampton Court Conference of 1604. James clearly enjoyed the theological chess-game of the Conference, and proved himself more than a match for his learned bishops. James was more a professor than a prince, a pacifist and not a soldier. He enjoyed the scholarly mantle thrust upon him, seeing his role as chief conciliator and chairman, inviting the representatives of the two factions to state their views. But when, on the second day, a Puritan mentioned the word 'presbyter', the hackles of King James were raised, and from that point the Conference became a charade. Thereafter, none of the Puritans' hopes were fulfilled, and the King declared, "I shall make them conform themselves, or I will harry them out of the land." At a stroke, James, the intellectual Calvinist, had isolated the Puritans and supported the High Church bishops. Indeed, James did not visit Cambridge University until 1615 because of his reluctance to visit the seedbed of Puritanism.

There were other factions that were disappointed in the early days of this Stuart king. The Roman Catholic recusants* were hoping for a relaxation of the recusancy laws which had been imposed during the reign of Elizabeth. James had declared that it was against his conscience "that the blood of any man shall be shed for diversity of opinions in religion", but now he imposed even stricter measures against priests and recusants. He urged his Protestant bishops to be more "careful, vigilant, and diligent than you have been to win souls to God". These anti-Catholic laws served only to spur on the conspirators of the Gunpowder Plot of 1605. Twice, attempts had been made upon the King's life, "to teach me," he declared, "that it was the same devil that still persecuted me, so it was one and the same God that still mightily delivered me." Following the failed plot, the oath of allegiance was required of all his Roman Catholic subjects, whereby they recognised their sovereign as their lawful king, repudiating such claims of the pope.

The Jacobean age was one of the most immoral, corrupt ages in English history, but it did produce greatness in literature and art, as in the tragedies of William Shakespeare. In *Macbeth,* Shakespeare pays constant tribute to the Scottish King and to Banquo, the mythical ancestor of the Stuarts. Shakespeare was familiar with King James's

---

* A Roman Catholic who did not attend the services of the Church of England, as was required by law.

book on demonology written in Scotland, and he was well aware of the King's great interest in witches. In addition to Shakespeare, the early seventeenth century saw the genius of Francis Bacon. However, when Bacon presented a copy of his great work, *The Novum Organum,* to James in 1620, the King said it reminded him of the peace of God, in that "it passeth all understanding"! There were also the comedies of Ben Jonson, the poetry of John Donne (of whom James was a patron), and the work of George Herbert, who wrote the most exquisite sacred poetry in our language (upon whom James conferred a sinecure worth £120 per annum); not to mention the magnificent spectacles, glorious dresses and buildings designed by Inigo Jones. It was James who introduced horse-racing to Newmarket, and indulged himself in the 'sports' of bear-baiting and cock-fighting.

In 1604, James published his classic work against tobacco-smoking. The King described tobacco-smoking as a

> custom loathsome to the eye, hateful to the nose, harmful to the braine, dangerous to the lungs ... resembling the horrible Stigian-smoke of the pit that is bottomless.

By 1616 James was fifty years of age, in poor health and in the hands of his chief physician, Theodore Turquet de Mayerne. James was suffering from gout and arthritis, and was in great pain particularly during the hours of darkness. Such was his physical weakness that he had to lean upon the young Earl of Buckingham, Sir George Villiers, prompting further speculation amongst twentieth century historians that James had homosexual tendencies: "How far this was a sexual relationship is hard to say;" and James's leaning upon Villiers for support is interpreted as "James would embrace him in public".[24] In 1617 he frankly admitted to his Council:

> I, James, am neither a god nor an angel, but a man like any other. Therefore I act like a man, and confess to loving those dear to me more than any other men. You may be sure that I love the Earl of Buckingham more than anyone else, and more than you who are here assembled ... for Jesus Christ did the same, and therefore I cannot be blamed. Christ had his John, and I have my George.[25]

In 1619 Anne lay gravely ill at Hampton Court Palace and James visited her three times, though he himself was ill. He was suffering from a painful fit of the stone and from arthritis, and many thought he was dying. His pains became more acute on account of ulcers on his hips, diarrhoea and other serious ailments. Nevertheless, he made the long journey from Newmarket to Hampton Court to see his 'Heartie'. The King was unable to be with her during her last earthly hours, nor could he attend her funeral in Westminster Abbey on 13 May, 1619. After his wife's death, James became increasingly lonely, his daughter Elizabeth being far distant in a foreign country. The last five years of the King's life were years of loneliness and pain, riddled and tormented by arthritis, so much so that he could no longer sign his own name. On 5 March 1625 he fell ill with the ague. Anthonia Fraser suggests that James had developed the 'royal disease', that is, porphyria. The symptoms were clearly evident in James's condition: colic, vomiting and diarrhoea, and abdominal pains. His urine was sometimes the purple colour of Alicante wine. Some have speculated that the King had been poisoned by Buckingham, but there is little evidence to substantiate such a theory. The King died on the Lord's Day of March 27, 1625, just before noon.

He was given a magnificent funeral costing upwards of £50,000! His body was brought to Denmark House where Dr John Donne, Dean of St Paul's, preached beside the bier as it lay in state. His catafalque* was designed by Inigo Jones. On May 7, 1625, the funeral procession, headed by the new King Charles as chief mourner walking behind the hearse, and followed by lords, privy councillors, foreign ambassadors and officials of Court, entered the Abbey of Westminster. Bishop Lancelot Andrewes was a very sick man and unable to visit the King in his dying hours. James highly esteemed Bishop Andrewes and kept sermons of the Bible translator under his pillow. The funeral sermon was therefore preached by Bishop John Williams, taking as his text 1 Kings 11:41-43 with its final verse, *And Solomon slept with his fathers and was buried in the city of David his father.* James's coffin was placed in the magnificent vault containing the remains of Henry VII and his consort, Elizabeth of York.

---

* A decorated bier on which a coffin rests in state during a funeral.

Four hundred years later, James should be remembered for his achievements in his earlier years and not for the humiliation of his final years. He was before his time in his passionate love of peace. His mind was ablaze with ideas. King James was a successful King of Scotland, maintaining his throne against all odds with intelligence and sagacity. He was the most human of our kings. To the early years belong the 'Jewel in the King's crown', the commissioning of the translation of the Bible known as the Authorised or King James Version. The Authorised Version of the Bible was the direct result of James's *via media* policy. It would be the means of uniting a divided Church, and giving to the Church one Bible. His object was to unite the rival factions of the English church, the high-church Anglicans and the low-church Puritans.

As early as 1601 he had urged a new translation upon the Kirk at Burntisland Parish Church. When the matter was raised at the Hampton Court Conference, the King was eager to respond, "I could never yet see a Bible well-translated." The translation was to be made by the most learned linguists in the universities, reviewed by the bishops and other learned churchmen, and then presented to the Privy Council, and finally ratified by royal authority.

> It is evident that James's prime motive in his instructions and care he took in his consultative work, was that the Bible should be easily understood by the ordinary people of the day. For the new Bible was above all an ornament to the English language, over ninety per cent of the words being of English derivation. It was an appropriate gift to the country from the new Arthur.[26]

> Great and manifold were the blessings, most dread Sovereign, which Almighty God, the Father of all mercies, bestowed upon us the people of England, when first he sent Your Majesty's Royal Person to rule and reign over us.
>
> ... But among all our joys, there was no one that more filled our hearts, than the blessed continuance of the preaching of God's sacred Word among us; which is that inestimable treasure, which excelleth all the riches of the earth; because the fruit thereof extendeth itself, not only to the time spent in this transitory world, but directeth and disposeth men unto that eternal happiness which is above in heaven.

> … Your Majesty did never desist to urge and to excite those to whom it was commended, that the work might be hastened, and that the business might be expedited in so decent a manner, as a matter of such importance might justly require.
>
> And now at last, by the mercy of God, and the continuance of our labours, it being brought unto such a conclusion, as that we have great hopes that the Church of England shall reap good fruit thereby; we hold it our duty to offer it to Your Majesty, not only as to our King and Sovereign, but as to the principal Mover and Author of the work.' [27]

Whilst the word "Author" owes something to sycophancy, the word "Mover" does not. James was the principal Mover, and the Authorised Version was indeed 'The Jewel in the King's crown'.

Elizabeth I , 1533-1603
Attributed to George Gower,c.1588
National Portrait Gallery, London

Sir William Cecil, who was created Baron Burghley in 1571.

Queen Elizabeth rallying her troops at Tilbury
on the eve of the Spanish Armada

Portrait of James Sixth of Scotland and First of England wearing the State robes by Daniel Mytens, 1621.

Anne of Denmark in hunting attire;
painting by Paul van Somer, 1617.

Queen Mary's room in Edinburgh Castle
where James was born on the morning of 19 June 1566.

Interior of Queen Mary's room in Edinburgh Castle.

Exterior of Queen Mary's room in Edinburgh Castle.

Henry Stuart, Lord Darnley with his younger brother, Charles Stuart; Painting by Hans Eworth, 1563.

Mary Queen of Scots in a double portrait with her son, James VI of Scotland, painted in 1583 from imagination by an unknown artist. She had not seen her son since his infancy.

A coloured drawing of the execution of Mary Queen of Scots, which took place at Fotheringhay Castle on 8 February 1587.

George Buchanan

Esmé Stuart, James's cousin and his first favourite,
created Duke of Lennox in 1580.

Mary Queen of Scots by an unknown artist.

Title page of the Works of James the First

The King and his family listening to a sermon at St. Paul's Cross. They are seated in the canopied box of the cathedral.

CHAPTER 3

Puritan Hopes and Recusant Dreams

THE first of the Stuart kings began his reign with a Pageant of Royal Progress from Berwick to London. During a month of spring weather James rode south. The land seemed bursting into bud to welcome him, growing greener each day as the ever-increasing train of courtiers wound slowly down out of the north country into the midland valleys, through excited market-places and by ancient steeples rocking with the clash of bells, and along open roads hedged with countrymen who had come in pilgrimage across whole counties. There was stag hunting through neighbouring parks, while at night, in private mansions, the regal entertainment witnessed to the solid magnificence and free loyalty of England.

The man on whom the English thus first set eyes was by no means contemptible in person, in spite of grossly course manners. He was in the prime of life, over middle height, a good horseman who was devoted to the chase, drinking hugely but never overcome by his liquor. He employed a pithy wit and a wealth of homely images and learned conceits in free and familiar discourse with all.

On his journey to the 'Promised Land', the new King had been presented with two petitions. The first was presented to him in York on the Lord's Day of the 17 April, on behalf of the English Roman Catholics. The petitioner was a Roman Catholic priest in disguise, Father Hill. His petition asked for the removal of all the penal laws against his co-religionists. Unfortunately for him, it contained a threatening biblical reference, for he reminded the new king that when the Israelites sought relief from King Jeroboam and none was granted they took "just occasion" to refuse to obey him in the future. Such threatened rebellion was too much for James, and Father Hill was placed in secure accommodation in the town jail.

The second was the Millenary Petition, so called because it pretended to express the opinion of a thousand clergy of the Established Church. Several hundred conformist Puritan clergy had met the King in the hope that the doubtful toleration afforded them within the Elizabethan establishment might under the new regime be changed for a secure and legalised framework for reform. They were serving the Episcopal Church with sufficient loyalty to her form of government and her Prayer Book service, and with a missionary zeal and pastoral energy, to which no other Church sector could pretend. The petitioners suggested that a clergyman should be allowed to choose for himself whether he would wear cap and surplice, and that he should not be required to declare his belief in the absolute truth of the whole Prayer Book, provided he signed the Articles and used the service.

The royal response would be a test of much besides for, if the new king was ready to tolerate Puritanism within the pale of the national Church, he would be ready to leave optional other matters. The Millenary Petition raised these: the disuse of the sign of the cross in baptism and the bowing at the name of Jesus, the abridgement of the service, the simplification of music and chanting, the encouragement of preaching and sermons, the prevention of ecclesiastical pluralities and sinecures, the observance of the Lord's Day, and the non-observance of saints' days. These were such as a wise monarch might have refused or left unanswered, on the grounds that any strict order favouring the Puritans on these points would give offence to many clergy and to many congregations. But the moderation of even these requests, so different from the demand for the abolition of the episcopate haughtily advanced by the Brownists, shows the humble and conformist spirit of Puritanism at this auspicious moment. Here was an opportunity that James, the peacemaker, was fated to throw away. The Petition was worded as follows:

> THE HUMBLE PETITION OF THE MINISTERS OF THE CHURCH OF ENGLAND, DESIRING REFORMATION OF CERTAIN CEREMONIES AND ABUSES OF THE CHURCH.
>
> To the most Christian and excellent prince, our gracious and dread sovereign, James by the grace of God, &c. We, the ministers of the church of England that desire reformation, wish a long,

prosperous, and happy reign over us in this life, and in the next everlasting salvation.

Most gracious and dread sovereign, seeing it hath pleased the Divine Majesty, to the great comfort of all good Christians, to advance your Highness, according to your just title, to the peaceable government of this church and commonwealth of England; we, the ministers of the Gospel in this land, neither as factious men affecting a popular party in the church, nor as schismatics aiming at the dissolution of the state ecclesiastical; but as the faithful servants of Christ, and loyal subjects to your majesty, desiring and longing for the redress of divers abuses of the church, could do no less, in our obedience to God, service to your majesty, love to his church, than acquaint your princely majesty with our particular griefs. For, as your princely pen writeth, “The King, as a good physician, must first know what peccant humours his patient naturally is most subject unto, before he can begin his cure.” And, although divers of us that sue for reformation have formerly, in respect of the times, subscribed to the Book, some upon protestation, some upon exposition given them, some with condition, rather than the church should have been deprived of their labour and ministry; yet now, we, to the number of more than a thousand, of your majesty’s subjects and ministers, all groaning as under a common burden of human rites and ceremonies, do, with one joint consent, humble ourselves at your majesty’s feet to be eased and relieved in this behalf. Our humble suit, then, unto your majesty is, that [of] these offences following, some may be removed, some amended, some qualified:

I. *In the church-service:* That the Cross in baptism, interrogatories ministered to infants, Confirmation, as superfluous, may be taken away: baptism not to be ministered by women, and so explained: the cap and surplice not urged: that examination may go before the communion: that it be ministered with a sermon: that divers terms of *priests* and *absolution,* and some other used, with the ring in marriage, and other such like in the Book, may be corrected: the longsomeness of service abridged: church-songs and music moderated to better-edification: that the Lord’s day be not profaned, the rest upon holy-days not so strictly urged: that there be an uniformity of doctrine prescribed: no popish opinion to be any more taught or defended: no ministers charged to teach their people to bow at the name of Jesus: that the canonical Scriptures only be read in the church.

II. *Concerning church-ministers:* That none hereafter be admitted into the ministry but able and sufficient men; and those to preach diligently, and especially upon the Lord's day: that such as be already entered, and cannot preach, may either be removed, and some charitable course taken with them for their relief; or else to be forced, according to the value of their livings, to maintain preachers: that non-residency be not permitted: the King Edward's statute for the lawfulness of ministers' marriage be revived: that ministers be not urged to subscribe but, according to the law, to the Articles of Religion, and the king's supremacy only.

III. *For church-livings and maintenance:* That bishops leave their commendams; some holding prebends, some parsonages, some vicarages with their bishoprics: that double-beneficed men be not suffered to hold, some two, some three benefices with cure: and some two, three, or four dignities besides: that impropriations annexed to bishoprics and colleges be demised only to the preachers incumbents, for the old rent: that the impropriations of laymen's fees may be charged with a sixth or seventh part of the worth, to the maintenance of the preaching minister.

IV. *For church-discipline:* That the discipline and excommunication may be administered according to Christ's own institution; or, at the least, that enormities may be redressed: as, namely, that excommunication come not forth under the name of lay persons, chancellors, officials, &c. That men be not excommunicated for trifles, and twelve-penny matters: that non be excommunicated without consent of his pastor: that the officers be not suffered to extort unreasonable fees: that none having jurisdiction, or registers' places, put out the same to farm: that divers popish canons (as for restraint of marriage at certain times) be reversed: that the longsomeness of suits in ecclesiastical courts, which hang sometimes two, three, four, five, six, or seven years, may be restrained: that the oath *ex officio,* whereby men are forced to accuse themselves, may be more sparingly used: that licences for marriage, without bans asked, be more cautiously granted.

These, with such other abuses yet remaining, and practised in the church of England, we are able to show not to be agreeable to the Scriptures, if it please your Highness farther to hear us, or more at large by writing to be informed, or by conference among the learned to be resolved. And yet we doubt not but that, without any farther process, your majesty, of whom Christian judgment we have received so good a taste already, is able of yourself to judge of the equity of this cause. God, we trust, hath appointed your Highness our physician to heal these diseases. And we say with Mordecai to Esther, "Who knoweth, whether you are come to the kingdom for such a time?" Thus your majesty shall do that which, we are persuaded, shall be acceptable to God; honourable to your majesty in all succeeding ages; profitable to his church, which shall be thereby increased; comfortable to your ministers, which shall be no more suspended, silenced, disgraced, imprisoned for men's traditions; and prejudicial to none, but to those that seek their own quiet, credit, and profit in the world. Thus, with all dutiful submission, referring ourselves to your majesty's pleasure, for your gracious answer, as God shall direct you; we most humbly recommend your Highness to the Divine Majesty; whom we beseech for Christ's sake to dispose your royal heart to do herein what shall be to his glory, the good of his church, and your endless comfort.

Your majesty's most humble subjects, the ministers of the Gospel, that desire not a disorderly innovation, but a due and godly reformation.

When Elizabeth died, Protestantism was so firmly rooted in the intelligence and passions of the city populace that there was not an important town in England where a Catholic priest could prudently have shown himself in the streets; but the English rustics, especially north of the Trent and west of Avon, had less understanding of the religious questions that divided Europe, and were ready to swallow any opinion provided for them by their betters. They preferred the ancestral forms of religion, but the vast majority were unable to afford the expensive privilege of recusancy. By the Act of Uniformity, passed at the beginning of Elizabeth's reign, every person over the age of sixteen was compelled to attend his or her local church on the

Lord's Day or holy days. Protestant communion had also to be taken at least twice a year. Failure to do so involved fines of a shilling a week in 1559, which was a considerable sum in those days when a yeoman by definition was a man with an annual disposable income of forty shillings.

A recusant, strictly speaking, was a Roman Catholic who refused to attend church, and was fined for that 'privilege'. The numerical strength of the Roman Catholics was quite unknown, and in any case the 'recusants' were only part of the Roman Catholic body. The recusants became a prime source of revenue for the Exchequer!

'Church Papists', as those were called who consented to attend the national worship but secretly considered themselves to be Roman Catholics, could not legally be distinguished from Protestants, and were therefore a wholly incalculable force. Some made no pretence of loyalty to the established order, attended church merely to avoid the fines, walked out ostentatiously before the sermon, and alarmed their Protestant neighbours with blood-curdling announcements that the good times of Queen Mary were coming back, when "faggots should be deere" yet. On the other hand many of these 'Church Papists' were slowly adapting themselves to the English communion.

Scattered throughout the land whole villages adhered to the old religion, under the protective and coercive influence of a Catholic squire or nobleman. In some of the northern counties, half the landowners attended the Mass. The central tenet of Rome's teaching was, and is, that her adherents hear Mass every Sunday and holy day. But nowhere in England could Mass be legally celebrated. To hear Mass was a felony punishable by heavy fines and jail. The ancient halls were maintained by Roman Catholic squires as asylums for priests, yeoman farmers and labourers, who decidedly preferred the old forms of worship. In these Roman Catholic estates, despite writs from vigilant magistrates, the priests were safely stowed with the pyx and chasuble in the passage between the great chimney and outer wall. Thus the priest would hide in his 'priest-hole', but at night would emerge to perform his nefarious enchantments under the thatch of the cottages around. In such a climate how could the government know exactly who was and who was not a Papist at heart? All recusants were Roman Catholics, but not all Catholics came out into the open.

To save England from the recovery by Rome, the only alternative to Penal Laws would have been the confiscation of Roman Catholic estates. The object of the loosely administered Penal Code, passed by Elizabeth's Parliaments, was three-fold. *First*, in order to prevent the papal party from seizing political power, or spreading the personal authority of Roman Catholics in the land, recusants were made to confine their activity and influence to their own estates, by laws which excluded them from any post in national or local government, and even forbade them to travel five miles from their place of residence without licenses signed by neighbouring magistrates.

The *second* policy was to penalise even those Roman Catholics who stayed quietly at home, by fines for not attending church. The fines were collected in different ways from different classes. The richest men in England were liable to pay £20 a month for the 'privilege' of staying away from church on the Lord's Day; lesser Roman Catholic landowners could purchase the same immunity by giving up two-thirds of their yearly rental; but heavy fines were also collected from farmers and cottagers. And yet the levy of these fines was very irregular. In 1606 only one hundred and sixty-two gentlemen paid the two-thirds of their rental, and less than £5,000 from all classes together reached the treasury. Scarcely one recusant in five was named. Moreover, it was almost impossible to impose a fine upon a recusant woman, since the 'weaker vessel' had no rights in law. Thus Roman Catholic women who ran large households played a vital part in hiding Rome's priests. It was the women who nurtured and protected the Jesuit missionaries and spread Catholic dogma through their households.

Two women stand out, and both were to play a prominent part in the Gunpowder Treason. Elizabeth Vaux was the sole head of a large Roman Catholic household, Harrowden Hall, near Wellingborough. She felt a call to protect and nurture the Roman Catholic priesthood. In the extensive rebuilding of Harrowden Hall, she had hiding places constructed within the fabric of the building, so that she was able to maintain a Jesuit college in the heart of England. In her many priest holes, men like Father John Gerard were sequestered away. Then, there was the spinster Anne Vaux, the sister-in-law of Elizabeth. Anne posed as Mistress Perkins, the sister of Father Henry Garnet, the Superior of the Jesuits. Thus

Mistress Perkins used her considerable fortune to rent houses in which Garnet's Jesuits might gather in safety. Baddesley Clinton was one such house, a secluded Tudor mansion in Warwickshire surrounded by a moat, in which she was able to conceal twelve or more priests. Another house she rented was White Webbs on Enfield Chase. 'Visitors' to White Webbs included her two first cousins, Robert Catesby and Francis Tresham. There is no doubt that the continuance of the Roman Catholic faith in England was due to the courage of its women, and in particular to Elizabeth and Anne Vaux.

The *third* method by which the spread of Roman Catholic principles was checked was the proscription of the Mass and priesthood. While every priest who exercised his functions in England and every layman who abetted him, was doomed by the statute to die the death of a traitor, in practice these bloody laws were kept suspended over the heads of the priests and their congregations, serving only to check the boldness of their propaganda and the publicity of their worship. While no Roman Catholic service was openly held, except in the chapels of the foreign ambassadors at the capital, every day Mass was heard in garrets and libraries by hundreds of little congregations, none of whom had to fear the penalties incurred, as long as they did not parade their breach of the law. Similarly, no systematic attempt was made to hunt the priests out of England. When in 1604 King James heard that his judges had taken upon themselves to hang several priests and their abettors in the western counties, where the Roman Catholics had seemed to them too prominent, he at once put a stop to these legalised atrocities, and would not allow them to be renewed even after the Gunpowder Plot. But as long as the laws themselves remained unrepealed, every zealous Roman Catholic, holding his life and property at the mercy of the Government, felt the restraint implied.

The political strength of the Roman Catholics as a danger to the state was even harder to calculate than their numbers as a religious body; for, on the question of loyalty to the state, they were divided between two parties and policies, and none knew to which side the bulk of the laity, recusants and conformists alike, would in the hour of trial adhere. The two parties were the Jesuits and the secular clergy.

In the middle of Elizabeth's reign, the secular priests, then in sole charge of the English flock, had bowed to the Protestant 'storm' and sought safety in diminished vigour; but it was then that the

Jesuits had landed in England and imposed themselves on clergy and laity alike with their zeal as missionaries and their authority as the Pope's messengers. Their influence was further enhanced by their connection with the Hispanic political conspiracies. When their policy of rebellion, assassination, and foreign conquests brought down the Penal Laws upon the whole Roman Catholic body, it merely confirmed to the Jesuits the need to overthrow the 'heretical' state!

The conspirators in England, whose hopes had been dashed by James's strong declaration of his Protestantism, had applied to Pope Clement VIII to put a bar in the way of his mounting the English throne. He sent over to Garnet, Provincial of the Jesuits in England, two bulls of his apostolic authority—one addressed to the Romish clergy, the other to the nobility and laity—and both of the same tenor. The bulls enjoined those to whom they were directed, in virtue of their obedience, at whatever time "that miserable woman", for so he called Elizabeth, should depart this life, to permit no one to ascend her throne, how near soever in blood, unless he swore, according to the example of the former monarchs of England, not only to tolerate the Roman Catholic faith, but to the utmost of his power to uphold and advance it.

At the time of James I's accession, this struggle for authority was at its height. The nominal head of the English papists was Blackwell, who stood midway between the two parties, but owed his position to Parsons, the founder of Jesuit power in England. The Jesuit plan was the overthrow of the State by the use of war and persecution. To the Jesuit, Protestantism would involve all the English in damnation, and therefore was it unpatriotic to save them by introducing Spanish spearmen into their homes, and driving James from the throne in favour of a Roman Catholic prince? It was unsafe for the Government to rely on the loyalty of the secular priests for, though their leaders opposed the Jesuit schemes, nearly all the rank and file who had now replaced the old Marian priesthood had been educated at Jesuit Colleges on the continent, and learned the Spanish theory of propaganda by sword and stake. The Jesuit policy induced statesmen to prevent the spread of Catholicism by the Penal Laws; but the Penal Laws, because they prevented the spread of Catholicism, could well justify to any whole-hearted Papist the Jesuit policy. Until Protestantism was either overthrown or firmly established in the land, attempts at toleration would defeat their own ends.

But James, whilst still James VI of Scotland, made the mistake of renewing diplomatic relations with the Pope, and made promise of toleration and State preferment for 'Church Papists'; but his promise was widely misinterpreted by the wider Catholic body as a pledge to remit recusancy fines. Therefore, when Elizabeth died, James received an enthusiastic welcome from many Roman Catholic households who were anticipating better days. Even the Jesuits led by Garnet drew back from opposing James's accession because Philip III of Spain hoped to secure peace between Spain and England.

In the last year of Queen Elizabeth's life, rumours were rife that King James VI had made promises of toleration once he ascended the English throne, and many were hopeful of his own conversion to the historic 'Mother Church'. Father Oswald Tesimond, a Jesuit priest in Northumberland, declared that James would free Rome's subjects from bondage and would admit them to every kind of office and honour in the state. Thus Tesimond filled the hearts of Roman Catholics with the highest hopes. But King James never had any plans to become a Roman Catholic. In his correspondence with Robert Cecil, he laments 'the daily increase that I hear of popery in England'. And again, 'I condemn their doctrine, I detest their conversation,' and of the Jesuits he says, 'that generation of vipers trading in the blood and crowns of Princes.' Yet as much as he loathed the Catholic priests and the dangers they posed, he shrank back from seeing them 'die by the dozen'. James, likewise, would rather have them exiled from the land than executed.

> I will never allow in my conscience that the blood of any man shall be shed for diversity of opinions in religion, but I should be sorry that Catholics should so multiply as they might be able to practise their old principles upon us.[1]

No sooner had James reached London, than the hopes of many Roman Catholics were thwarted. Fines continued to be collected from recusants, and many of the secular priests were involved in plots and conspiracies to seize the person of the King. One of the plots, known as the 'treason of the Bye', was hatched by Father Watson and involved capturing the King and holding him prisoner in the Tower of London until he granted a wide series of demands to the Roman Catholics including, of course, full toleration. Another plot, known as 'the treason of the Main', involved Lord Cobham and in some way Sir Walter Raleigh, whereby they intended to eliminate the King and his offspring and elevate Lady Arabella Stuart to the throne. These plots were reported to Cecil by the Jesuits, who thus temporarily gained favour with James. Those involved in both the Bye and Main plots were arrested in July, held prisoner and then tried in the autumn. All were sentenced to death, but Lord Cobham and Sir Walter Raleigh were later reprieved. This betrayal by the two Jesuits, Fathers Gerard and Garnet, deceived James into believing that the time was ripe for his scheme of toleration and conciliation. King James was grateful and, as part of his coronation festivities, he allowed pardons to recusants and remitted their fines for a year.

James now saw an opportunity to exercise his own broader philosophy of kingcraft. His plan was to tolerate the private exercise of religion, on condition, first that all the Roman Catholics should transfer their loyalty from pope to king; and secondly, that there should be no increase in their numbers. Thus, he would grant to Roman Catholics the privilege of a tolerated minority status. He would allow them to have "a Mass in a corner", that is, in a private house. But this scheme was doomed to fail, for the granting of toleration would most certainly increase their numbers. The Church Papists would reveal their Romish hearts! As soon as the recusancy fines were remitted, the number of Roman Catholics seemed to double. The sleeping Church Papists immediately disappeared from the parish church, and now that laws against the Mass were no longer enforced, vast numbers gathered to celebrate their repeated sacrifice of Christ, which to Protestants was an abomination and a denial of the Gospel. The priests who had for long been hidden in the homes of wealthy Catholics and had operated under the cloak of darkness, now emerged from their dark sequestrations and crept from home to home to secure converts to the 'old religion'. It was not long before James saw the plan had utterly failed.

Within weeks of the Hampton Court Conference, on 19 February 1604, under the direction of Cecil, a proclamation appeared ordering all Roman Catholic priests to quit the country. He announced his "utter detestation" of the Papist religion, which he condemned as "superstitious". In November the levy of fines from lay recusants was re-introduced. He had effectively crushed those Roman Catholic hopes of liberty of conscience. Letters were intercepted from Rome granting a dispensation to Roman Catholics to profess the Protestant faith for a time, provided they cherish in their hearts a loyalty to Rome, and let slip no opportunity their disguise might offer them for advancing her interests. A crisis was evidently approaching, indeed a crisis within the Roman Catholic priesthood within England. Father Tesimond declared that the King,

> protested most vehemently that he would take it as an extreme insult if anyone imagined that either then or at any time in the past, he had entertained the slightest intention of tolerating their religion.[2]

And all the while, his own wife, the pro-Spanish Queen, still wrote adoringly to the Pope and continued to hear mass in private!

On the one hand, there were some of the Jesuits who held to the sacred tenets of Rome and spread them wherever possible, and would die for the cause. Chief of their number was Father Robert Parsons, who supported the power of the Pope to depose sovereigns. On the other hand, there were the Appellants, who believed in establishing some kind of compromise with the state and pledging their loyalty to the government, even to the extent of painting the Jesuits to the government as treacherous emissaries of the Pope. Both parties sought to preserve Roman Catholicism within England.

The Jesuit party regarded James as a heretic, and they had not the least intention of pledging loyalty to King James. The English Jesuits were left with the two bulls of Clement VIII and the good wishes of Philip II as their only weapons for carrying out their general enterprise of restoring their church to its former supremacy in England. They did not despair, however. The Jesuits are never more formidable than when they are stripped of all external means of doing harm. At such times of dire extremity they devise the vastest schemes, and execute them with the most daring courage. They would inflict upon England a ruin sudden and terrible, like that which Philip's fleet would have inflicted had not the "winds become Lutheran". Those recusant dreams and Jesuit plots would continue to fester throughout the early months of James' reign, and reach their fruition in the Gunpowder Treason, to which we shall return in chapter six.

Hampton Court Palace

Hampton Court Palace

Great Hall, Hampton Court

Royal Chapel, Hampton Court

CHAPTER 4

Royal Charades—
The Hampton Court Conference

On his way to London, King James I had been presented with the 'Millenary Petition', as of a thousand—though indeed there were but seven hundred and fifty preachers' hands involved from some twenty-five counties of England. This was presented by Arthur Hildersham and Stephen Egerton on behalf of the Presbyterian and Puritan parties in England.

It is not certain whether the Hampton Court Conference was called by the King's favour, by the mediation of the lords of his council, by the bishops, or by the 'Millenary Petition'. It is thought the last is most probable. And, by whatever means the conference was called, it had been set for 1 November 1603, but had to be deferred because of the ravages of the plague. Throughout May and June, between 112 and 158 deaths per week were being reported, and by the end of the year some 30,000 souls had fallen victim. Thus the conference was delayed until the New Year, and the venue chosen, Hampton Court, was far from the pestilent stench of plague-stricken London.

Prince Henry accompanied his father to the conference. King James, wrapped in furs against the cold, presided over a series of theological discussions which were intended to silence the Puritan element in the Protestant Church.

The bishops were determined to oppose all compromise. When Cartwright had made his Presbyterian attack on the authority of the bishops, they had countered with the loftier pretensions that Episcopal government is of Divine origin! Bancroft, Bishop of London, the champion of the new theory, took the lead at Hampton Court. On the second day of the session, when the principal demands of the Millenary Petition were to be discussed, he began by asking James to silence the Puritan divines on the high ground that Canon Law forbade schismatics to be heard against their bishops, and then tried to raise a silly laugh against the 'Turkey gowns' in which the Puritans had thought fit to appear at the conference. But James was not going to lose the chance of a disputation. Rebuking Bancroft's unfairness, he assumed the part of a good-humoured and talkative umpire of debate, hearing all in full, but deciding point after point against the Puritan spokesman, Dr Reynolds. The session, however, came to a stormier close. Reynolds proposed that the lower clergy should have the right of meeting in conference, and that the bishops should consult the synod of their diocese. At the word synod, redolent to James of the daily humiliations of his youth among the rude lieutenants of Knox, the petulance that was always chafing under the crust of his learning burst out in his native fury. "If you aim at a Scottish Presbytery," he cried, "it agreeth as well with monarchy, as God and the devil." Seizing up his hat to dismiss the assembly, he vented his spleen against the Scottish Presbyterians: "How they used the poor lady, my mother, is not known, and how they dealt with me in my minority. I thus apply it … No bishop, no king … Well, Doctor, have you anything more to say?" "No more, if it please your Majesty." "If this be all your party hath to say, I will make them conform themselves, or else I will harry them out of the land." Thus, in two minutes he had sealed his own fate and that of England.

The following account of the conference is taken from William Barlow's, *The Summe and Substance of the Conference,* London, 1608,[1] which is perhaps prejudiced against the Puritans. The account is supportive of the bishops, cringingly sycophantic, and damaging to the credibility of the Puritan delegation. Nevertheless it is the chief and fullest account of the verbal exchanges between the King and the Puritan representatives. It is reproduced in full, because the transcript of the proceedings clearly show that King James was an astute theologian and erudite debater, and more than a match for his sycophantic bishops.

The date for conference was now fixed for 14 January, and the following persons were involved:

FOR CONFORMITY: Archbishop of Canterbury, Whitgift; the Bishops of London, Bancroft; of Durham, Matthews; of Winchester, Bilson; of Worcester, Babington; of St David's, Rudd; of Chichester, Watson; of Carlisle, Robinson; of Peterborough, Dove. The Deans of the Chapel; of Christ-Church; of Worcester; of Westminster, Andrews; of St Paul's, Overall; of Chester, Barlow; of Salisbury, Bridges;[2] and of Windsor, Drs. Field and King.

AGAINST CONFORMITY: Dr Reynolds and Dr Sparks; Mr. Knewstubs and Mr. Chaderton. These remaining in a room outside, were not called in the first day.

MODERATOR: King James I;

OBSERVERS: All the lords of the Privy Council.

THE FIRST DAY OF THE CONFERENCE was opened by King James himself. His majesty began the Conference with these remarks:

> It is no novel device, but according to the example of all Christian princes, for kings to take the first course for the establishing of the church, both in doctrine and policy, ... in this land, King Henry VIII toward the end of his reign, altered much, King Edward VI more, Queen Mary reversed all, and, lastly, Queen Elizabeth (of famous memory) settled religion as now it standeth.
>
> Herein I am happier than they, because they were fain to alter things they found established; whereas I see yet no such cause to change, as to confirm what I find well-settled already. For, blessed be God's gracious goodness, who hath brought me into the promised land, where religion is purely professed, where I sit amongst grave, learned, and reverend men, not as before, elsewhere, a king without state, without honour, without order, where beardless boys would brave us to face.
>
> And, I assure you, we have not called this assembly for any innovation; for we acknowledge the government ecclesiastical, as now it is, to have been approved by manifold blessings from God himself, both for the increase of the Gospel, and with a most happy and glorious peace. Yet because nothing can be absolutely ordered, but that something may be added thereunto, and corruption in any state (as in the body of man) will insensibly grow either through time or persons; and because we have received many complaints since our first entrance into this

kingdom, of many disorders and much disobedience to the laws, with a great falling away to popery; our purpose therefore is, like a good physician, to examine and try the complaints, and fully to remove the occasion thereof if scandalous, cure them if dangerous, and take knowledge of them if but frivolous; ... For this cause we have called you, bishops and deans, in, severally by yourselves, not to be confronted by the contrary opponents; that if anything shall be found meet to be redressed, it might be done without any visible alteration.

Particularly, there be some special points herein I desire to be satisfied, and which may be reduced to three heads:

1. Concerning the Book of Common Prayer, and Divine Service used in the church.
2. Excommunication in ecclesiastical courts.
3. The providing of fit and able ministers for Ireland.

In the Common-Prayer Book I require satisfaction about three things:

First, about Confirmation. For the very name thereof, if arguing a confirming of baptism, as if this sacrament without it were of no validity, is plainly blasphemous. For though at the first use thereof in the church it was thought necessary that baptised infants, who formerly had answered by their *patrini,* should, when come to years of discretion, after their profession made by themselves, be confirmed with the blessing of the bishop, I abhor the abuse wherein it is made a sacrament, or corroboration to baptism.

Second, as for Absolution, I know not how it is used in our church, but have heard it likened unto the Pope's pardons. There be indeed two kinds thereof from God: One *general;* all prayers and preaching importing an absolution: The other *particular,* to special parties, having committed a scandal, and repenting. Otherwise where excommunication precedes not, in my judgment there needs no absolution.

Third, Private Baptism is the third thing wherein I would be satisfied in the Common-Prayer. If called *private,* that any beside a lawful minister may baptise, I utterly dislike it.

And here his majesty grew somewhat earnest in his expressions, against the baptising by women and laics (laymen).

> In the second head of Excommunication, I offer two things to be considered of: First, the matter; Secondly, the persons.
>
> For the First: I would be satisfied whether it be executed (as it is complained of to me) in light causes, and that too commonly, which causeth the undervaluing thereof.
>
> For the persons: I would be resolved, why chancellors and commissaries, being laymen, should do it, and not rather the bishops themselves, or some minister of gravity and account, deputed by them for the more dignity to so high and weighty a censure. As for providing ministers for Ireland, I shall refer it, in the last day's Conference, to a consultation.

Archbishop of Canterbury, addressing himself to the King on his knees, replied:

> Confirmation hath been used in the catholic church ever since the apostles; and it is a very untrue suggestion (if any have informed your Highness), that the church of England holds baptism imperfect without it, as adding to the virtue and strength thereof.

Bishop of London responded:

> The authority of Confirmation depends not only on antiquity, and the practice of the primitive church, but is an apostolic institution, named in express words, 'Of the doctrine of baptisms…'(Hebrews 6.2), and so did Mr. Calvin expound the very place, earnestly wishing the restitution thereof in the Reformed churches.

The Bishop of Carlisle is said gravely and learnedly to have urged the same, and the Bishop of Durham noted something out of St Matthew for the imposition of hands on children.

The conclusion was this, "For the fuller explanation *that we make Confirmation neither a sacrament nor a corroboration thereof,* their lordships should consider whether it might not without alteration (whereof his Majesty was still very wary) be entitled *an Examination with a confirmation.*

Archbishop of Canterbury:

> As for the point of Absolution, wherein your majesty desires satisfaction: it is clear from all abuse or superstition, as it is used in our church of England, as will appear on the reading

both of the Confession and Absolution following it, in the beginning of the Communion Book.

Here the King perused both, and returned.

HIS MAJESTY:

I like and approve them, finding it to be very true what you say.

BISHOP OF LONDON:

It becometh us to deal plainly with your majesty. There is also in the book a more particular and personal Absolution in the *Visitation of the sick.*

Here the Dean of the Chapel turned unto it and read it.

BISHOP OF LONDON:

Not only the Confessions of Augusta, Boheme, and Saxon, retain and allow it, but Mr. Calvin also doth approve both such a general and such a private (for so he terms it) Confession and Absolution.

HIS MAJESTY:

I exceedingly well approve it, being an apostolic and godly ordinance, given in the name of Christ, to one that desireth it, upon the clearing of his conscience.

The conclusion was this, that the bishops should consult, whether unto the Rubric of the General Absolution, these words, "Remission of sins," might be added for explanation-sake.

ARCHBISHOP OF CANTERBURY:

To the point of Private Baptism: the administration thereof by women and lay persons is not allowed in the practice of the church, but inquired of, and censured by bishops in their visitations.

HIS MAJESTY:

The words of the book cannot but intend a permission of women and private persons to baptise.

Bishop of Worcester:

> The doubtful words may be pressed to that meaning; yet the compilers of the book did not so intend them, as appeareth by their contrary practice. But they propounded them ambiguously, because otherwise (perhaps) the book would not (then) have passed the parliament. To this he cited the testimony of the Archbishop of York.

Bishop of London:

> Those reverend men intended not by ambiguous terms to deceive any, but thereby intended a permission of private persons to baptise, in case of necessity. [Here he produced the letters of some of those first compilers.] This is agreeable to the practice of the ancient church, when three thousand being baptised in a day, Acts ii.41, (which for the apostles alone to do, was the least improbable,) some, being neither priests nor bishops, must be presumed employed therein; and some Fathers are of the same opinion.

Here he spake much, and earnestly about the necessity of baptism.

His Majesty:

> That in the Acts was an act extraordinary, and done before a church was settled and grounded; wherefore no sound reasoning thence to a church stablished and flourishing. I maintain the necessity of baptism, and always thought the place, John iii.5, "Except one be born again of water,"&c. was meant thereof. It may seem strange to you, my lords, that I think you in England give too much to baptism, seeing, fourteen months ago, in Scotland, I argued with my divines there for attributing too little unto it; insomuch that a pert minister asked me, if I thought baptism so necessary, that, if omitted, the child should be damned. I answered, "No: but if you, called to baptise a child, though privately, refuse to come, I think you shall be damned." But this necessity of baptism I so understand, that if necessary to be had, if lawfully to be had; that is, ministered by lawful ministers, by whom alone, and no private persons in any case, it may be administered: though I utterly dislike all re-baptisation on those whom women or laics (laymen) have baptised.

BISHOP OF WINCHESTER:

> To deny private persons to baptise in case of necessity, were to cross all antiquity, and the common practice of the church; it being a rule agreed on amongst divines, that the minister is not of the essence of the sacrament.

HIS MAJESTY:

> Though he be not of the essence of the sacrament, yet is he of the essence of the right and lawful ministry thereof, according to Christ's commission to his disciples, "Go preach, and baptise," &c. Matt. xxviii.19.

The result was this, to consult, whether in the Rubric or Private Baptism, which leaves it indifferently to all, these words, "Curate or lawful minister," may be inserted..

For the point of Excommunication, his majesty propounded, whether in cases of lesser moment the name might not be altered, and the same censure retained? Secondly. Whether, in place thereof, another coercion, equivalent thereunto, might not be invented. Which all sides easily yielded unto, as long and often desired; and so was the end of the first day's Conference.

THE SECOND DAY OF THE CONFERENCE at Hampton Court, began on Monday, January 16. They all met in the same place, with all the deans and doctors mentioned above. Patrick Galloway, minister of Perth, in Scotland, was also allowed to be present; and Prince Harry, the King's son, sat on a stool by his father.

The King made a pithy speech to the same purpose that he had made the first day, differing only in the conclusion thereof. It was an address to the four opposers of conformity, there present, whom he understood the most grave, learned, and modest of the aggrieved sort, professing himself ready to hear at large what they could object, and willed them to begin.

DR REYNOLDS:

> All things disliked or questioned may be reduced to these four heads:

1. That the doctrine of the church might be preserved in purity, according to God's word.
2. That good pastors might be planted in all churches to preach the same.
3. That the church-government might be sincerely ministered according to God's word.
4. That the Book of Common-Prayer might be fitted to more increase of piety.

For the First: May your majesty be pleased, that the Book of Articles of Religion, concluded on 1562, may be explained where obscure, enlarged where defective; namely, whereas it is said, article XVI "After we have received the Holy Ghost, we may depart from grace"; those words may be explained with this or the like addition, "Yet neither totally nor finally." To which end it would do very well, if the nine orthodoxal assertions concluded at Lambeth might be inserted into the Book of Articles.

Secondly. Whereas it is said in article XXIII that it is not lawful for any *in* the congregation to preach, before he be lawfully called; these words ought to be altered, because implying one *out of* the congregation may preach, though not lawfully called.

Thirdly. In article XXV there seemeth a contradiction, one passage therein confessing Confirmation to be a depraved imitation of the apostles, and another grounding it in their example.

BISHOP OF LONDON:

May your majesty be pleased, that the canon may be remembered: *Schismatici contra episcopos non sunt audiendi.* And there is another decree of a very ancient council, that no man should be admitted to speak against that whereunto he hath formerly subscribed. And as for you, Dr Reynolds, and your sociates, how much are ye bound to his majesty's clemency, permitting you, contrary to the statute *primo Elizabathae,* so freely to speak against the Liturgy and discipline established! Fain would I know the end you aim at, and whether you be not of Mr. Cartwright's mind, who affirmed, that we ought in ceremonies to conform to the Turks than to the papists. I doubt you approve his position, because here appearing before his majesty in Turkey-grograins[3], not in your scholastic habits, according to the order of the universities.

HIS MAJESTY:

My Lord Bishop, something in your passion I may excuse, and something I must mislike. I may excuse you thus far, that I think you have just cause to be moved, in respect that they traduce the well-settled government, and also proceed in so indirect a course, contrary to their own pretence, and the intent of this meeting. I mislike your sudden interruption of Dr Reynolds, whom you should have suffered to have taken his liberty; for there is no order, nor can be any effectual issue of disputation, if each party be not suffered, without chopping, to speak at large. Wherefore, either let the Doctor proceed, or frame your answer to his motions already made, although some of them are very needless.

BISHOP OF LONDON:

Upon the first motion concerning falling from grace, may your majesty be pleased to consider how many in these days neglect holiness of life, presuming or persisting in grace upon predestination: "If I shall be saved, I shall be saved." A desperate doctrine, contrary to good divinity, wherein we should reason rather *ascendedo* than *descendendo,* from our obedience to God and love to our neighbour, to our election and predestination. As for the doctrine of the Church of England touching predestination; it is in the very next paragraph, namely, "We must receive God's promises in such wise as they be generally set forth to us in Holy Scripture, and in our doings the will of God is to be followed which we have expressly declared unto us in the word of God."

HIS MAJESTY:

I approve it very well, as consonant with the place of Paul, "Work out your salvation with fear and trembling." Yet let it be considered of, whether any thing were meet to be added for clearing of the doctor's doubt, by putting in the word "often", or the like. Mean time, I wish that the doctrine of predestination may be tenderly handled, lest on the one side God's omnipotency be questioned by impeaching the doctrine of his eternal predestination, or on the other side a desperate presumption arreared (raised), by inferring the necessary certainty of persisting in grace.

Bishop of London:

> The second objection of the doctor's is in vain; it being the doctrine and practice of the Church of England, that none but a licensed minister may preach, nor administer the Lord's Supper.

His Majesty:

> As for Private Baptism, I have already with the bishops taken order for the same.

Then came they to the second point of Confirmation: and, upon the perusal of the words of the article, his majesty concluded the pretended contradiction a cavil.

Bishop of London:

> Confirmation is not so much founded on the place in the Acts of the Apostles, but upon Hebrews vi.2; which was the opinion (beside the judgment of the Fathers) of Mr. Calvin, on Hebrews vi.2; and Dr Fulk, on Acts viii.17; neither needeth there any further proof, seeing (as I suppose) he that objected this holds not Confirmation unlawful; but he and his party are vexed that the use thereof is not in their own hands, for every pastor to confirm his own parish; for then it would be accounted an apostolic institution, if Dr Reynolds were pleased but to speak his thoughts therein.

Dr Reynolds:

> Indeed, seeing some dioceses of a bishop hath therein six hundred parishes, it is a thing very inconvenient to permit Confirmation to the bishop alone; and I suppose it impossible that he can take due examination of them all which come to be confirmed.

Here the Bishop of London thought himself touched, because there were about six hundred and nine in his diocese.

Bishop of London:

> To the matter of fact, I answer, that bishops in their visitations appoint either their chaplains, or some other ministers, to examine them which are to be confirmed, and lightly confirm none but the testimony of the parsons and curates, where the children are bred

and brought up. To the opinion I answer, that none of all the Fathers ever admitted any to confirm but bishops alone. Yea, even St Jerome himself (otherwise no friend to bishops) confesseth the execution thereof was restrained to bishops only.

BISHOP OF WINCHESTER:

Dr Reynolds, I would fain have you, with all your learning, show where ever Confirmation was used in ancient times by any other but bishops. They used it, partly to examine children, and, after examination, by imposition of hands, (the Jewish ceremony of blessing,) to bless and pray over them: and partly to try whether they had been baptized in the right form or no. For in former ages some baptized (as they ought) "in the name of the Father, Son, and Holy Ghost". Some (as the Arians) "in the name of the Father" as the greater, "and the Son" as the less. Some "in the name of the Father, by the Son, in the Holy Ghost". Some not in the name of the Trinity, but only "in the death of Christ". Whereupon catholic bishops were constrained to examine them who were baptized *in remotis,* concerning their baptism, if right, to confirm them, if amiss, to instruct them.

HIS MAJESTY:

I dissent from the judgment of St Jerome in his assertion that bishops are not of divine ordination.

BISHOP OF LONDON:

Unless I could prove my ordination lawful out of Scripture, I would not be a bishop four hours longer.

HIS MAJESTY:

I approve the calling and use of bishops in the church; and it is my aphorism, "No bishop, no king;" nor intend I to take Confirmation from the bishops, which they have so long enjoyed; seeing as great reason that none should confirm, as that none could preach without the bishop's licence. But let it be referred, whether the word "examination" ought not to be added to the Rubric in the title of Confirmation in the Communion-Book. And now, Dr Reynolds, you may proceed.

Dr Reynolds:

> I protest I meant not to gall any man, though I perceive some took personal exceptions at my words and desire the imputation of schism may not be charged upon me.[4] To proceed on article XXXVII wherein are the words, "The bishop of Rome hath no authority in this land:" these are not sufficient, unless it were added, "nor ought to have any."

His Majesty:

> *Habemus jure quod habemus;* and, therefore, insomuch as it is said "he hath not," it is plain enough *that he ought not to have.*

Here passed some pleasant discourse betwixt the King and lords about Puritans, till, returning to seriousness, the Bishop of London began:

Bishop of London:

> May it please your majesty to remember the speech of the French ambassador, Monsieur Rognée, upon the view of our solemn service and ceremony; namely, that if the Reformed Churches in France had kept the same order, there would have been thousands of Protestants more than there are.

Dr Reynolds:

> It were well if this proposition might be added to the Book of Articles, "The intention of the minister is not of the essence of the sacrament;" the rather, because some in England have preached it to be essential: and here again I could desire that the nine "Orthodoxal Assertions", concluded at Lambeth may be generally received.

His Majesty:

> I utterly dislike the first part of your motion, thinking it unfit to thrust into the Book of Articles every position negative; which would swell the book into a volume as big as the Bible, and confound the reader. Thus one Mr. Craig in Scotland, with his, "I renounce and abhor," his multiplied detestations and abrenunciations, so amazed simple people, that, not able to conceive all their things, they fell back to popery, or remained in

their former ignorance. If bound to this form, the confession of my faith must be in my table-book, not in my head.

Because you speak of intention, I will apply it thus: If you come hither with a good intention to be informed, the whole work will sort to the better effect; but if your intention be to go as you came, (whatsoever shall be said,) it will prove the intention is very material and essential to the end of this present action.

As for the nine "Assertions" you speak of, I cannot suddenly answer, not knowing what those propositions of Lambeth be.

BISHOP OF LONDON:

May it please your majesty, this was the occasion of them: By reason of some controversies arising in Cambridge about certain points of divinity, my Lord's Grace assembled some divines of special note to set down their opinions, which they drew into nine "Assertions", and so sent them to the university for the appeasing of their quarrels.

HIS MAJESTY:

When such questions arise amongst scholars, the quietest proceedings were to determine them in the university, and not to stuff the Book of Articles with all conclusions theological.

Secondly. The better course would be to punish the broachers of false doctrine, than to multiply Articles; which, if never so many, cannot prevent the contrary opinions of men till they be heard.

DEAN OF ST PAUL'S:

May it please your majesty, I am nearly concerned in this matter, by reason of a controversy betwixt me and some other in Cambridge, upon a proposition, which I there delivered, namely, that "whosoever (though before justified) did commit any grievous sin, as adultery, murder, &c. do become, *ipso facto,* subject to God's wrath, and guilty of damnation, *quoad praesentem statum,* until they repent; yet so that those who are justified according to the purpose of God's election, (though they might fall into grievous sin, and thereby into the present estate of damnation,) yet never totally nor finally from justification; but were in time renewed by God's Spirit unto a lively faith and repentance." Against this doctrine some did oppose, teaching that persons once truly justified, though falling into grievous sins, remained still in the state of justification, before they actually repented of these sins; yea, and, though they never repented of them through forgetfulness or sudden death, they nevertheless were justified and saved.

His Majesty:

I dislike this doctrine, there being a necessity of conjoining repentance and holiness of life with true faith; and that is hypocrisy, and not justifying faith, which is severed from them. For although predestination and election depend not on any qualities, actions, or works of man which are mutable, but on God's eternal decree; yet such is the necessity of repentance, after known sins committed, that without it no reconciliation with God, or remission of sins.

Dr Reynolds:

The Catechism in the Common-Prayer Book is too brief, and that by Mr. Nowell, (Late Dean of Paul's,) too long for novices to learn by heart. I request, therefore, that one uniform Catechism may be made, and none other generally received.

His Majesty:

I think the doctor's request very reasonable; yet so, that the Catechism may be made in the fewest and plainest affirmative terms that may be, not like the many ignorant Catechisms in Scotland, set out by every one who was the son of a good man; insomuch that what was Catechism-doctrine in one congregation was scarcely received as orthodox in another. And herein I would have two rules observed: First. Those curious and deep questions should be avoided in the fundamental instruction of a people. Second. That there should be not be so general departure from the papists, that everything should be accounted an error wherein we agree with them.

Dr Reynolds:

Great is the profanation of the Sabbath-day, and contempt of your majesty's proclamation; which I earnestly desire may be reformed.

This motion found an unanimous consent.

DR REYNOLDS:

May your majesty be pleased that the Bible be new translated, such as are extant not answering the original. And he instanced three particulars:

Galatians 4:25, in the original συτοιχεϊ is ill translated, "Bordereth." Psalm 105:28, in the original, "They were not disobedient," is ill translated, "they were not obedient." Psalm 106:30, in the original, "Phineas executed judgment," is ill translated, "Phineas prayed."

BISHOP OF LONDON:

If every man's humour might be followed, there would be no end of translating.

HIS MAJESTY:

I profess I could never yet see a Bible well translated in English; but I think, that, of all, the Geneva is the worst. I wish some special pains were taken for a uniform translation, which should be done by the best-learned in both universities, then reviewed by the bishops, presented to the Privy Council, lastly, ratified by royal authority, to be read in the whole church, and none other.

BISHOP OF LONDON:

But it is fit that no marginal notes should be added thereunto.

HIS MAJESTY:

That caveat is well put in; for in the Geneva translation, some notes are partial, untrue, seditious, and savouring of traitorous conceits: As, when from Exodus 1:19, disobedience to kings is allowed in a marginal note; and 2 Chronicles 15:16, King Asa taxed in the note for only *deposing* his mother for idolatry, and not *killing* her. To conclude this: let errors in the matter of faith be amended, and indifferent things be interpreted, and a gloss added unto them. For as Bartolus de Regno saith, that "a king with some weakness is better than still a change"; so, rather a church with some faults than an innovation. And surely, if these were the greatest matters that grieved you, I need not have been troubled with such importunate complaints.

[The marginal note in the Geneva Bible at Exodus 1:19 comments on the refusal of the Hebrew midwives to obey Pharaoh and kill the Hebrew babies. The note reads: "Their disobedience herein was lawful, but their dissembling evil." Likewise in 2 Chronicles 15:16 where Asa, having deposed Maachah his mother for idolatry, destroyed the idol. The Geneva note reads: "Or grandmother: and herein he showed that he lacked zeal: for she ought to have died both by covenant, as v.13, and by law of God: but he gave place to foolish pity, and would also seem after a sort to falsify the law." Such comments were anathema to King James' belief in the divine right of kings.]

Dr Reynolds:

> May it please your majesty, that unlawful and seditious books be suppressed, such as Ficlerus, a papist, *De Jure Magistratûs in Subditos,* applied against the late queen for the Pope.

Bishop of London:

> There is no such licentious divulging of those books: and none have liberty, by authority, to buy them, except such as Dr Reynolds, who was supposed, would confute them. And if such books come into the realm of secret conveyances, perfect notice cannot be had of their importation. Besides, Ficlerus was a great disciplinarian; whereby it appears what advantage that sort gave unto the papists, who *mutatis personis*, apply their own arguments against princes of their religion, though for my part I detest both the author and applier alike.

The Lord Cecil:

> Indeed, the unlimited liberty of dispersing Popish and seditious pamphlets in Paul's Church-yard, and both the Universities, hath done much mischief; but especially one called *Speculum Tragicum.*

His Majesty:

> That is a dangerous book, indeed.

Lord H. Howard:

> Both for matter and intention.

LORD CHANCELLOR:

Of such books, some are Latin, some are English; but the last dispersed do most harm.

SECRETARY CECIL:

But my Lord of London (and no man else) hath done what he could to suppress them.

HIS MAJESTY:

Dr Reynolds, you are a better college-man than a states-man, if meaning to tax the Bishop of London for suffering these books, between the Secular Priests and Jesuits, to be published; which he did by warrant from the Council, to nourish a schism betwixt them.

LORD CECIL:

Such books were tolerated, because by them the title of Spain was confuted.

LORD TREASURER:

And because therein it appears, by the testimony of the priests themselves, that no papists are put to death for conscience only, but for treason.

DR REYNOLDS:

Indeed, I meant not such books as were printed in England, but only such as came from beyond the seas. And now, to proceed to the second general point, concerning the planting of learned ministers: I desire they be in every parish.

HIS MAJESTY:

I have consulted with my bishops about it, whom I have found willing and ready herein. But, as *subita evacuatio* is *periculosa;* so *subita mutatio.* And yet they afford more learned men than the realm doth maintenance; which must be first provided. In the mean time, ignorant ministers, if young, are to be removed, if there be no hope of amendment; if old, their death must be expected, because Jerusalem cannot be built up in a day.

Bishop of Winchester:

Lay-patrons much cause the insufficiency of the clergy, presenting mean clerks to their cures; (the law admitting of such sufficiency); and, if the bishop refuseth them, presently a *quare impedit* is sent out against him.

Bishop of London:

Because this, I see, is a time of moving petitions, [this he spake, kneeling,] may I humbly present two or three to your majesty? First. That there may be amongst us a praying ministry, it being now come to pass, that men think it is the only duty of ministers to spend their time in the pulpit. I confess, in a church newly to be planted, preaching is most necessary, not so, in one long-established, that prayer should be neglected.

His Majesty:

I like your motion exceedingly well, and dislike the hypocrisy of our time, who place all their religion, in the ear, whilst prayer (so requisite and acceptable, if duly performed) is accounted and used as the least part of religion.

Bishop of London:

My second motion is, that, until learned men may be planted in every congregation, godly Homilies may be read therein.

His Majesty:

I approve your motion, especially where the living is not sufficient for the maintenance of a learned preacher. Also, where there be multitudes of sermons, there I would have Homilies read divers times. [Here the King asked the assent of the plaintiffs, and they confessed it.] A preaching ministry is best; but, where it may not be had, godly prayers and exhortations do much good.

Lord Chancellor:

Livings rather want learned men, than learned men livings; many in the universities pining for want of places. I wish, therefore, some may have single coats [one living] before others have doublets [pluralities]. As this method I have observed in bestowing the King's benefices.

BISHOP OF LONDON:

I commend your honourable care that way; but a doublet is necessary in cold weather.

LORD CHANCELLOR:

I dislike not the liberty of our church, in granting to one man two benefices, but speak out of mine own purpose and practice, grounded on the aforesaid reason.

BISHOP OF LONDON:

My last motion is, that pulpits may not be made pasquils,* wherein every discontented fellow may traduce his superiors.

HIS MAJESTY:

I accept what you offer; for the pulpit is no place of personal reproof. Let them complain to me, if injured.

BISHOP OF LONDON:

If your majesty shall leave yourself open to admit of all complaints, your Highness shall never be quiet, nor your under-officers regarded; whom every delinquent, when censured will threaten to complain of.

HIS MAJESTY:

I mean, they shall complain to me by degrees. First, to the ordinary; from him to the Archbishop; from him to the lords of Council; and, if in all these no remedy be found, then to myself.

DR REYNOLDS:

I come now to subscription, as a great impeachment to a learned ministry; and therefore entreat it may not be exacted as heretofore; for which many good men are kept out, though otherwise willing to subscribe to the statutes of the realm, Articles of Religion, and the king's supremacy. The reason of their backwardness to

* An abusive lampoon or satire.

subscribe is, because the Common-Prayer enjoineth the Apocrypha-books to be read in the church, although some chapters therein contain manifest errors repugnant to Scripture. For instance: Ecclesiasticus xlviii.10, Elias in person is said to come before Christ, contrary to what is in the New Testament of Elias in resemblance, that is, John the Baptist, Matthew xi.14; Luke i.17.

Bishop of London:

Most of the objections against these books are the old cavils of the Jews, renewed by St Jerome, who first called them Apocrypha; which opinion, upon Ruffinus's challenge, he, after a sort, disclaimed.

Bishop of Winchester:

Indeed, St Jerome saith, *Canonici sunt ad informandos mores, non ad confirmandam fidem.*

His Majesty:

To take an even order betwixt both: I would not have all canonical books read in the church:[5] nor any chapter out of the Apocrypha, wherein any error is contained. Wherefore, let Dr Reynolds note those chapters in the Apocrypha-books wherein those offences are, and bring them to the Archbishop of Canterbury against Wednesday next. And now, doctor, proceed.

Dr Reynolds:

The next scruple against subscription, is, because it is twice set down in the Common-Prayer Book, "Jesus said to his disciples," when by the text in the original, it is plain, that he spake to the Pharisees.

His Majesty:

Let the word "disciples" be omitted, and the words, "Jesus said," be printed in a different letter.

Mr. Knewstubs:

I take exception at the Cross in baptism; whereat the weak brethren are offended, contrary to the counsel of the apostle, Romans xiv.; 1 Corinthians viii.

HIS MAJESTY:

Distingue temporar, et concordabunt Scripturæ, great the difference betwixt those times and ours. Then, a church not fully settled; now, ours long established. How long will such brethren be weak? Are not forty-five years sufficient for them to grow strong in? Besides, who pretends this weakness? We require not subscriptions of laics and idiots, but of preachers and ministers, who are not still (I trow) to be fed with milk, being enabled to feed others. Some of them are strong enough, if not headstrong: conceiving themselves able enough to teach him who last spake for them, and all the bishops in the land.

MR. KNEWSTUBS:

It is questionable whether the church hath power to institute an outward significant sign.

BISHOP OF LONDON:

The Cross in baptism is not used otherwise than a ceremony.

BISHOP OF WINCHESTER:

Kneeling, lifting up the hands, knocking of the breast, are significant ceremonies, and these may be lawfully used.

DEAN OF THE CHAPEL:

The Rabbins write, that the Jews added both signs and words at the institution of the Passover; namely, when they ate sour herbs, they said, "Take and eat these in remembrance," &c. When they drank wine, they said, "Drink this in remembrance," &c. Upon which addition and tradition, our Saviour instituted the sacrament of his last supper, thereby approving, a church may institute and retain a sign significant.

HIS MAJESTY:

I am exceeding well satisfied in this point, but would be acquainted about the antiquity of the use of the Cross.

Dr Reynolds:

It hath been used ever since the apostles' time. But the question is, How ancient the use thereof hath been in baptism?

Dean of Westminster:

It appears out of Tertullian, Cyprian, and Origen, that it was used *in immortali lavacro.*

Bishop of Winchester:

In Constantine's time it was used in baptism.

His Majesty:

If so, I see no reason but that we may continue it.

Mr. Knewstubs:

Put the case, the church hath power to add significant signs, it may not add them where Christ hath already ordained them; which is as derogatory to Christ's institution, as if one should add to the Great Seal of England.

His Majesty:

The case is not alike; seeing, the sacrament is fully finished, before any mention of the Cross is made therein.

Mr. Knewstubs:

If the church had such a power, the greatest scruple is, how far the ordinance of the church bindeth, without impeaching Christian liberty.

His Majesty:

I will not argue that point with you but answer as kings in parliament, *Le Roy s'avisera.* This is like Mr. John Black, a beardless boy, who told me, the last Conference in Scotland,[6] that he would hold conformity with his majesty in matters of doctrine; but every man, for ceremonies, was to be left to his own liberty. But I will have none of that; I will have one doctrine, one discipline, one religion, in substance and in ceremony. Never speak more to that point,—how far you are bound to obey.

DR REYNOLDS:

Would that the Cross (being superstitiously abused in popery) were abandoned, as the brazen serpent was stamped to powder by Hezekiah, because abused to idolatry.

HIS MAJESTY:

Inasmuch as the Cross was abused to superstition in time of popery, it doth plainly imply that it was well used before. I detest their courses who peremptorily disallow of all things which have been abused in popery; and know not how to answer the objections of the papists, when they charge us with novelties, but by telling them, we retain the primitive use of things, and only forsake their novel corruptions. Secondly. No resemblance betwixt the brasen serpent, (a material, visible thing,) and the sign of the Cross, made in the air. Thirdly. Papists, as I am informed, did never ascribe any spiritual grace to the Cross in baptism. Lastly. Material Crosses, to which people fell down in time of popery, (as the idolatrous Jews to the brazen serpent,) are already demolished, as you desire.

MR. KNEWSTUBS:

I take exception at the wearing of the Surplice, a kind of garment used by the priests of Isis.

HIS MAJESTY:

I did not think, till of late, it had been borrowed from the heathen, because commonly called "a rag of popery". Seeing now we border not upon heathens, neither are any of them conversant with or commorant amongst us, thereby to be confirmed in paganism; I see no reason but for comeliness-sake it may be continued.

DR REYNOLDS:

I take exception at these words in the marriage, "With my body I thee worship."

HIS MAJESTY:

I was made believe, the phrase imported no less than Divine adoration, but find it an usual English term; as when we say "a gentleman of worship;" and it agreeth with the Scriptures, "giving honour to the wife." As for you, Dr Reynolds, [this the King spake with a leery grin,] many men speak of Robin Hood, who never shot in his bow: If you had a good wife yourself, you would think all worship and honour you could do her were well bestowed on her.

Dean of Sarum:

Some take exception to the ring in marriage.

Dr Reynolds:

I approve it well enough.

His Majesty:

I was married with a ring, and think others scarce well-married without it.

Dr Reynolds:

Some take exceptions at the churching of women, by the name of "purification".

His Majesty:

I allow it very well. Women being loath of themselves to come to church, I like this or any other occasion to draw them thither.

Dr Reynolds:

My last exception is against committing ecclesiastical censures to lay-chancellors, the rather, because it was ordered, *anno* 1571, that lay-chancellors, in matters of correction, and *anno* 1589, in matters of instance, should not excommunicate any, but be done only by them who had the power of the keys, though the contrary is commonly practised.

His Majesty:

I have conferred with my bishops about this point, and such order shall be taken therein as is convenient. Meantime, go on to some other matter.

DR REYNOLDS:

I desire that according to certain provincial constitutions, the clergy may have meetings every three weeks:
First, in rural deaneries, therein to have prophesying, as Archbishop Grindal and other bishops desired of her late majesty.
Second, that such things as could not be resolved on there, might be referred to Archdeacons' visitations.
And third, to the episcopal synod, to determine such points before not decided.

HIS MAJESTY:

If you aim at a Scottish presbytery, it agreeth as well with monarchy, as God and the devil. Then Jack, and Tom, and Will, and Dick shall meet and censure me and my Council. Therefore I reiterate my former speech, *Le roy s'avisera.* Stay, I pray, for one seven years, before you demand; and then if you find me grow pussy and fat, I may, perchance, hearken unto you; for that government will keep me in breath, and give me work enough. I shall speak of one matter more, somewhat out of order, but it skilleth not. Dr Reynolds, you have often spoken for my supremacy, and it is well. But know you any here or elsewhere, who like the present government ecclesiastical, and dislike my supremacy?

DR REYNOLDS:

I know none.

HIS MAJESTY:

Why, then, I will tell you a tale: After that the religion restored by King Edward VI was soon overthrown by Queen Mary here in England, we in Scotland felt the effect of it. For, thereupon, Mr. Knox writes to the Queen Regent, a virtuous and moderate lady; telling her, that she was the supreme head of the church, and charged her, as she would answer it to God's tribunal, to take care of Christ's Evangel, in suppressing the popish prelates, who withstood the same. But how long, trow you, did this continue? Even till, by her authority, the popish bishops were repressed, and Knox, with his adherents, being brought in, made strong enough. Then began they to make small account of her supremacy, when, according to that *more light* wherewith they were illuminated, they made a further reformation of themselves. How they used the poor lady my mother, is not unknown, and how they dealt with me in my minority. I thus apply it: my lords the bishops, [this he said, putting his hand to his hat,] I may thank you that these men plead thus for my supremacy. They think they cannot make their party good against you, but by appealing unto it. But if once you were out and they in, I know what would become of my supremacy; for, "No bishop, no king"! I have learned of what cut they have been, who, preaching before me since my coming into England, passed over, with silence, my being supreme governor in causes ecclesiastical. Well, doctor, have you anything else to say?

Dr Reynolds:

No more, if it please your majesty.

His Majesty:

If this be all your party hath to say, I will make them conform themselves, or else I will harry them out of the land, or else do worse.

Thus ended the second day's Conference; and the third began on Wednesday following, January 18, many knights, civilians, and doctors of the law, being admitted thereunto, because the High Commission was the principal matter in the debate.

The third day of the Conference at Hampton Court.

His Majesty:

I understand, that the parties named in the High Commission are too many, and too mean; and the matters they deal with, base, such as ordinaries at home in their courts might censure.

Archbishop of Canterbury:

It is requisite their number should be many, otherwise I should be forced often-times to sit alone, if, in the absence of the lords of the Council, bishops, and judges at law, some deans and doctors were not put into that Commission, whose attendance I might command with the more authority. I have often complained of the meanness of matters handled therein, but cannot remedy it. For though the offence be so small, that the ordinary may—the offended oft-times is so great and contumacious that the ordinary dare not—punish him; and so is forced to crave help at the High Commission.

A NAMELESS LORD:

The proceedings in that Court are like the Spanish Inquisition; wherein men are urged to subscribe more than law requireth; and, by the oath *ex officio,* forced to accuse themselves, being examined upon twenty or twenty-four articles on a sudden, without deliberation, and for the most part against themselves.

In proof hereof, he produced a letter of an ancient honourable Counsellor, *anno* 1584, verifying this usage to two ministers in Cambridgeshire.

ARCHBISHOP OF CANTERBURY:

Your Lordship is deceived in the manner of proceeding. For, if the article touch the party for life, liberty, or scandal, he may refuse to answer. I can say nothing to the particulars of the letter, because twenty years since; yet doubt not but at leisure to give your Lordship satisfaction.

LORD CHANCELLOR:

There is necessity and use of the oath *ex officio,* in divers courts and causes.

HIS MAJESTY:

Indeed, civil proceedings only punish facts; but it is requisite that fame and scandals be looked unto in courts ecclesiastical; and yet great moderation is to be used therein.

In gravioribus criminibus.

In such whereof there is a public fame, caused by the inordinate demeanour of the offender.

And here he soundly described the oath *ex officio,* for the ground thereof, the wisdom of the law therein, the manner of proceeding thereby, and profitable effect from the same.

Archbishop of Canterbury:

Undoubtedly your majesty speaks by the special assistance of God's Spirit.

Bishop of London:

I protest, my heart melteth with joy, that Almighty God, of his singular mercy, hath given us such a king, as, since Christ's time, the like hath not been. [This he spake on his knee.]

Then there passed much discourse between the King, the bishops, and the lords, about the quality of the persons and causes in the High Commission, rectifying excommunication in matters of less moment, punishing recusants, providing divines for Ireland, Wales, and the northern borders. Afterward the four preachers were called in, and such alterations in the Liturgy were read unto them, which the bishops, by the King's advice, had made, and to which, by their silence, they seemed to consent.

His Majesty:

I see the exception against the Communion-Book are matters of weakness; therefore if the persons reluctant be discreet, they will be won betimes, and by good persuasions; if indiscreet, better they were removed; for by their factions many are driven to be papists. From you, Dr Reynolds, and your associates, I expect obedience and humility, the marks of honest and good men; and that you would persuade others abroad by your example.

Dr Reynolds:

We here do promise to perform all duties to bishops, as reverend fathers, and to join with them against the common adversary for the quiet of the Church.

Mr. Chaderton:

I request, the wearing of the Surplice, and the Cross in baptism, may not be urged on some godly ministers in Lancashire, fearing, if forced unto them, many won by their preaching of the Gospel will revolt to popery; and I particularly instance in the Vicar of Rochdale. [This he spake kneeling.]

ARCHBISHOP OF CANTERBURY:

You could not have light upon a worse; for, not many years ago, (as my Lord Chancellor knows,) it was proved before me, that, by his unreverent usage of the eucharist, (dealing the bread out of a basket, every man putting in his hand, and taking out a piece,) he made many loathe the communion, and refuse to come to church.

HIS MAJESTY:

It is not my purpose, and I dare say it is not the bishops' intent, presently and out of hand, to enforce these things without fatherly admonitions, conferences, and persuasions promised. But I wish it were examined, whether such Lancashire ministers, by their pains and preaching, have converted any from popery, and withal be men of honest life and quiet conversation. If so, let letters be written to the Bishop of Chester[7] (who is a grave and good man,) to that purpose, that some favour may be afforded unto them, and let the Lord Archbishop write the letters.

BISHOP OF LONDON:

If this be granted, the copy of these letters will fly all over England; and then all nonconformists will make the like request, and so no fruit follow of this Conference, but things will be worse than they were before. I desire, therefore, a time may be limited, within the compass whereof they shall conform.

HIS MAJESTY:

I assent thereunto; and let the bishop of the diocese set down the time.

MR. KNEWSTUBS:

I request [here he fell down on his knees] the like favour of forbearance to some honest ministers in Suffolk. For, it will make much against their credits in the country, to be now forced to the surplice, and cross in baptism.

ARCHBISHOP OF CANTERBURY:

Nay, sir –

His Majesty:

Let me alone to answer him. Sir, you show yourself an uncharitable man. We have here taken pains, and, in the end, have concluded on unity and uniformity; and you, forsooth, must prefer the credits of a few private men before the peace of the Church. This is just the Scotch argument, when any thing was concluded which disliked some humours. Let them either conform themselves shortly, or they shall hear of it.

Lord Cecil:

The indecency of *ambling* communions is very offensive, and hath driven many from the church.

Bishop of London:

And, Mr. Chaderton, I could tell you of *sitting* communions in Emmanuel College.

Mr. Chaderton:

It is so, because of the seats so placed as they be; and yet we have some kneeling also in our chapel.

His Majesty:

No more hereof for the present, seeing they have jointly promised hereafter to be quiet and obedient.

Whereat he rose up to depart into an inner chamber.

Bishop of London:

God's goodness be blessed for your majesty, and give health and prosperity to your Highness, your gracious queen, the young prince, and all the royal issue!

Thus ended the three days of the Conference.

On many points James was not out of sympathy with the Puritans. Unlike Charles I, he was not brought up in the atmosphere of Anglicanism. He cared nothing for ritual, for he was a Calvinist in doctrine. But the one point, on which he differed completely from the Puritans, was the relative authority of the bishops and their clergy. It was not for religious, but for political reasons that he distanced himself from the Puritans. He saw in them the Scottish Presbyterians, who had made his youth one long humiliation, and his manhood one long struggle—men who would take the Lord's anointed by the sleeve and call him "God's silly vassal". The English Puritans were of a milder temper: but the policy of suppression by which James sought to "harry them out of the land", served to arouse in them the instincts which he most feared, and led them indeed to abolish bishops and to put his son to death.

When his first Parliament met in the spring of 1604, the House of Commons supported the Millenary Petition and the arguments of Dr Reynolds. It escaped the King how ominous was the alliance; how considerable the fact that the Puritan divines, who had picked up their Turkey gowns and scurried from his presence amid the laughter of bishops, represented the religion of the gentry and the towns of England. It was enough for him to lecture Parliament on "Puritans and novelists (innovators), ...which I call a sect rather than a religion,... who do not differ from us on points of religion as in their confused form of policy and parity." In that last comment James summed up the mistake of his life. Because the Puritan leaders of the previous generation had desired a Presbyterian 'policy' of Church government, and had a 'parity' of clergy with their bishops, the services and merits of all Puritans were to be overlooked. They were at once to be deprived of their benefices, and finally, together with all their adherents, "harried out of the land." James did not perceive that, if they were allowed to continue their work in the Church and to take their place on the Episcopal Bench, the desire for 'parity' would be kept in the background; while on the other hand, if they were driven out by the bishops, the Presbyterian 'policy' would revive, with the arm of the House of Commons for its support.

As soon as Parliament had risen in July, the King informed the clergy by proclamation that unless before December they were ready to conform to all existing rules of Church service, they would be deprived of their livings. When the fatal month came round, Bancroft, now Archbishop of Canterbury, eagerly set himself to carry out the orders of the King's Council. All curates and unbeneficed preachers were required to sign a statement that the Prayer Book contained nothing contrary to the Word of God; and the beneficed clergy, while excused the severer test, were required to obey the rubric in every detail. Three hundred refused and were ejected. Many of the most influential and conscientious of the servants of the Church were driven into the position of separatists. Those thus forcibly expelled gathered round them large congregations of devoted adherents. Nevertheless, this was the religious and political climate in which the most excellent of English translations of the Bible was shaped. The Authorised Version of the Bible was the one precious jewel in the King's sullied crown.

CHAPTER 5

All The King's Men

THE first half of the seventeenth century, when the King James Bible was completed, was the golden age of biblical and oriental scholarship in England. Never before, nor since, have these studies been pursued by scholars with such zeal, industry and success. This in itself is a remarkable attestation of God's providential care of His Word.

There has never been a group of men of the calibre of the translators, who not only had the character and moral qualifications, but were truly spiritual men as well! For such a high and holy work, it is doubtful whether any other age could produce such a body of men equally qualified.

The King James Bible was the jewel which resulted from the accumulated labour and pious care bestowed upon it by so many zealous and erudite scholars. It is this rare and unique blending of co-operate scholarship which gives to this version alone intrinsic excellence and lasting popularity. Barlow writes,

> Whereupon his highness wished that some especial pains should be taken in that behalf for one uniform translation (professing that he could never yet see a Bible well translated in English; but worst of all his Majesty thought the Geneva to be), and this to be done by the best learned in both the universities, after them to be reviewed by the Bishops and the chief learned men of the Church, from them to be presented to the Privy Council, and lastly to be ratified by his Royal authority; and so the whole Church to be bound unto it and none other.[1]

Not only had the English language ripened to its full perfection, but the study of Greek, and of the oriental tongues, and of rabbinical lore, had then been carried to a greater extent in England than ever before, or since. This particular field of learning has never been as highly cultivated among English divines as it was at that day. Indeed, we do not hesitate to say, that all the colleges of Great Britain and North America could not bring together in our day the same number of divines equally qualified by learning and godliness, for such a great undertaking.

It would be impossible to convene out of any one Christian denomination, or out of all, a body of translators, on whom the whole Christian community would bestow such confidence as is reposed upon that illustrious company.

The translators little foresaw the vast results and immeasurable influence of what they had done, both for time and eternity. Venerated men indeed! Their very names are scarcely known to more than a few, yet, in the providence of God, the fruits of their labours have spread to far distant lands. They have afforded to multitudes the strength to endure adversity, and grace to resist the temptations of Satan; and only the revelations of the Judgment Day itself can disclose how many countless millions, through the instrumentality of their labours, have been made wise unto salvation.

There were difficulties, and there was much opposition to the work, but they melted away, as if the scheme had Divine approval. The choice of translators was undertaken by Edward Lively, Regius Professor of Hebrew at Cambridge. The King asked Bishop Richard Bancroft, fierce opponent of Puritanism (Appendix 3), to write to the translators in June 1604,

Richard Bancroft

> His Majesty, being made acquainted with the choice of all them to be employed in the translating of the Bible in such sort as Mr. Lively can inform you, doth greatly approve of the said choice. And forasmuch as his Highness is very anxious that the same so religious a work should admit of no delay, he has commanded me to signify unto you in his name that his pleasure is, you should with all possible speed meet together in your University and begin the same.[2]

On the twenty-second of July, Bancroft wrote another letter on behalf of the King, but this time circulated to all the bishops of the realm,

> Right trusty and well beloved we greet you well. Whereas we have appointed certain learned men to the number of four and fifty, for the translating of the Bible ... Furthermore, we require you to inform yourselves of all such men within your several dioceses as having especial skill in the Hebrew and Greek tongues, having taken pains in private studies of the Scriptures for clearing of any obscurities either in Hebrew or Greek, or touching any difficulties or mistakings in the former English translations which we have now commanded to be thoroughly viewed and amended, and thereupon to write unto them earnestly charging them that they send such observations, either to Mr. Lively, our Hebrew reader at Cambridge, or to Dr Harding our Hebrew reader at Oxford, or to Dr Andrews, Dean of Westminster, to be imparted to the rest of their several companies; so that our said intended translation may have the help of all our principal learned men within this our kingdom.[3]

Some fifty-four translators were selected and appointed, although seven are not officially listed. Such men as William Thorne were evidently involved in the translation of the First Oxford Company, but for various reasons neither he nor the other six are included. Perhaps they acted in a consultancy role. The forty-seven men were divided into six companies: two at Westminster, two at Oxford, and two at Cambridge. The list of translators was completed by mid–July. All the translators commissioned by James Stuart were ripe and critical scholars, profoundly versed in all the learning required. Most of the forty-seven were Fellows of Oxbridge colleges, a dozen being heads. The Regius Professors of Hebrew and Greek in both universities were present. Both parties in the Church were represented by some of their best men. There has never yet been a time when a better qualified company could have been collected for the purpose. A few have left us but little more than their names, but their association with so many other scholars of the greatest eminence is proof that they were fit companions of those who, under God, produced this most noble monument of learning and piety. Moreover, though the King designed to employ in this work the highest and ripest talents in his realm, there were still many men in England distinguished for their learning, like Broughton and Bedell, who were not included on the list of translators.

In the marginal notes of the Douai-Rheims Bible, the Romanist translators speak somewhat disparagingly of King James' learned men, "They will be abhorred in the depths of hell!" Well, they may be abhorred there, but not in heaven! It is to the brief biographical portraits of those eminent and godly men that we now turn. These were the men entrusted with the task of cutting by the lapidary of their godly learning, the gem which was to become the King James Bible.

FIRST WESTMINSTER COMPANY:—
PENTATEUCH, JOSHUA – 2 KINGS.

The Westminster group of the Old Testament was directed by Lancelot Andrewes and met in the Jerusalem Chamber, which was part of Andrewes' pleasant deanery. This fourteenth century room had been the abbot's lodgings at Westminster. As Henry IV lay dying in this very room he thought he was in Jerusalem, and thereafter it was known as the Jerusalem Chamber!

There is a strong Cambridge connection and an emphasis on academic brilliance. None of the men chosen in the First Westminster Company could be accused of Puritan sentiment.

Lancelot Andrewes	Dean of Westminster
John Overall	Dean of St Paul's
Hadrian Saravia	Prebendary of Westminster & Vicar of Lewisham
Richard Clarke	Vicar of Minster, Thanet
John Layfield	Rector of Clement Danes, London
Robert Tighe	Vicar of All Hallows, Barking

Westminster Abbey, 1600

The Jerusalem Chamber

Lancelot Andrewes

Francis Burleigh	Fellow of Chelsea College
Geoffrey King	Fellow of King's College, Cambridge
Richard Thompson	Fellow of Clare Hall, Cambridge
William Bedwell	Rector of St Ethelburga's

LANCELOT ANDREWES was born in the London parish of All Hallows, Barking, in 1555. From his earliest years he was totally addicted to learning, and had no interest in the fooleries of childhood. His one recreation was walking, which he would use to cultivate the minds of studious boys and students who accompanied him on these scholarly walks. He was trained chiefly at Merchant Taylor's school in his native city, till he was appointed to one of the first Greek Scholarships of Pembroke Hall, Cambridge, when sixteen years of age, then later appointed catechist at Pembroke Hall, after which he was to be appointed Master of the Hall.

Once a year, in the spring, he would walk the thirty miles home to Barking to pass a month with his parents. During his vacation he would find a tutor from whom he learned some language. In this way, after a few years, he acquired most of the modern languages of Europe. At the University, he gave himself chiefly to the oriental tongues and to divinity. He was made a catechist; that is to say, a lecturer in divinity.

His formidable talents soon gained him powerful patrons. Henry, Earl of Huntingdon, took him to the north of England where he was the means of converting many papists by his preaching and disputations.

Whilst at Pembroke he gave lectures at three o'clock on Saturdays and the Lord's Day on the Ten Commandments. He associated with such Puritans as Lawrence Chadderton and obtained the ministry of St Giles, Cripplegate. He was often described as "an angel in the pulpit". Thomas Fuller says that he was, "an inimitable preacher in his way; and such plagiarists as have stolen his sermons could never steal his preaching." His sermons were ranked with the finest English prose of their time or any time. He had a guileless simplicity both of manner and of mind, an unaffected modesty, and a rare sense of humour.

In 1586, when he was only thirty-one, he was appointed chaplain to the Queen. She found Andrewes humane, cordial, gracious, benign, and took delight in the grave manner of his preaching. Andrewes was present at her death on 24 March 1603, and then preached her funeral sermon. In one of his greatest sermons, preached in 1588, he proved to be a staunch defender of the Church of England against Romanism, quoting Master Calvin with praise and affection. In another sermon, preached in November 1600 on the theme of justification, he demolished the Romish myth of the 'real presence' in the wafer and the wine.

In 1601 he became Dean of Westminster and headmaster of Westminster School. Thrice a week he called the uppermost scholars to his lodgings from eight till eleven at night, unfolding to them the rudiments of Greek and the elements of Hebrew grammar. The young students were his special care:

> What pains Dr Andrewes did take both day and night ... He did often supply the place both of the head school master and usher for the space of a whole week at a time, and gave us not an hour of loitering from morning to night ... He caused our exercises in prose and verse to be brought to him, to examine our style and proficiency ... He never walked to Chiswick for his recreation without a brace of this young fry, and in this wayfaring leisure had a singular dexterity to fill those narrow vessels with a funnel.[4]

In 1604, between February and June, he joined with Harding of Oxford and Lively of Cambridge in drawing together the scholars who were able and willing to serve as translators, and by November he was leading the First Westminster Company of translators. With King James, Dr Andrewes stood in even higher favour than he had done with Elizabeth. The King had published a *Defence of the Rights of Kings*, in opposition to the arrogant claims of the popes. He was answered most bitterly by the renowned Cardinal Bellarmine. The King requested that Andrewes refute the cardinal, which he did and thus silenced the Pope's cardinal. For this service the King promoted Andrewes to the bishopric of Chichester, two days before the failed Gunpowder Plot of 5 November 1605. Prior to this he had refused promotion to the bishops' bench, but on this occasion, and with great humility, he accepted the position, but graven into his Episcopal seal were the solemn words, "And who is sufficient for these things." In 1609, he was transferred to the bishopric of Ely and was called to his majesty's privy council; then, in 1618, he was promoted to the bishopric of Winchester.

Andrewes always conducted himself with great ability and solemnity, so that even the King was forced to desist from his profaneness and levity in his presence.

The learned bishop was fluent in fifteen modern languages and six ancient, gifted with a musical understanding of English, which is responsible for much of the final effect of the translation. It was said of him that, "the world wanted learning to know how learned this man was." One remarked that, such was his skill in all languages, especially the oriental, that, had he been present at the confusion of tongues at Babel, he might have served as Interpreter General. He was a man with an extraordinarily tender relationship with his God, praying five hours every morning, and was said to have been in tears for most of them. His *Private Devotions* have been translated from the Greek and Latin, and reprinted many times.

Father, the Creator
Son, the Redeemer,
Spirit, the Regenerator,
destroy me not,
whom Thou hast created redeemed,
regenerated.
Remember not, Lord, my sins,...

Spare ... Thy servant,
Who is redeemed with Thy precious blood;
And be not angry with us for ever.
Be merciful, be merciful; spare us Lord,
And be not angry with us for ever.
Be merciful, be merciful; have pity upon us, Lord,
And be not angry with us to the full.
Deal not, O Lord,
Deal not with me after mine iniquities,
Neither recompense me according to my sins;
But after Thy great pity,
Deal with me.

Bishop Andrewes, Private Devotions.

Following the Gunpowder Plot of 5 November 1605, when half a dozen violent Papists conspired to blow up king and parliament, Andrewes preached at Whitehall in cheerful jubilation on Psalm cxviii.23: *This is the LORD's doing, it is marvellous in our eyes.* The Lord had saved Protestant England once more from the tyrannical forces of papistical darkness! Therafter, until his death, Andrewes preached an annual commemorative sermon (Appendix 5). It was to be, "consecrated to perpetual memory, by a yearly acknowledgment to be made throughout all generations."

Lancelot Andrewes died at Winchester House, in Southwark, London, September 25, 1626, aged seventy-one years. He was buried in the Church of St Saviour.

JOHN OVERALL was born on March 2, 1560, in the cloth-making village of Hadleigh in Suffolk, and orphaned at an early age. At Hadleigh Grammar School he was a sizar, or poor student, who served the master for his board and lodging. Two or three years later he went up to St John's College, Cambridge accompanied by John Bois, a fellow student of Latin and Scripture. His tutor in Greek was the translator Andrew Downes. In 1592 he was appointed Vicar at

John Overall by Wenceslaus Hollar

Epping in Essex, and then in 1596, Overall became Regis Professor of Divinity and then Master of Catherine Hall in 1598. Later, in 1602, the Queen made him the Dean of St Paul's whilst still retaining his post at Cambridge.

On April 16, 1604, at the age of forty-four, and just before he began work on the translation of the Holy Scriptures, he married the lovely Anne Orwell of Christ Church, London. Anne was regarded as, "the greatest beauty of her time in England," but before the work of translation was completed her flirtatious conduct would occasion much gossip. She left the marital home and eloped with Sir John Selby, a Yorkshire squire, but the Dean had her escorted back to the Deanery at St Paul's.

He was an accomplished Latin linguist, but not regarded as a great Hebrew scholar. All of his university teaching had been in Latin, and this proved to be an advantage in Bible translation where all discussion was in that ancient tongue. This brilliant linguist, and perhaps the foremost Latin scholar of the age, nevertheless struggled to speak for any length in English! "Being appointed," says Thomas Fuller, "to preach before the Queen, he professed ... that he had spoken Latin so long, it was troublesome to him to speak English in a continued oration." Nevertheless, in Overall there was the heart of a true pastor of the flock. Whilst at Epping he says,

> I was requested to come visit some of my parish that were sick, and coming I found them sicker in mind than body. The thing that troubled their minds, so they said, was this. They could not be persuaded that Christ died for them. Wherein, having by the comforts of the gospel, as I thought best, somewhat eased and persuaded them, I took occasion afterward in my sermon, for their sakes, to handle this point ... Christ died for all men sufficiently, for the believer only effectually, as the sun shineth sufficiently to give light to all, though it doth it effectually only to them that open their eyes; as water that is sufficient to quench all the thirsty, but doth it only to them that drink it; as physic that is sufficient to cure all maladies, but doth it effectually only where it is applied. So Christ, the sun of righteousness, the water of life, the heavenly medicine.[5]

Soon after the enthronement of King James, Dr Overall became speaker of the lower house of Convocation. To this body he presented a volume of canons, in which he vindicated the divine right of kings. This was adopted by Convocation, but then suppressed by King James, because Overall taught that, after a revolution, a new government or dynasty then formed, could also claim the obedience of the people as a matter of duty toward God. This book was published after the death of James, and indeed had the very effect which King James was afraid of, for when James II was expelled from the soil and throne of England, many bishops and other clergymen refused through conscience to swear allegiance to the new government of William and Mary, but upon reading Overall's treatise were convinced by his argument.

None but Andrewes was better fitted to discern the sense of the sacred original. The Dean of St Paul's was a man of prodigious learning. As a translator, Overall could either walk the two miles from St Paul's to Westminster, or he could take the Thames river boat.

He was made Bishop of Lichfield and Coventry, in 1614, and then in 1618 was transferred to the see of Norwich, where he died at the age of sixty in 1619. The psalms of David were constantly upon his lips, particularly the thirty-ninth: *When thou with rebukes dost correct man for iniquity, thou makest his beauty to consume away like a moth: surely every man is vanity. Selah.*

Of all the translators, none were more distinguished than the two Deans of Westminster and St Paul's.

DR HADRIAN SARAVIA was driven to these shores by persecution and at seventy-three was the oldest of the translators. Born in 1530 at Hesdin, Artois, Saravia had a father of Spanish descent and a Flemish mother. Both his parents had become Protestants, so he had no popish childhood to outgrow. He was trained in theology at Antwerp and became pastor of a Calvinist Walloon church in Brussels, where he drew up a Reformed Confession of Faith. Copies of the Confession were given to the Prince of Orange and to Count Egmont, the leaders of the Low Countries' Protestants, on behalf of the Calvinists.

When Philip of Spain set up the Inquisition and began that fearful persecution of Dutch Protestants, Saravia fled to Guernsey where he laboured in a twofold capacity, doing the work of an evangelist and teaching at a newly established school, Elizabeth College. It was through his tireless ministry that the preaching of God's Word was firmly planted there. From this island retreat, he was recalled to the continent by the Belgian churches in 1577. He was invited to become Professor of Divinity at the University of Leyden in 1582; and soon after was also made preacher of the French church in that city. He received the degree of Doctor of Divinity whilst at Leyden.

In 1587 he came to England with the Earl of Leicester, and became master of the grammar-school in Southampton, where, he trained many distinguished pupils. He then served as Vicar of Lewisham in Kent. He received a Doctor of Divinity from Oxford in 1590 and he became Prebend at Gloucester, then Canterbury in 1595, and Westminster in 1601, and was chosen by Andrewes to serve on the First Westminster Company. Whilst he was Prebend at Canterbury he made acquaintance with Richard Hooker, who was Rector of the village of Borne some three miles from Canterbury. Izaak Walton said that, "those two excellent persons began a holy friendship increasing daily to so high and holy affection that their two wills seemed to be but one and the same; and their designs, both for the glory of God, and peace of the church, still assisting and improving each other's virtues, and the desired comforts of a peaceable piety." Saravia was Hooker's confidential adviser while the latter was preparing his books *Of the Laws of Ecclesiastical Polity.*

Like Andrewes and Overall, he approved the divine right of kings and the august function of bishops, and was "a terribly high churchman". His zeal for episcopacy led him to publish several Latin treatises against Beza, Danæus, and other Presbyterians. He also published a treatise on papal primacy against the Jesuit Gretser. He maintained the authority of the bishops by apostolic warrant, and in his *Treatise on the Different Degrees of the Christian Priesthood,* published in 1590, he declared that "by apostles are meant bishops", with Titus and Timotheus created bishops by divinely authorised ordination. Any attempt to overthrow this primitive authority would result in a deformed church, not a reformed church! He was therefore a man of the established order of things, and disliked change and was opposed to novelty.

In 1609 he became Rector of Great Chart in Kent. He is said to have been "educated in all kinds of literature in his younger days, especially in several languages". Archbishop Whitgift held him in the highest esteem, and relied much on Dr Saravia's Hebrew learning in his contests with Hugh Broughton, that formidable Puritan divine.

In 1611 he had published a portfolio of treatises called *Diversi Tractatus Theologi,* and on the 11 May 1612 he attended his last Chapter Meeting at Westminster Abbey. At the end of that month he had an audience with King James and noted that he was impressed with the King's knowledge of theology.

These were the last occasions on which he visited London. He died in Canterbury on the 15 January 1613 at the age of eighty two, and he was buried in the cathedral, with his first wife Catherine, on the 19 January. He ended his life with an estate estimated to be in the region of £1,366, which was truly an enormous sum for those days. His second wife, Margaret, erected the following plaque in his memory, and it can be seen in the cathedral near the north west door of the nave:

Dilecto conivgi Hadriano de Seravia
Margareta Wiits adhuc svperstes
Qvacvm ille nuptias secundo iniit
annosq. sex pie et feliciter vixit
Memoriale hoc syncervm, Licet
exigvvm Amoris svi qvasi pignvs
ponendvm coravit. Fvit is dvm vixit
Theologiae Doctor egregivs, Cathe-
dralis hvius ecclesiae Praebendarivs
meritissimus vir in omni literarum
Genere eximivs; pietate, probitate,
gravitate, svavitate, morvm Insignis:
scriptis clarvs, Fide plenvs, et bonis
operibus dives valde. Natione Belga
natvs Hedinae Artesiae. Rexit
Qvondam Lvgdvni Batavorvm Angliam
Petit primo svb initivm Regni beatae
Memoriae Elizabethae. Doctor
(Lvgdvni ante creatvs) Oxoniae
Post incorporatvs est.
In memoria aeterna erit Ivstvs.
1612

The following is a translation:

> To Hadrianus de Saravia, a beloved husband, Margaret Wiits, surviving to the present, whom he married as his second wife and with whom he lived piously and happily for six years, arranged for this memorial to be set up as an, albeit small, but sincere token of her love. Whilst he lived he was a distinguished Doctor of Theology, a most worthy prebendary of this cathedral church, an outstanding man in all branches of letters, remarkable for the piety, uprightness, sobriety and sweetness of his conduct, renowned for his writings, full of faith and abounding richly in good works. He was a native of the Netherlands born at Hesdin in Artois. Sometime Rector of Leiden, he first came to England at the beginning of the reign of Elizabeth of blessed memory. Doctor, first of Leiden, and afterwards incorporated at Oxford. The righteous man will be remembered forever. 1612.

The introductory passage to his will reveals an interesting insight into his beliefs.

> First of all I confess that I die in the faith delivered to the church by the apostles of our Lord Jesus Christ and the prophets which form the contents of the canonical books of the Old and New Testament and which is presently accepted in the English Church by public authority. These fifty years, after I had quitted and renounced the errors of tyranny and idolatry which hold sway in the Roman Church, I have taught and professed this faith privately and in public. I accept and greatly esteem the so called Apostles' Creed, the Creed of Nicea and of the other three ecumenical Councils with that of Athanasius, because they are gathered from God's Word. To these I add the Confession of the English Church together with that which the German princes presented to the Emperor at Augsburg in the year of our Lord 1530. I am not aware of any errors which have been condemned by God's Word or by the Fathers of the Church's earliest days. I therefore condemn all heresies and teachings which are contrary to the written Word of God and particularly those which were condemned by those four renowned councils, that of Nicea, of Constantinople, the first of Ephesus and that of Chalcedon. When God shall once summon me out of this life, then, certain of the

> salvation proclaimed to me by Christ the Lord, I entrust my soul into his hands and I leave my body to be committed to the earth without ostentatious funeral.

The Secretary of State to King James I, Sir Thomas Lake, a former pupil of Hadrian Saravia, described him in these words: "He is a Minister of State fit to serve the greatest prince in Europe."

JOHN LAYFIELD a former Fellow and Lecturer at Trinity College, Cambridge. He became Rector of St Clement Danes in the Strand in 1602. He was not only a skilled linguist, proficient in Greek and Hebrew, but was an adventurer, explorer and architect. He had ventured to the West Indies as chaplain and chronicler to the third Earl of Cumberland. The voyage to Puerto Rico was made in the spring of either 1596 or 1598. It was a dangerous and tragic expedition, in which hundreds died. Cumberland himself was very nearly drowned in his armour as he lay wounded under Spanish fire, unable to lift himself from the shallow waters of a Puerto Rican rio (river). He has left in *Purchas, His Pilgrims,* one of the most wonderful accounts of the arrival of the English in the Caribbean. Layfield had a gift for rich and dramatic narrative. His chronicle is a heart-gripping narrative of adventure and discovery. In May, at the island of Dominica, he wrote:

> By two in the afternoon we were come so near abroad the shore that we were met with many canoes manned with men wholly naked, saving that they had chains and bracelets and some bodkins in their ears, or some strap in their nostrils or lips ... They are men of good proportions, strong and light limbed, but few of them tall, their wits able to direct them to things bodily profitable ... They have wickers platted something like a broad shield to defend the rain, they that want use a very broad leaf for that purpose. They provide shelter against rain because it washeth off their red painting, laid so on that if you touch it you find it on your fingers ... They saw their women as naked as we had seen their men and alike attired even to the boring of their lips and ears. Yet in that nakedness they discovered some sparks of modesty, not willingly coming in the sight of strange apparelled

> men, and whom they did come busy to cover what should have been better covered …
>
> The soil is very fat, even in the most neglected places matching the garden plats in England for a rich black mold; so mountainous that the valley may better be called pits than plains, and withal so impassably wooded that it is marvellous how those naked souls can be able to pull themselves through them without renting their natural clothes … These hills are apparelled with very good trees of many sorts. The tallness of these unrequested trees makes the hills seem more hilly than of themselves happily they are; for they grow so like good children of some happy civil body, without envy or oppression, as that they look like a proud meadow about Oxford, when after some eruption Thames is again couched low within his own banks, leaving the earth's mantle more rugged and flaky than otherwise it would have been …
>
> A wolvish kind of wild dogs which are bred in the woods and there do go in great companies together … live off crabs … an animal, a living and sensible creature … these woods are full of those crabs … Parrots and parakeets are here … I have ordinarily seen them fly in flocks …
>
> A woody pine apple is of an exceeding durance and lasting. The taste of this fruit is very delicious, so as it quickly breedeth a fulness. For I cannot like it in the palate to any (me thinks) better than to very ripe strawberries and cream, the rather if a man hath already eaten almost his belly full … It growth upon a bush like an artichoke … coming near to the relish of an Apple-john [a new word when Layfield wrote and describing the banana] … that hath been kept till it is over-ripe, saving that methought I still found some taste of a root in it, the meat of it is lapped up in a thin skin, which being scored the long way with a knife, delivereth what is within it.[6]

There are many words in this account that are found in the King James Bible, and there are rhythms here which are echoed in those Hebrew passages that he was called upon to translate. Layfield was among the men who translated the opening chapters of the book of Genesis. His experience of the Caribbean isles, and in particular the breathtaking forests of Dominica, where "the trees do continually maintain themselves in a green-good liking", and "of many fine rivers, which do requite the shadow and coolness they receive from the trees, give them back again, a continual refreshing of every sweet and tasty water", was a picture of Paradise itself with its all-enveloping lushness! Layfield would have had a hand in writing these wonderful words:

> *And out of the ground made the LORD God to grow every tree that is pleasant to the sight, and good for food: the tree of life also in the midst of the garden, and the tree of knowledge of good and evil. And a river went out of Eden to water the garden.*

As an architect, his judgment was much relied upon for the fabric of the tabernacle (Exodus xxvi.) and the temple (1 Kings vi.), as all the fine woodcut engravings found in the Geneva Bible were forbidden in the King James Bible. Few things are more difficult, than the giving of architectural details in such a manner as to be intelligible to the unprofessional reader, but in this Layfield excelled:

> *And the house which King Solomon built for the LORD, the length thereof was threescore cubits, and the height thereof thirty cubits. And the porch before the temple of the house, twenty cubits was the length thereof, according to the breadth of the house; and ten cubits was the breadth thereof before the house. And for the house he made windows of narrow lights.*
>
> 1 Kings vi.2-4.

Layfield died at his rectory in 1617.

RICHARD THOMPSON was born in Holland to English parents. In 1587 he was awarded his bachelor's degree at Clare Hall, and in that year became the Rector of Upwell. He received his M.A. degree from both Cambridge and Oxford. By 1604 he had been awarded a Doctor of Divinity degree, and had become a graduate of both universities. He believed in the freedom of the will, and the Presbyterian divines called him "the grand propagator of Arminianism". In his later years he used that 'free will' to indulge himself both with food and wine, for he was a most corpulent fellow. Prynne said he was, "a debauched drunken English-Dutchman who seldom went to bed one night sober." This assessment is both vindictive and exaggerated. Few divines of that day were averse to drinking, and very few wholly abstained from it. But if he had what others may have thought too much by night, he arose in the morning with his head clear enough to go forward competently with the day's work. He was, however, one of the foremost Hebraists of that day. When Andrewes became Bishop of Ely in 1609, he gave Thompson the living of Snailwell, a few miles from Newmarket. One can hardly envisage a godly man like Andrewes rewarding a drunkard with such a living!

William Bedwell was born in 1562 and was educated at St John's College, Cambridge. He was Vicar of Tottenham High Cross, and then, from 1601, of St Ethelburgh's in Bishopsgate Street, London. He was regarded as an eminent oriental scholar, "for the Eastern tongues, as learned a man as most lived in these modern times." He published in quarto an edition of the epistles of St John in Arabic, with a Latin version, printed at the press of Raphelengius, at Antwerp, in 1612. He also left many Arabic manuscripts to the University of Cambridge. His fame for Arabic learning was so great that, when Erpenius, a most renowned orientalist, resided in England, in 1606, he was much indebted to Bedwell for direction in his studies. Bedwell was rightly regarded as the father of Arabic studies. It was Bedwell who promoted and revived the study of the Arabic language and literature in Europe. For many years Bedwell was engaged in producing an Arabic lexicon in three volumes, but proceeding very slowly, from a desire to make his work as perfect as possible, Golius forestalled him, by the publication of a similar work.

After Bedwell's death at the age of seventy on May 5, 1632, the voluminous manuscripts were loaned by the University of Cambridge, to aid Dr Castell's colossal work, the *Lexicon Heptaglotton.* He also commenced a Persian dictionary, which is still preserved in the Bodleian Library at Oxford. In 1615 he published his book, *A Discovery of the Impostures of Mohamet and of the Koran.*

This remarkable linguist was also a mathematician! He invented a geometric ruler that was named after him and had a notable library of books on mathematics and astronomy.

Richard Clarke was a Fellow of Christ's College, Cambridge. He was regarded as a very learned clergyman and eminent preacher. He was Vicar of Minster and Monkton in Thanet, and one of the six preachers of the cathedral church in Canterbury. He died in 1634, and three years after his death a folio volume of his learned sermons was published. Preaching on atheism he said:

> There are two sorts of atheism, mental and vocal ... I pardon the mouth atheist. For he that shall openly say, There is no God, will *ipso facto* be thought beside himself. Or if he seem to have his wits, yet they that hear him will abhor him; they will stop their ears against his blasphemy, they will hiss at him, they will spit at him; his impious assertion shall not stumble any one. But the heart atheist that saith God is, but thinks it not, and lives accordingly, ungodly, unrighteously, unsoberly ... his sin is greater than his hypocrisy.[7]

ROBERT TIGHE was born at Deeping, Lincolnshire; and was educated at both Oxford and Cambridge. He was Archdeacon of Middlesex and Vicar of the Church of All Hallows, Barking, London, the church where Lancelot Andrewes had been baptised. He is described as "an excellent textuary and profound linguist". He died in 1620 leaving to his son an estate of one thousand pounds a year.

FRANCIS BURLEIGH, of whom we know even less than Robert Tighe. He had been a scholar at Pembroke, Andrewes's own college, and was made Vicar of Bishop's Stortford in 1590, which benefice he held at the time of his appointment to the important service of Bible translation.

GEOFFREY KING was a Fellow of King's College, Cambridge, and succeeded Mr. Spalding as Regius Professor of Hebrew at Cambridge.

The Westminster Hebrew group appears to have been a well balanced team. They were all from the south of England, most of them holding livings in or near London. Andrewes was the scholarly linguist with an irenic spirit; Overall, the studious and diligent workman; Saravia, with his analytical understanding of Calvinistic doctrine tempering Thomson's free will novelties; Thomson, the Arminian and master of word roots; Bedwell, the renowned Arabic and Persic scholar, versed in the oriental tongues; and Clarke, the fiery preacher. These, with the lesser men of the company, could sit down in the Jerusalem Chamber and discuss the books of the Bible they were called upon to translate. These eminent scholars with all their shades of doctrine bore with each other. They united in their desire to produce a good and accurate translation of the Old Testament passages ascribed to them. Whilst it is true that Andrewes had written to the secretary of the Society of Antiquaries in late 1604, that, "most of our company are negligent," there is nothing negligent about the translation that was finished in 1608. The Westminster Company was driven on by their inimitable Director to produce a work of simple and matchless grandeur, like the opening scene of some grand opera:

> *In the beginning God created the Heaven, and the Earth.*
> *And the earth was without form, and void, and darkness was upon the face of the deep: and the Spirit of God moved upon the face of the waters.*

Of these verses, when compared to Tyndale and to the Geneva, Nicholson writes,

> These are slight and marvellous changes. Some are almost purely rhythmic. To say 'the Heaven' and 'the Earth', which he borrowed from the Genevans, allows an easier run than Tyndale's harsher and more naked substantives. The commas after 'Heaven' and in the second verse are signs to pause in the reading of it, and the colon after 'deep' marks a slightly longer rest. In these slightest of ways, Andrewes introduces two new qualities to add to Tyndale's: an aural fluency and the sense of ease which comes from that; and, allied to that ease, a pace of deliberate and magisterial slowness, no hurry here, pausing in its hugeness, those bass colours in the vocabulary matched by a heavy, soft drumming of the rhythm. It is as solemn and orderly as the beginning of a steady and majestic march … The face of the waters carries a subliminal suggestion that the face of God is reflected in them.[8]

The part of the Bible assigned to this group was Genesis to 2 Kings inclusive. Tyndale had translated literally from the original Hebrew of the Old Testament from Genesis to Nehemiah, and this provided a remarkable basis for Andrewes and the First Westminster Company. They also had the Geneva Bible, and frequently a Hebrew text cited in the Geneva margin reappeared in the King James text, for example:

- At Genesis ii. v. 22, where the King James says that of Adam's rib God *made … a woman*, the Geneva, and AV have a marginal note saying, "Hebrew: builded."
- Genesis iii. v.7, where the Geneva has *breeches*, we find that Coverdale, Bishops', and King James have *aprons*. The Geneva has a marginal note, "Ebr.* Things to gird about to hide the privities." The Authorised Version includes the Genevan footnote, *Or things to gird about.*

SECOND WESTMINSTER COMPANY:— THE NEW TESTAMENT EPISTLES

William Barlow	Bishop of Rochester
William Dakins	Professor of Gresham College
Roger Fenton	Vicar of Chigwell
Ralph Hutchinson	President of St John's, Oxford
Michael Rabbett	Caius College, Cambridge
Thomas Sanderson	Rector of All Hallows
John Spenser	President of Corpus Christi

With the exception of William Barlow, this was a relatively undistinguished company. Two of its members died before the completion of the task and were not replaced. Their task was to translate the Epistles, which included the majestic writings of the Apostle Paul with their profound theology, fiery polemic, and tender pastoral counsel.

WILLIAM BARLOW had been the recorder at the Hampton Court Conference. He was born in 1564 and gained the patronage of Dr Richard Cosin, who paid for his education at Trinity Hall, Cambridge where he gained his BA in 1583, his MA in 1587, and was admitted as a Fellow in 1590. He completed his BD in 1594 and his DD in 1599 at the age of thirty-five. Archbishop Whitgift made him sinecure Rector of Orpington in Kent. Shortly before Cosin's death, Barlow was appointed as a chaplain to Archbishop Whitgift, then Rector of St Dunstan's in the East, and a prebendary at St Paul's Cathedral, Chiswick; later he was chosen as one of the twelve chaplains to Queen

* Hebrew.

Westminster Abbey,
Jerusalem Chamber to the right of the West Gate.

Emmanuel College, Cambridge

Lawrence Chaderton commemorated in a stained glass window in the Chapel, Emmanuel College.

Elizabeth. It was Barlow who was appointed by the old and heartbroken queen to attend her last and dearest favourite, Robert Devereux, the Earl of Essex, during his confinement in the Tower under sentence of death, and to be present at his excessively gory execution within its ramparts in semi-privacy on Ash Wednesday 25 February 1601. Devereux, so tall, so youthful, so blond, clad in scarlet, lay down and after a moment gave the sign for the end by thrusting out his scarlet arms. The mighty axeman thrice raised the axe in a mighty curve and thrice smashed it down. He was so frightened that he first slashed the Earl through the shoulder, then through the head, and at last through the neck in a fashion most grisly. Stooping, he lifted the bloodied head, held it high for all to see, and roared as was his final duty, "God save the Queen!"

On top of this ordeal Barlow was required by royal command to preach at St Paul's Cross under special instruction from Robert Cecil, Secretary of State (followed most exactly by the preacher) to make known to the world at large the Earl's confession of guilt, sincere repentance of his treason, and his recital of the Apostles' Creed on the scaffold (Appendix 4). Then, in 1606, he was asked to inter the one-day-old body of the King and Queen's daughter, Princess Sophia, in Henry VII's Chapel, Westminster Abbey. Barlow believed in the royal-cum-divine prerogative: "It is the prudence of a prince which swayeth the sceptre as the stern guides the ship." The king's body, he said, is "sacred by holy unction ... their authority sacred; that is, free from touch of disgrace, or dismay of terror by any human power." No wonder he was greatly approved of by King James.

In 1601 he resigned his Prebend at Chiswick in favour of another at Westminster, and the Deanery of Chester, and later the bishopric of Rochester. As one with a sycophantic tendency, he was one of the prelates assembled on the King's side to overcome the arguments of the Puritans at the Hampton Court Conference, and it was Barlow who drew up a report of the encounter. Barlow's account is no doubt jaundiced, for he records how the Puritans were brow-beaten and hectored in the most abusive manner by the monarch and his minions. The King was in his element, trampling with such fury on the claims of the Puritans that his lordly prelates were in raptures of ecstasy, going down on their knees, and blessing God extemporaneously, for "such a king as had not been seen since Christ's day"! These men of the Prayer Book praying without the Prayer Book!

He was the obvious choice to lead the Second Westminster Company. In 1605, along with other Bible translators, he had preached after the failed Gunpowder Plot. He preached his first Guy Fawkes sermon at Westminster from Psalm 18:50: *Great deliverance giveth he to his king*, saying that, if the plot had succeeded, "this whirling blast would have been unto our sacred king the fiery chariot of Elias to carry his soul up to Heaven."[10] He was appointed Bishop of Lincoln in June 1608, but died suddenly at the age of fifty in 1613, and was buried at the Midland village of Buckden, where the bishop's palace had been situated.

WILLIAM DAKINS was born in 1570 at Ashwell in Herfordshire, and was educated at Westminster, and then at Trinity College, Cambridge, obtaining his BA, then MA, and finally BD in 1601. He was chosen as Greek Lecturer in 1602 and in 1603 became Vicar of Trumpington in Cambridgeshire. Then, in 1604, he was chosen to succeed Dr Hugh Gray as Professor of Divinity at Gresham College when only thirty-five years of age. Even the King acknowledged that Dakins was a learned Grecian, and he was renowned on account of "his skill in the original languages". In 1606, Dakins was chosen Dean of Trinity College; he died, however, in February 1607 at the tender age of thirty-seven.

ROGER FENTON was a native of Lancashire, and born in 1567. He was Fellow of Pembroke Hall, Cambridge. For many years he was the "painful, pious, learned, and beloved minister" of St Stephen's, Walbrook, London, to which he was admitted in 1601. He succeeded Roger Andrewes to the vicarage of Chigwell in Essex in 1606. He was a gifted preacher, and preached against simony; against usury in 1611 (later issued in three volumes); and then shortly before his death in 1616 he preached upon 'oathes'. A series of sermons were also printed posthumously against "dependence on Rome". His "judgment was admired on every hand, his naked innocency, and majesty of style, like a master bee without a sting."[11] He died on the 16 January 1616, aged fifty years. He lies, buried beneath the communion table in St Stephen's, Walbrook, where there is a monument erected to his memory with an inscription expressing his parishioners affection toward him as their faithful pastor, eminent for piety and learning. His closest friend, Bishop Felton, said of him, "None was fitter to dive into the depths of school divinity ... Never a more learned hath Pembroke Hall brought forth, with but one exception"—that one exception being Lancelot Andrewes.

Ralph Hutchinson was born in 1553 and was educated at St John's College, Oxford, where he obtained his DD before being elected as president of the College. He became Vicar of Cropthorne in Worcestershire, Charlebury in Oxfordshire, and then Prebendary at St Paul's Cathedral. Appointed to work in the Second Westminster Company, he died before the work was completed in 1606 at the age of forty-three. John Bois, however, used the notes he left behind in the meetings of the General Committee (see Appendix 6). His notes on 1 Corinthians 6:4 were incorporated into the King James translation, *If then ye have judgments of things pertaining to this life, set them to judge who are least esteemed in the church.*

Michael Rabett was born in 1552 and died at the age of eighty in 1632. He was educated at Westminster School and Trinity College, Cambridge, and then Gonville and Caius, from which he obtained his DD and served as proctor. He was fifty-two years of age when called upon to serve on the Second Westminster Company and was at the prime of his powers as a master of Greek.

Of Thomas Sanderson little is known, other than he was Rector of All Hallows the Great, London, and later the Archdeacon of Rochester.

However, we know far more of John Spenser who was born in 1559 in the County of Suffolk. His father, Thomas Spencer, is listed among the members of the English Church in Geneva, where he had married his wife, Alice, in 1557. Thomas Spencer had worked upon the Genevan Bible and, upon his return to England, was appointed Rector of Hadleigh in Suffolk where he died in 1571. His son, John, was educated at that 'hive of bees' for learning Latin and Greek, Corpus Christi, where at the age of nineteen he was appointed reader of Greek and obtained his BD in 1590. Upon leaving Oxford, he had a succession of livings at Aveley and Ardleigh, both in Essex; and then at Faversham in Kent. His wife was a great-niece of Archbishop Thomas Cranmer, whom Queen Mary burnt at the stake for his Protestantism.

Upon the death of Richard Hooker, the Fellows of Corpus Christi immediately elected Spenser president of their College on June 9 1607. It was Spenser who edited and rendered fit for the press the last three volumes of Hooker's work, *The Laws of Eccesiastical Polity.* His death took place on 3 April 1614, when he was fifty-five years of age.

The Second Westminster Company began work in November 1604 and completed its task by May 1607, having worked for some 125 weeks and revised 116 chapters.

FIRST CAMBRIDGE COMPANY

TRANSLATED THE BOOKS FROM 1 CHRONICLES THROUGH TO ECCLESIASTES, AND THE SONG OF SOLOMON.

Dr Edward Lively	Regius Professor of Hebrew
Dr John Richardson	Regius Professor of Divinity
Dr Lawrence Chaderton	Master of Emmanuel College (1581-1622)
Mr. Francis Dillingham	Fellow of Christ's Church College
Dr Thomas Harrison	Vice-Master of Trinity College
Mr. Roger Andrewes	Master of Jesus College, and brother of Lancelot
Mr. Robert Spalding	Fellow of St John's College
Dr Andrew Bing	Fellow of Peterhouse

At Cambridge the Hebrew group had as Director EDWARD LIVELY, the father of thirteen children. Lively was born sometime in 1545, had studied Hebrew under Drusius the famous Flemish scholar, who in turn had been instructed by the Italian, Tremellio. His wife, Catherine died sometime in 1604, leaving our translator with the thirteen children to support. A patient, humble, and diligent man, he died the next year before the translation was completed, but not before he had passed on to the other translators his assiduous methods of Hebrew study. He is commemorated as "one of the best linguists in the world". He was a student, and afterwards a Fellow, of Trinity College, Cambridge, and King's Professor of Hebrew. He was actively employed in the preliminary arrangements for the translation, and appears to have stood high in the confidence of the King. Much dependence was placed on his surpassing knowledge of the oriental tongues. But his death, in May 1605, disappointed all such expectations, and is said to have considerably retarded the commencement of the work. He was buried at St Edward's, Cambridge, May 7 1605, only seven months after he had received the good living of Purleigh, Essex. It was said that "too earnest study and pains about the translation hastened his death".

His stipend had been small and, after many troubles and the loss of his dear wife, the mother of his thirteen children, he was well provided for by Dr Barlow that he might be enabled to devote himself to the business of translation. He died of quinsy after four days' illness, leaving eleven orphans, "destitute of necessaries for their maintenance, but only such as God, and good friends, should provide." He was the author of a Latin exposition of five of the Minor Prophets. He is regarded as second only to Pococke, as "the greatest of our Hebraists".

Dr John Richardson. This profound divine was born at Linton, seven miles from Cambridge, around 1564. One fact that stands out about Dr Richardson is that he was somewhat corpulent. The Calvinists often referred to him as that "fat-bellied Arminian"! He went to Clare Hall, Cambridge, where he must have known well "Dutch" Thompson, the other Arminian. He became Rector of Upwell in Norfolk in 1595, and then chosen a Fellow at that most puritan of colleges, Emmanuel, in 1585. After obtaining his Doctor of Divinity, he was appointed the Regius Professor of Divinity, and in 1609 became Master of Peterhouse, then in 1615 Master of Trinity, and eventually Vice-Chancellor of the University in 1617. He died in 1625, and was buried in Trinity College Chapel.

He was noted "as a most excellent linguist", as every good theologian must be, for, as Coleridge says, "language is the armoury of the human mind; and at once contains the trophies of its past, and the weapons of its future conquests."

In those days it was the custom at seats of learning for the ablest men to hold public disputes in the Latin tongue, with a view to displaying their skill in the weapons of logic and the "dialectic defence". As the ancient knights delighted to display and exercise their skill and strength in running at tilt and amicably breaking spears with one another, so the great scholars used to grapple with each other in the arena of public argument and strive for literary 'masteries'. Those scholastic tournaments were sure to be got up whenever the great halls of learning were visited by the King; and the logical conflicts, always conducted in the Latin tongue, were attended with as much absorbing interest as were the shows of gladiators among the Romans.

On such an occasion, when James I was visiting Cambridge, "an extraordinary act in divinity was kept for His Majesty's entertainment. Dr John Davenant, later Bishop of Salisbury, was 'respondent'. His task was to fend off all who might choose to assail the point he was to defend, namely, that kings might never be excommunicated. Well did Dr Davenant conduct the war of words, till Dr Richardson cited the example of Ambrose, the famous Bishop of Milan, who, to the admiration of the whole Christian world, excommunicated the emperor Theodosius the Great. King James, who was always very sensitive on the subject of royal prerogative, saw that Davenant was staggering under that stunning fact, and to save him, cried out in a frenzied passion, "Profecto fuit hoc ab Ambrosio insolentissime factum" ("Verily, this was a great piece of insolence on the part of Ambrose"). To this, Dr Richardson calmly rejoined, "Responsum vere regium, et Alexandro dignum, hoc est non argument dissolvere, sed desecare" ("A truly royal response, and worthy of Alexander! This is cutting our knotty arguments, instead of untying them"). And so the King took his seat and desisted from further discussion. The mild dignity of this remonstrance, in which independence and submission are happily combined, is about all we know of the personal character of the man. Clearly he was a wise, faithful, and learned translator of the Word of God.

LAWRENCE CHADERTON was a staunch Puritan, brave and godly, learned and laborious. He was born at Lees Hall near Bolton in Lancashire, in the year 1537. His family were wealthy and addicted to popery, in which religion he was carefully nurtured. Being destined to the bar, he was sent to the Inns of Court, at London, where he spent some years in the study and practice of the law. Here he became a Protestant; and, forsaking the law, entered as student at Christ's

College, Cambridge, at the age of twenty-six in 1564. Mr. Chaderton wrote to his father asking for some pecuniary aid, but the wrathful old papist replied,

> Son Laurence, if you will renounce this new sect you may expect all the happiness which the care of an indulgent father can assure you. Otherwise, I enclose a shilling to buy a wallet. Go and beg! [9]

Disinherited of a large estate, Laurence was resolved to continue his studies at Christ's College, and became an outstanding scholar in Hebrew, Latin, Greek, French, Spanish, and Italian, as well as indulging in a taste for botany. He never had recourse to beg. His mind was sustained by the promises of the Saviour, for whose sake he had "endured the loss of all things". He took his first degree in 1567, and was then chosen one of the Fellows of his college. He became a Master of Arts in 1571; and Bachelor of Divinity in 1584, receiving his doctorate in 1613.

He was thoroughly skilled with the Latin, Greek, and Hebrew tongues, and was a most diligent student of all the Rabbinical writings. This is evident from the copious annotations in his Bomberg Hebrew Bible, which had been printed in Venice in 1518.

He was appointed lecturer at St Clement's Church, Cambridge. He was a grave, pious, and excellent preacher. There he started a series of afternoon lectures or sermons that continued for fifty years. His biographer, and fellow translator, Dr Dillingham, recounts how his sermons were timed by an hour glass on the pulpit, which on one occasion he turned twice, and then, fearing he had wearied his congregation, he determined to finish his sermon, whereupon the entire congregation cried out, "For God's sake, go on! We beg you, go on!" He then continued for a further hour! He preached at St Clements for fifty years and, when he finally intimated his intention to resign, some forty clergymen who had been converted under his ministry pleaded with him to reconsider his decision. He had a pastor's heart and was greatly venerated. During the fifty-three years of his married life, he never suffered any of his servants to be detained from public worship by the preparation of food or other household chores. He used to say, "I desire as much to have my servants know the Lord as myself."

In 1576 Chaderton had to choose between his Cambridge fellowship and marriage. He resigned in order to marry Cecilia, daughter of Nicholas Culverwell, the Queen's wine merchant. It was a long and happy union, with one daughter.

In 1578 he delivered a sermon at St Paul's Cross, London, which appears to have been his only printed sermon. Here it was that Tyndale's Bible had been burned. In that sermon, he lamented the state of the Gospel ministry,

> There are swarms of idle, ignorant and ungodly curates who neither can nor will go before the flock of Christ in sound doctrine and integrity of life ... but serve mortal and sinful men with simony, flattering words, and servile obedience, not lawfully to obtain one room in the vineyard of the Lord, but two, three, four or more places.[10]

In the year 1584, Sir Walter Mildmay, one of Queen Elizabeth's noted statesmen, founded Emmanuel College, Cambridge. The Queen charged him with having "erected a Puritan foundation". In reply, he said, "No, madam, far be it from me to countenance anything contrary to your established laws, but I have set an acorn, which, when it become an oak, God only knows what will become of it." Sir Walter chose Chaderton as its first Master. The modesty of Mr. Chaderton made him refuse the offer, to which Sir Walter Mildmay responded, "If you will not be the Master, I will not be the Founder." Upon this Chaderton accepted the position and filled it with zeal, and industry, and high repute, for thirty-eight years. It was during his mastership of Emmanuel College, that Dr Chaderton was engaged in the Bible translation. He was in his late sixties, his ripe knowledge was fully digested and matured by experience while "his natural force was not abated", and his faculties burned with inextinguishable blaze.

At the Hampton Court Conference, in 1604, Dr Chaderton was one of the four divines appointed by the King as being "the most grave, learned, and modest of the aggrieved sort", to represent the Puritan interest. Dr Chaderton, however, took no part in the debates, perceiving that the Conference was merely a royal charade, got up to give the Royal Scot an opportunity to avow his bitter hostility to Puritanism. James equated Puritanism with Scottish Presbyterianism and its refusal to be subject to his arbitrary royal power!

Emmanuel was a truly Puritan foundation, and many godly and zealous men were trained within its portals, men who were to carry the Gospel light to New England. Dr Chadderton was a resolute Calvinist and, whilst stressing the need for the new birth, he laid great emphasis upon the sovereignty of divine grace.

In 1622, having reached the ripe old age of eighty-five, he resigned his office and Dr Preston, the very champion of the Puritans, was inducted as Dr Chaderton's successor. The patriarch, however, lived to survive Dr Preston and to see Dr Sancroft, and after him Dr Holdsworth, in the same position. It was Dr Holdsworth who preached Dr Chaderton's funeral service. Dr Holdsworth used to tell him that, as long as he lived, he should be master *in* the house, though he himself was forced to be master *of* the house. The aged saint was always consulted as to the affairs of the college. Right up to his death at the age of 103 in 1640, he was able to read his small print Greek New Testament without the aid of spectacles!

His epitaph is to be found on a monumental stone, at the entrance of Emmanuel College chapel,

Here
Lies the body of
Lawrence Chaderton, D.D.,
Who was the first Master of this College.
He died in the year 1640,
In the one hundred and third
Year of his age.

Francis Dillingham entered Christ's College, Cambridge, in 1583, gaining his MA in 1590, and was elected Fellow in 1594. He was Vicar of Deane (his birthplace) in Bedfordshire, and then of Wilden in the same county. He, along with Thomas Harrison, was a Puritan admirer of Chaderton. His brother and heir, Thomas Dillingham, also minister of Deane, was chosen one of the famous Assembly of Divines at Westminster, but on account of age and illness did not take his seat. Francis was an excellent linguist and renowned as "the great Grecian". He was also a prolific author, writing three major anti-Romish tracts, including a dispute with Cardinal Bellarmine on the nature of true repentance.

In 1603, just before he started work on the Bible, he replied to a scurrilous attack on married ministers by Dr Hill, an arch Romanist. Dr Hill had accused Protestant ministers of, "being too much occupied about wooing, wenching, and wiving, taking upon them to be doctors of divinity and husbands too." Though he never married, Dillingham writes of the joys of those ministers who had married godly wives, wives who learned submission to their husbands in mutual love, according to the biblical pattern.

> That a man may obtain a wife that will be in subjection unto him, he must choose a prudent and wise wife, for prudence and wisdom respecteth persons, place, and manner of doing a thing … Prudence teacheth the wife that her husband is her head, and so subjecteth herself unto him. No marvel then though many men have not their wives in subjection, for they have married fools which know not their place … A wise woman, saith Solomon … buildeth the house, but the foolish destroyeth it with her own hands … A man of religion that matcheth with an irreligious woman is unequally matched, and therefore his yoke needs be heavy … The misery of this age is that … men inquire after wealth, not after religion in a woman. Hence it is that some live discontentedly, and come in the end to great misery.[11]

No doubt Dillingham's views were shaped by the Hebrew Scriptures in Proverbs 31, which he translated into the English.

He died on February 14, 1625, and was buried at Wilden, Bedfordshire.

THOMAS HARRISON was born at London in 1555, and as a biblical scholar was second only to Lancelot Andrewes with whom he was a contemporary at Merchant Taylor's School. He was part of the radical Puritan movement with Chaderton in the 1580s. Harrison was not ashamed to be associated with that ardent Puritan, Thomas Cartwright, even though the latter was imprisoned for his *Admonition to Parliament.* A graduate of St John's College, he had a distinguished academic career as a Greek and Hebrew scholar at Trinity College, one of the most prestigious colleges in Cambridge, where he became Vice-Master. On account of his profound skill in the Hebrew and Greek idioms, he was one of the University's chief examiners of those who sought to be public professors of these languages. He was also a renowned poet, though none of his poems have survived. Such a man would have been of great service in the work on the Psalms.

Robert Spalding was Fellow of St John's College, Cambridge. He succeeded Edward Lively as Regius Professor of Hebrew. Dr Spalding "slept with his fathers", in 1626.

Andrew Bing was a tall, affable young man. Born in Cambridge in 1574, he went to Peterhouse, Cambridge, and became Professor of Hebrew in Trinity College, Cambridge. In course of time he succeeded Geoffrey King, who was Dr Spalding's successor, as the Regius Professor of Hebrew. Dr Bing was Subdean of York in 1606, and was installed as Archdeacon of Norwich in 1618. He was only thirty when King James chose him to work on the Bible, outliving nearly all his fellow workers. He died during the time of the Commonwealth, in 1652.

Roger Andrewes had been Fellow in Pembroke Hall, and became Master of Jesus College, Cambridge. He also became Prebendary of Chichester and Southwell. Like his brother, Lancelot, he was a skilled linguist.

The King James Bible was grounded on a wide range of learning. The translators were men of different persuasions, but the several sides joined in a work that would produce a masterpiece to transcend their age. Their own age honoured them as true scholars of the first rank.

SECOND CAMBRIDGE COMPANY:—
THE PRAYER OF MANASSES AND THE REST OF THE APOCRYPHA

Dr John Duport	Master of Jesus College
Dr William Branthwaite	Fellow of Emmanuel College; Master of Gonville and Caius
Dr Jeremiah Ratcliffe	Fellow of Trinity College
Mr. Samuel Ward	Fellow and Master of Sidney Sussex College; Royal Chaplain
Mr. Andrew Downes	Fellow of St John's; Regius Professor of Greek
Mr. John Boyes	Fellow of Clare Hall; Dean of Canterbury
Mr. Robert Ward	Of King's College

It is surprising that this collection of spurious, unreliable and non-canonical writings should find their inclusion in Jacobean Bibles. Its errors were exposed by Reformed learning, and thereafter a tradition began of separating the books from the rest of the text of Holy Scripture, as in Luther's German, Coverdale's, and Geneva Bibles. This was carried on in the Bishops' and the King James translation. The Puritans were deeply concerned at the retention of these "Popish dregs", and there is increasing evidence that they were omitted from some early editions of the King James Bible.[12] Archbishop Abbot in 1615, however, forbad the publication of Bibles without the Apocrypha, so that from 1615 onwards it was more usual to find the Apocrypha included in the King James Bible. The reasons for not admitting the apocryphal books into the canon of Scripture are briefly the following:

- Not one of them is in the Hebrew language, which alone was used by the inspired historians, prophets and poets of the Old Testament.
- Not one of the writers lays any claim to inspiration.
- These books were never acknowledged as sacred Scriptures by the Jewish church, and therefore were never sanctioned by our Lord.
- They were not allowed a place among the sacred books during the first four centuries of the Christian church.

- They contain incredible statements that contradict not only the canonical Scriptures, but themselves; as when, in the two books of Maccabees, Antiochus Epiphanes is made to die three different deaths in as many different places.
- It inculcates doctrines at variance with the Bible, such as prayers for the dead and sinless perfection.
- It teaches immoral practices, such as lying, suicide, assassination and magical incantations.

For these and other reasons, the apocryphal books, which are all in Greek, except one that is extant only in Latin, are valuable only as ancient documents, illustrative of the manners, language, opinions and history of the East.

John Duport's ancestors had emigrated from Caen in Normandy during the early part of the fifteenth century. John was born at Shepshed, Leicestershire, in 1555, and was educated at Jesus College, Cambridge, where he became a Fellow, and obtained his Doctor of Divinity in 1590. He was then chosen as Master of Jesus College, a position he was to hold for thirty years. He was elected as Vice-Chancellor of the University on no less than four occasions! Duport was chosen as Director of this Company of scholars.

He was a man who adhered rigidly to the doctrine and discipline of the Church of England. In 1595 he became Precentor at St Paul's. He was at various times the Rector of Harlton, Cambridgeshire, Bosworth in Middlesex, and Fulham. Such frequent 'preferments' indicate that he was held in high esteem by wealthy and influential friends who controlled vacant benefices. He married Rachel Cox, the daughter of the Bishop of Ely, by whom he had two sons, one of whom, James, became a distinguished Greek professor. John Duport was a learned man of high standing throughout England, going to his grave in December 1617.

William Branthwaite of Wymondham in Norfolk entered Clare Hall and was awarded his BA in 1582. He was then elected Fellow of Emmanuel College, the newly established Puritan foundation for the training of evangelical preachers and lecturers. He was awarded his MA in 1586, his BD in 1593, and his DD in 1598. He was elected

Master of Gonville and Caius College, and was in that position when named in the royal commission as one of the translators. In 1619 he became Vice-Chancellor of the University. He had a vast library which he bequeathed to his College and that today occupies one bay of the library at Gonville and Caius. Adam Nicholson quotes a modern historian of the College describing viewing Branthwaite's bequest,

> As the eye roams up from the folios below to the tiny octavos among the ceiling joists, one seems to follow a course in the history of learning, from the medieval Bible and its glossators to the continental Protestant divines of the late sixteenth century.[13]

These books marked the rarefied atmosphere in which these learned men lived and breathed.

JEREMIAH RATCLIFFE was the brother of Edward, Physician to King James I. He was educated at Trinity College between 1567 and 1582, from which he obtained his Doctor of Divinity in 1582. He had several livings in the Church, more notably at Trumpton a few miles from Cambridge, Heversham in Westmorland, Evehsam in Worcestershire, and Orwell in Cambridgeshire. He was Vice-Master of his College in 1597. He died in 1612.

SAMUEL WARD was born in 1577 and therefore, along with Dr Fairclough, one of the youngest of the translators. He was a native of Middleham in the county of Durham.

He obtained his BA from Christ Church in 1597, where he had come under the puritan influence of William Perkins. Like many godly men of his age, Ward kept a diary of temptations where he "bewailed his overmuch desire for preferment" and, "my wandering regard at chapel" and, "my gluttony, and sleeping without remembering my last thought should be of God." He deplored, "my hardness this day in hearing God's word," and, "sluggishness in hearing a sermon."[14] After obtaining his MA he was elected Fellow of Emmanuel, where he studied and taught. He was elected a Royal Chaplain. As a translator he worked on the Prayer of Manasses and 1 and 2 Maccabees. He received his Doctorate after he had finished his translation in 1610 and then became Master of Sidney Sussex College where members had to, "abhor popery, bull baiting, bear baiting and bowling greens, together with long curls, huge ruffs, velvet pantaloons, taverns and cards!"[15] He remained Master of Sidney Sussex College for thirty-four years. Under Ward's direction the College flourished, four new fellowships were founded and a new chapel and buildings were erected.

When work commenced on the translation, Ward wrote in his diary:

> Remember, on Wednesday, January 18, was the day when the surplice was first urged by the Archbishop to be brought into Emmanuel College. God grant that worse things do not follow the so strict urging of this indifferent ceremony. Alas, we little expected that King James would have been the first permitter of it to be brought into our college to make us a derision to so many that bear us no good will.[16]

From such entries we get a glimpse of the fears of the Puritans. On the one hand, men like Ward were working on the translation of the Scriptures, and yet, on the other hand, those self-same Scriptures gave no sanction to the ceremonies and ritualism that were now being imposed upon them.

He was distinguished for the gravity of his deportment and for the integrity with which he discharged the duties of his Mastership. He was appointed chaplain to Bishop Montague, who promptly made Ward Archdeacon of Taunton in 1615 and also Prebendary of Wells. In 1617, Dr Toby Matthew, Archbishop of York, made him Prebendary of Ampleford in the cathedral church of York, a position he held until his death.

King James sent Ward, together with three other delegates, in 1618, to the Synod of Dort, in Holland. There the Church of England delegates sat in solemn assembly with those other true churches of Jesus Christ. The object of the Synod was to settle the doctrinal disputes which then were tearing the heart out of the established Church of the Netherlands. The Synod sat for some five months between 3 November 1618 and 29 April 1619, to resolve the long contested dispute between the doctrines of Calvin and those innovations of Armenius. The points in dispute related to divine predestination, the nature and extent of the atonement, the corruption of man, his conversion to Christ, and the perseverance of the saints. These five points are explained in some sixty 'canons', which were, "confirmed by the unanimous consent of all and each of the members of the whole Synod." They represent the most exact statement of Calvinistic belief. Whilst there, Samuel Ward gave an account of the translation of the King James Bible.

On his return, Dr Ward resumed his duties as Master of Sidney Sussex College, and then, in 1621, he was appointed Vice-Chancellor of the University and at the same time appointed Lady Margaret's Professor of Divinity, a post he was to hold for twenty years.

In 1629, and again in 1638, Ward was also involved in correcting the printer's errors which had crept into Robert Barker's editions of the King James Bible. He was summoned as a member of the Westminster Assembly in 1643, but he never attended. He was a decided Puritan in doctrine, but in politics he was a Royalist. In the tumultuous days of the Civil War, he was deemed by some to be a lover of popery because he supported the tyrannical Charles Stuart. In consequence of sending the college-plate to be melted for the King's use, the parliamentary party deprived Dr Ward of his professorships and mastership, and confiscated all his goods. He was, for a short time imprisoned in St John's College, where he contracted the illness that proved fatal. Because of this illness he was released and died at the age of sixty-six in 1643. He was the first person buried in Sidney Sussex Chapel. Dr Goad said of this godly scholar:

None thy quick sight, grave judgment, can beguile,
So skilled in tongues, so sinewy in style;
Add to all these that peaceful soul of thine,
Meek, modest, which all brawling doth decline.

Fuller's *History of the University of Cambridge* describes Dr Ward thus,

> He was a Moses, not only for slowness of speech, but otherwise meekness of nature. Indeed, when in my private thoughts, I have beheld him and Dr Collins, I could not but remember the running of Peter and John to the place where Christ was buried. In which race, John came first, as youngest and swiftest; but Peter first entered the grave. Dr Collins had much speed of him in quickness of parts; but let me say … the other pierced the deeper into underground and profound points of divinity. Now as high winds

> bring some men the sooner into sleep, so, I conceive, the storms and tempests of these distracted times invited this good old man the sooner to his long rest, where we leave him, and quietly draw the curtains about him.[17]

Andrew Downes was born in 1549 and was admitted to St John's College in 1567. He obtained his BA in 1570, elected Fellow in 1571, admitted as a Senior Fellow in 1581, obtained his BD in 1582, and appointed Regius Professor of Greek in 1585, a post which he held until 1627 when he resigned at the age of seventy-seven. Downes was a member of the final Company, which was chosen to review the whole work at the Stationer's Hall. According to Bois's notes, Downes was "a most subtle weigher of words".[15] He was tall, long-faced, with a ruddy complexion and bright eyes. He died on 2 February 1625, at the great age of eighty-one years.

John Bois was born on January 4, 1561. His father William was born and brought up in Halifax. He had studied music and surgery and went to Cambridge with a view to the Church until he broke with Rome. Thereafter he settled on a farm at Nettlestead, near Hadleigh, in Suffolk. Hadleigh would ever be remembered for the martyrdom of Doctor Rowland Taylor (Appendix 2). William Bois joined the Church of England and was presented to the Rectory of West Stow, also in the County of Suffolk. He had married Mirabel Poolye, a godly woman, who had read the Bible twelve times, and the *Book of Martyrs* twice, besides other books.

John's father had taught him to read and write Hebrew and Greek when he was but five years old! John was educated at Hadleigh School, where he became acquainted with John Overall, later to become a member of the First Westminster Company and Dean of St Paul's. He went up to St John's College in 1575, where Dr John Still, Rector of Hadleigh, was Master. Such was John Bois' proficiency in Greek that he had passed through the two-year Greek course within the first month! The chief lecturer in Greek was Andrew Downes, who plied him with the twelve hardest Greek authors. Bois was a diligent and studious learner, frequently spending sixteen hours (from four in the morning until eight at night) in the university library. He was Chief Lecturer in Greek, and gave lectures at four in the morning, which were always well attended by Fellows sitting round by candlelight.

John's father had studied surgery and, whilst at Cambridge, John too determined to become skilled in medicine and purchased a whole library of medical books. Thankfully, he soon discovered that "whatsoever disease he read of, he was troubled with the same himself", and so Bois the hypochondriac put medicine aside and devoted himself to the Bible.

In 1591 he succeeded his father as Rector of West Stow, but resigned that living when his mother went to live with her brother.

In October 1596 he became Rector of Boxworth and married the daughter of the previous incumbent. Apparently, the previous rector, Mr. Holt, had bequeathed the advowson* of that living to his daughter, and therefore whichever minister succeeded him had to marry his daughter first! He hoped his successor might be John Bois and had friends approach him with prospect of Boxworth rectory and a wife. Bois did take the trouble to drag himself away from his Greek manuscripts in the university library, to go and "look her over" before he accepted, and the two took an instant liking to each other; and so it was that Bois accepted the key to the parsonage in October 1596. He married the good lady on February 7, 1598, and so resigned his beloved Fellowship at St John's.

Life on the farm in his youth had given him a strong and robust body. Frequently he would walk the twenty miles from his college to dine with his mother. When travelling on horseback, he would take some book to read or some grammar to study, leaving his horse to find his own way there! With his voracious appetite for learning, he was wedded to his books to the neglect of the financial affairs of his growing family. He left all domestic affairs to the management of his wife, whose want of skill in these matters reduced him to bankruptcy. His books were "his darling", and he boasted that every word of every Greek author was to be found on his shelves. His library was the most complete and costly collection of Greek literature that had ever been made, but, finding himself in debt, he had to sell the larger part of his extensive library in order to keep the creditors at bay. This cruel loss so disheartened him as almost

* The right in English law of presenting a nominee to a benefice.

to drive him from his family and his native country. He was, however, sincerely attached to his wife, with whom he lived in great happiness for forty-five years.

When chosen as part of the Second Cambridge Company, he would spend six days in Cambridge in the work of translation, travelling home on the Saturday evening to discharge his duties on the Sabbath Day. His wife bore him four sons and three daughters. He was a most careful, affectionate father and a loving husband. Five of his children died before he did, two dying within a month in the early summer of 1623 from smallpox. The death of his daughter Mirabel well-nigh broke his heart, as he wrote years later of the bitter night in which Mirabel died.

He only ever ate two meals a day, and never ate or drank anything between meals, unless he was troubled with wind for which he would take a little sugared brandy. After eating meat he would always pick and rub his teeth, esteeming that a special preservative to health, so that he carried to his grave a Hebrew alphabet of teeth. He would then sit or walk an hour or more to digest his meat before he would go into his study. He fasted twice a week. Later in life he never studied between supper and bed, but spent two hours with family and friends.

As a translator he was precise, unequalled in England for his understanding of the Greek, and unsurpassed for the long hours he devoted to the task. Upon finishing his work on the Apocrypha, he was intreated by the other Cambridge Company to give his assistance on their portion of the Old Testament, as he was equally distinguished for his skill in Greek and Hebrew. Their Director, Professor Lively, had died shortly after the work was undertaken and they were desperate for help.

Along with Downes, John Bois was chosen to review the whole work. The notes taken by John Bois were rediscovered after almost four hundred years by Gustavus Paine, and were printed in facsimile by Professor Ward Allen.[18] In 1628 Lancelot Andrewes, the Bishop of Winchester, bestowed the Prebend of Ely Cathedral upon him, a post he held until his death in 1643 at the age of eighty-three. Even in old age he would study for eight hours every day, employing his time in correcting old Greek manuscripts. He arrived at old age unwrinkled, with clear sight, perfect hearing, a fresh skin, a full head of hair, and his body sound. He attributed his health and longevity to the observance of three rules, given him by one of his college tutors, Dr Whittaker: First, always study standing; secondly, never study in a drafty air; and thirdly, never go to bed with his feet cold! He was:

> A most exact grammarian, he read nearly sixty grammars in Latin, Greek, Hebrew, Syriac and others. He wrote notes upon the Four Evangelists and Acts. ... He was a most loving husband. ... In prayer with his family he always kneeled upon the bare bricks. A reverent esteemer of Holy Scripture, in reading or hearing, he would uncover his head.[19]

Among his writings, was a voluminous commentary in Latin on the Gospels and Acts, which was published some twelve years after his death. His preaching was without notes, though not without much prayer and study. He sought at all times to make himself easily understood by the humblest and most ignorant of his hearers.

As his end approached he said, "There has not been a day for these many years, in which I have not meditated at least once upon my death." He met death, at last, with great joy, as an old acquaintance and long expected friend, having survived his wife by two years. He expired, on the Lord's Day of January 14, 1643 aged eighty-four. "He went unto his rest on the day of rest; a man of peace, to the God of peace."

JOHN WARD. All that we know of him is that he was Fellow of King's College, Cambridge; Prebendary of Chichester and Rector of Bishop's Waltham in Hampshire.

FIRST OXFORD COMPANY:—
ISAIAH – MALACHI

The first Oxford divines met in the chambers of Dr Reynolds at Corpus Christi.

Dr John Harding	Regius Professor of Hebrew and President of Magdalen Hall (now Hertford College)
Dr John Reynolds	President of Corpus Christi
Dr Thomas Holland	Regius Professor of Divinity
Dr Richard Kilbye	Rector of Lincoln College, Regius Professor of Hebrew
Mr. Miles Smith	Brasenose College, Prebendary of Hereford and Exeter Cathedrals
Mr. Richard Brett	Fellow of Lincoln College
Mr. Richard Fairclough	Fellow of New College

All of the above were Fellows of their respective Colleges, four of these men were the leading scholars in oriental languages, three were Royal (Regius) Professors of Hebrew, and one of Divinity. All of these men had Puritan sympathies, none of them were High Churchmen, and all were Calvinists. There is no doubt that the First Oxford Company had the most difficult task of all the translators, and the men chosen were equal to that task.

JOHN HARDING was the appointed Director of this esteemed Company. When commissioned by the King to take part in this great enterprise, Dr Harding was Rector of Halsey, in Oxfordshire, and at the same time he was also President of Tyndale's old college, Magdalen. Queen Elizabeth had attempted to reform the College of "the late decays and disasters", that is, the College's Puritan regime. When this failed, Harding was appointed to continue the Puritan tradition of that College, though his appointment was met with much opposition; nonetheless, his learning and piety entitled him to the position he occupied amongst this venerable company of scholars. At the time of his appointment he had been Regius Professor of Hebrew in the University for thirteen years. His occupancy of that chair, at a time when the study of sacred literature was pursued by thousands with a passionate zeal, is clear indication of the stature and fitness of the man for the task.

JOHN REYNOLDS, whom we may justifiably call the father of the King James Bible, was born in Penhoe, Devon, in the year 1549. He entered the University at the age of thirteen and spent all his days within its precincts. He first entered Merton College in 1562, but transferred the following year to Corpus Christi, and became a Fellow in 1566 at the tender age of seventeen. Six years later he was made Greek Lecturer in his College, and was undoubtedly one of the foremost Greek scholars of the day, writing his own introduction, synopsis, index, and copious notes on Aristotle. Unquestionably, Reynolds was the most learned man in Elizabethan and early Stuart England. Those who knew him held him to be learned, pious, courteous, modest, kind, and wholly honest, with a vast memory that made him "a walking library, a third university".

John Reynolds, however, had been a zealous papist, as was his father; his brother, William, though, had become a zealous Protestant. The two brothers were fellow students at Oxford and frequently met for discussion and disputation. Each, in fraternal anxiety for a brother's soul, laboured for the conversion of the other; and each of them was successful! William was so impressed by his brother John's argument for Romanism, that he became an inveterate papist, and so lived and died. John was equally affected by William's arguments for the Protestant faith, that he became a decided Protestant of the Puritan mould, and continued to his death a vigorous defender of the Protestant cause. Reynold's father remained a Roman Catholic. His brother William resigned his position as Rector of Lavenham, migrated to Douai and was received back into the Roman Church in 1575. He then held the Chair of Divinity at the English College in Rheims and helped Gregory Martin translate the Rheims New Testament of 1582!

In 1578, John Hart, a popish zealot, challenged all the learned men in the nation to a public debate. One of Queen Elizabeth's privy counsellors approached Dr Reynolds, who took up the challenge.

He stood with Luther in maintaining that the Authority of Holy Scripture is greater than that of the Church, writing:

> Avant all ye, who braine-sicke toyes and fancies vain defend,
> Who on humane tradition and Fathers' favors depend,
> The holy written Word of God doth show the perfect way
> Whereby from death to life arise, from curse to bliss ye may.[20]

After several public debates, the Pope's champion retired from the battlefield a defeated and broken man. The Queen appointed Reynolds to be the Royal Professor of Divinity in the University.

John Reynolds became a prolific author and disputant, frequently taking up cudgels with Rome's 'Goliath', Cardinal Bellarmine, on such themes as "Scripture and the Church", "Idolatry and the Roman Church," and "250 Censures on the Apocrypha". Reynolds placed himself in the very forefront of the battle against popery, and vicious words were daily shot at him. In 1602, as he walked in London in Finsbury Fields, "an arrow whether shot purposely by some Jesuit papist or at random, fell upon his breast but entered not his body"—and for that we can give thanks to the good providence of God, who spared our translator for the final work of his life.

In 1592 he began an assault on stage plays. In 1566, when Reynolds was a student at Oxford, Queen Elizabeth had paid a visit to the University. At Corpus Christi College a play composed for her was acted with Reynolds, then seventeen, playing the role of a female. The Queen enjoyed the performance, laughing much and thanking the author for his pains. Now, nearly thirty years after, Reynolds could not forgive himself for acting the part of a girl. Nearly all his pamphlet, *The Overthrow of Stage Plays,* was about how unbiblical it was for men to wear women's clothing and for people to see such shameful make-believe. The law of God, in Deuteronomy 22:5, expressly forbade a man to put on women's raiment, and so Reynolds laid the axe to the tree of fashionable plays so popular at Elizabethan and Stuart court life. Nevertheless, in spite of Reynolds's protestations, the English stage would continue to present boy actors in women's parts. Of the plays themselves, Reynolds declared,

> They meditate how they may inflame a tender youth with love, entice him to dalliance, to whoredom, to incest, inure their minds and bodies to uncomely, dissolute, railing, boasting, knavish, foolish, brainsick, drunken conceits, words and gestures.[21]

When the Queen visited Oxford in 1592, she sent for the heads of houses and others, and reprimanded Dr Reynolds for his obstinate preciseness, willing him to follow her laws and not run before them.[22]

From the time of his conversion, he was a most able and gifted preacher of the Word of God. He was wholly addicted to the study of the Scriptures in the original tongues, and read all the Greek and Latin Fathers, as well as all the ancient records of the Church. He had an incredibly retentive memory and could readily turn to any specific passage, in every leaf, page, column and paragraph of the numerous and voluminous works he had read. He was considered by many to be "the very treasury of erudition", "a living library." Among the students whom he tutored was Richard Hooker, who was to write *The Laws of Ecclesiastical Polity.*

He was renowned as a man of prodigious learning, sound judgment, marvellous memory, and lofty character. He was one of four eminent scholars chosen by James I to represent the Puritan cause at the Hampton Court Conference, and undoubtedly he was their leading spokesmen, for it was he who made the suggestion for a new translation of the Bible. He opposed episcopacy (graciously declining the Queen's offer of a bishopric), maintaining, with the Reformed churches of Europe, that bishops were but pastors who had equal authority and power with all true ministers of the Word of God. Of the church, he said it was,

> every faithful company, yea, every faithful body, a temple to serve God in. The presence of Christ among two or three, gathered together in his name, maketh any place a church, even as the presence of a king with his attendants maketh any place a court.[23]

This most distinguished of scholars, however, was not to see the full fruits of his suggestion as he died from consumption on 21 May 1607. By then though he had "perfected the work" of translation allotted to the First Oxford Company, which was completed within 125 weeks in May 1607. Throughout his prolonged illness, the company met regularly every week in his chamber to compare and perfect what they had done in their private studies: thus he was employed in translating the Word of Life till he himself was translated to life everlasting. His days were thought to have been shortened by too intense an application to study. When urged by friends to ease up, he would reply that, "for sake of life, he would not lose the very end of living!"[24] During his sickness, his time was wholly taken up in prayer and in hearing and translating the Scriptures.

Romanists reported that their fierce opponent had recanted his Protestant opinions and had returned to the true fold! This malicious falsehood reached the ears of the dying Reynolds and, though too weak to speak, he was able to sign the following declaration,

> These are to testify to all the world, that I die in the possession of that faith which I have taught all my life, both in my preachings and in my writings, with an assured hope of my salvation, only by the merits of Christ my Saviour.[25]

The next day, May 21, 1607, he passed into the presence of His Saviour in his sixty-eighth year. His remains lie buried in the chapel of his College. He had been a great pillar of Puritanism and supporter of non-conformity. Dr Crackenthorpe, his close friend, said of him:

> He turned over all writers, profane, ecclesiastical, and divine. He had a sharp and ready wit, a grave and mature judgment, and was indefatigably industrious. He was so well skilled in arts and sciences, as if he had spent his whole life in each of them. And as to virtue, integrity, piety, and sanctity of life, he was so eminent and conspicuous, that to name Reynolds is to commend virtue itself.[26]

THOMAS HOLLAND was born at Ludlow, Shropshire, in the year 1539, and was therefore one of the oldest of the translators. He was educated at Exeter College from which he graduated in 1570. Three years later he was made Chaplain and Fellow of Balliol College, from which he was awarded his Doctor of Divinity in 1584, becoming Regius Professor of Divinity in 1589. In in 1592 he was appointed by the Queen as the Rector of Exeter College, an office he filled with great reputation for twenty years, being regarded as a universal scholar and a prodigy of literature. His reputation extended to the continent where he was held in high esteem in the universities.

Like Reynolds, he was a man of ardent piety, a thorough Calvinist in doctrine, and a decided non-conforming Puritan in matters of ceremony and church discipline. He stood his ground against Queen Elizabeth when she visited the University in the autumn of 1592. He publicly maintained—in contrast with the views of Dr Hadrian Saravia and of Bishop Bancroft—that bishops were no different from presbyters or elders, and refused to provide himself with a scarlet gown and hood, which he regarded as "the rags of popery"! He was, however, left alone by the bishops, being regarded by many as some doddery eccentric, but harmless, old man.

He opposed any novel doctrines or ways of worship, preferring the ancient landmarks and the old paths. He stoutly resisted the popish innovations that Bancroft and Laud strove too successfully to introduce at Oxford. When Laud was going through his exercises as candidate for the Bachelor in Divinity in 1604, he contended that, "there could be no true churches without diocesan episcopacy." He was rebuked by Dr Holland, who presided on the occasion, as "one who sought to sow discord among brethren, and between the Church of England and the Reformed Churches abroad".[27]

When the King visited Oxford in 1605, Dr Holland took part in an argument on the theological question: "Do the saints and angels know the thoughts of the heart?" In essence it was a question which no one could answer, and therefore a perfect subject for a heated debate in the manner of the Schoolmen of the Middle Ages. Dr John Aglionby upheld one side and three other translators—Drs. Holland, Giles Thomson, and John Harding—argued in opposition. The moderator was to be Thomas Bilson, Bishop of Winchester, another translator.

As a preacher Dr Holland was both earnest and solemn. His extemporary sermons were usually better than his more elaborate preparations. His preaching had the unction of the Holy Spirit upon it. He took a prominent part in the translation of the King James Bible . This was the crowning work of his life. Even while he laboured on the Bible translation he gave much time to fervent prayers and meditations marked by an ever growing longing for heaven. The translation being finished, Dr Holland spent most of his time in prayer and meditation. Sickness and the infirmities of age ripened his desires for heaven. In the hour of his departure, he exclaimed, "Come, Oh come, Lord Jesus, thou bright and morning star! Come, Lord Jesus; I desire to be dissolved and be with thee." [28]

Whenever he took a journey, he first called together the fellows of his college for his parting farewell, which always ended with these words, "I commend you to the love of God, and to the hatred of popery and superstition."[29] He died at the age of seventy-three on March 16, 1612, a few months after this most excellent and noble version of the English Bible was completed and published. His funeral sermon was preached by a fellow translator, Dr Richard Kilbye. In the course of that sermon, Dr Kilbye said of Dr Holland,

George Abbot

Sir Henry Savile

Hugh Broughton by John Payne, line engraving, 1620

Corpus Christi College, Oxford

> He had a wonderful knowledge of all the learned languages, and of all arts and sciences, both human and divine. He was mighty in the Scriptures; and so familiarly acquainted with the Fathers, as if he himself had been one of them; and so versed in the Schoolmen, as if he were the Seraphic Doctor. He was, therefore, most worthy of the divinity-chair, which he filled about twenty years, with distinguished approbation and applause. He was so celebrated for his preaching, reading, disputing, moderating, and all other excellent qualifications, that all who knew him commended him, and all who heard of him admired him.[30]

His earthly remains lie in the chancel of St Mary's, Oxford.

RICHARD KILBYE was born of humble parents at Ratcliffe on the Wreake, in Leicestershire. He was educated at Lincoln College, Oxford, and was chosen Fellow of that college in 1577, becoming a Doctor of Divinity in 1596. He took 'holy orders', and became a fiery preacher of note throughout the University, one whom Latimer would have said "had the contemplation of hell before his eyes". He preached the all-sufficiency of Christ's redemptive work and urged sinners to repent and turn to Christ. In his sermon entitled "The Burden of a Loaden Conscience", Kilbye speaks of his reprobate heart, which

> being utterly hardened in sin, and void of repentance, causeth me to heap wrath upon wrath and vengeance upon vengeance to the increasing of mine everlasting torments in hell fire.

He pleaded,

> All manner of people, young and old, take heed by me. Have no more God but one.

For he continued,

> Consider well what He hath done for you. He made you at first like unto Himself, in wisdom and holiness, and when you were by sin made like the devil, and must therefore have been condemned to hell torments, God sent His only Son who taking unto Him a body and soul, was a man and suffered great wrong and shameful death, to secure your pardon, and to buy you out of the devil's bondage, that ye might be renewed to the likeness of God … to the end ye might be fit to keep company with all saints in the joys of heaven.[31]

In the same sermon he quoted his own nightly prayer,

> O most mighty and gracious Lord God, I, wretched man, the worst of the world, do cry Thy mercy for all my sins, which this day or at any time have come out of my heart, by the way of word, deed or thought. I heartily thank Thee for all the blessings which Thou hast graciously and plentifully given me.[32]

In 1590 he was chosen as Rector of his college, and made Prebendary of the cathedral church in Lincoln, and then in 1601 he was a Prebend at Westminster Abbey. He was considered most accurate in Hebrew studies, leaving a commentary on Exodus drawn chiefly from the writings of Rabbinical interpreters. He was chosen by Lively as part of the First Oxford Company to work on the translation of the Prophets, the spirit of which permeated his preaching. Kilbye was amongst the most precise translators, a stickler for the right word and phrase.

Izaak Walton, in his life of Bishop Sanderson, makes mention of one incident in connection with Dr Kilbye. The renowned angler writes,

> I must here stop my reader, and tell him that this Dr Kilbye was a man of so great learning and wisdom, and so excellent a critic in the Hebrew tongue, that he was made Professor of it in this University; and was also so perfect a Grecian, that he was by King James appointed to be one of the translators of the Bible; and that this Doctor and Mr. Sanderson had frequent discourses, and loved as father and son. The Doctor was to ride a journey into Derbyshire, and took Mr. Sanderson to bear him company; and they, resting on a Sunday with the Doctor's friend, and going together to that parish church where they then were, found the young preacher to have no more discretion, than to waste a great part of the hour allotted for his sermon in exceptions against the late translation of several words, (not expecting such a hearer as Dr Kilbye,) and showed three reasons why a particular word should have been otherwise translated. When evening prayer was ended, the preacher was invited to the Doctor's friend's house, where after some other conference, the Doctor told him, he might have preached more useful doctrine, and not have filled his auditors' ears with needless exceptions against the late translation; and for that word for which he offered to that poor congregation three

> reasons why it ought to have been translated as he said, he and others had considered all of them, and found thirteen more considerable reasons why it was translated as now printed.[33]

It was to the credit of the young preacher that he humbly received the gracious rebuke given to him by a father in Israel. But how rare is such humility and gracious submissiveness today. We hear preachers on occasions displaying their smatterings of Hebrew and Greek, deriding the King James Bible, and declaring how it ought better to have been rendered! It is good at such times to call to mind the rebuke of Dr Kilbye and the "thirteen other considerable reasons" why it was translated as it now is in the King James Bible.

Miles Smith, a Hereford fletcher's (maker of bows and arrows) son, was born in 1560. He entered Corpus Christi College in 1568, but afterwards moved to Brasenose College, receiving his Doctor of Divinity in 1594. He was a classicist, and then became one of the leading oriental scholars of his generation, studying Chaldaic, Syriac, Arabic, and Hebrew. So expert was he in these languages that they were almost as familiar as his native tongue. It was said that "Hebrew he had at his finger's tips." The author of the biographical preface to his published sermons (1632) enlarged on his skill in the biblical languages, and illustrated this with the story of what happened at evensong one day in Hereford Cathedral. Being requested by the Dean to read the first lesson, Smith had only his copy of the Hebrew Scriptures with him but, undaunted, he delivered the chapter from it in the English tongue plainly and fully to that learned and judicious auditory!

He was so versed in history and general literature that he was described by a fellow bishop, as "a living library", also noting that "he studies all the Greek and Latin Fathers, making his annotations on them all." He was well acquainted with the Targums and Rabbinical glosses and comments and was thus regarded by his contemporaries as an incomparable theologian. He became a chaplain of Christ's Church, and became a canon of the cathedral church at Hereford.

He had a four-fold share in the translation, not only serving in the First Oxford Company, but as one of the twelve selected to revise the work before it was referred to the final examination of Dr Smith and Dr Bilson. Last of all, Dr Smith was employed to write that most learned and eloquent preface, which has become so rare and is seldom seen by the readers of the King James Bible. Whilst the flattering and sycophantic dedication to the King is constantly reprinted, the noble preface, addressed by "the translators to the reader", in the first edition, "stands as a comely gate to a glorious city within." Those who take the trouble to read the preface will soon discover that these 'learned men', were masters of the art of sacred criticism. The translators felt a sense of unstoppable divine authority. Smith wrote,

> Translation it is that openeth the window, to let in the light … that breaketh the shell, that we may eat the kernel; that putteth aside the curtain, that we may look into the most Holy Place; that removeth the cover of the well, that we may come by the water.

Smith never sought promotion, but said of himself that he was "covetous of nothing but books", and keeping no books in his library that he had not read! Nevertheless, in 1612, the King appointed him Bishop of Gloucester. In this office he behaved himself with the utmost meekness and benevolence.

Smith played a prominent part in the final editing of the King James Bible, which included the new chapter and page headings. Because he was the final critic who looked for flaws and smoothed out the whole translation, there is perhaps more of Dr Miles Smith in the King James Version than of any other man. It was said of him, "He … set forth the new and exact translation … He delivered the Scriptures … to Englishmen in English." He also wrote the flowery and Latinised preface in the English of 1611, which stands in marked contrast to the Biblical and Saxon English of the King James Bible itself. Incidentally, in that preface he quotes, not from the new translation, but rather from the Geneva Bible!

Smith's heart was ever with the Puritan party, even though he wrote in his preface, "We have on the one side avoided the scrupulosity of the Puritans, as on the other we have shunned the obscurity of the Papists." He, like Reynolds, was a staunch Calvinist. On one notable occasion, as Bishop of Gloucester, he removed the 'high altar' from the east end. When William Laud, the Dean of the Cathedral, had it re-positioned in its 'rightful' place, Smith declared that he would not enter the Cathedral until the cause of offence had been removed! He died at the age of seventy-four in 1624.

RICHARD BRETT was born in 1560 and studied first at Hertford College, before being elected a Fellow at Lincoln College, where Richard Kilbye was President. By unwearied industry he became very eminent in the languages, divinity, and other branches of science. According to Wood,

> He set himself to perfect his acquaintance with the Classical and Eastern languages, becoming famous in his time for learning as well as piety, skilled and versed to a critical degree in the Latin, Greek, Hebrew, Chaldaic, Arabic and Ethiopic tongues.

He became in 1595 the Rector of Quainton in Buckinghamshire, some twenty miles from Oxford, where for the next forty-two years he ministered. As a member of the First Oxford Company, he worked at home for five days a week revising two chapters a day, then one day each week he would ride to Oxford for discussions with the other translators in John Reynolds's lodge at Corpus Christi. This studious and godly minister died on 15 April 1637 at the age of seventy. His mortal remains lie buried in the chancel of Quainton Church where his stone shows him, his widow, and his four daughters, all kneeling.

The identity of **MR. FAIRCLOUGH** remains obscure. McClure identifies him as Dr Daniel Featley (which is a corrupted pronunciation of Fairclough). This is distinctly asserted by his nephew, who wrote a life of his uncle, and printed it at the end of a book entitled *Dr Featley Revived.* The nephew states that his uncle was ordained deacon and priest under the name Fairclough. If so, he would have been one of the youngest of the translators at twenty-six years of age. This youthful, but distinguished, scholar was the one chosen to preach the funeral sermon of the great Dr Reynolds, who died shortly after the First Oxford Company had finished their work.

The birthplace of Daniel Fairclough was Charlton, in Oxfordshire, where he was born in 1578. He was admitted to Corpus Christi College in 1594 and was elected Fellow in 1602. He stood in such high esteem that Sir Thomas Edwards, ambassador to France, took him to Paris as his chaplain, where he spent two or three years in the ambassador's house. Here he held many disputes with the doctors of the Sorbonne and other papists. His opponents called him "the keen and cutting Featley".

Upon his return to England he went first to his college, Corpus Christi, where he remained until 1613, at which time he was appointed Rector of Northill, in Cornwall. Shortly after he became chaplain to Dr Abbot, Archbishop of Canterbury, who made him Rector of Lambeth. He held a succession of other livings including All Hallows in London, and Acton in Middlesex, and chaplain to King Charles I.

Featley, or Fairclough, leaned towards the Puritan party, and as Dr Featley he was appointed to be one of the Assembly of Divines who met at Westminster in 1643. However, he expressed some scruples about taking the "solemn league and covenant"; and for this was unjustly suspected of being a spy. He was arrested and imprisoned, and had his various rectories taken from him. With his failing health, he was released and removed to Chelsea College, where he spent his last days in prayer and meditation until his death on 17 April 1645. He was small of stature, "yet he had a great soul, and had all learning compacted in him." He published some forty books and treatises.

Such are the worthies in this noble Company of translators. Nothing can tend more to inspire confidence in their incomparable version than the knowledge of their immense acquirements, almost incredible compared with the superficial scholars and frothy pretenders that would foist their 'new versions' upon us!

While the scholars were busy with the translation, their royal patron was pursuing his usual interests. Twice a week at Whitehall there were cockfights, and in November of 1604 the King was with the guns at Royston. From sunrise to dusk, the King sat astride his horse shooting hare and deer. In April 1605 the King was enjoying the 'sport of kings' at Newmarket, which was starting its long sporting association with horse racing. In June, the royal revels continued as the King and his courtiers went to the Lion's Tower to watch live cocks thrown to lions to be torn to pieces—all of this while Lancelot Andrewes, Reynolds, and the other worthies were faithfully setting aside their days for "translation time". The work of translation continued peaceably amid the court activities in sports, gaming, and amateur theatricals. But, in August of 1605, their work was to be disturbed by the King himself. The King planned a visit to Oxford on 27 August. A month before the visit the following charge to the head of houses was issued:

- All doctors and graduates, scholars, fellows and probationers to provide before the first day of August next gowns, hood, and cape according to the statutes of their houses and orders of the University, and that all commoners and halliers do wear round caps, and colours and fashions in their apparel as the statutes do provide.
- That whosoever shall be seen by the Vice-Chancellor or protectors or other overseers appointed by the delegates in the street or any public place, during the King's Majesty's abode, otherwise apparelled than the statutes of their houses or the University appoint for their degree, shall presently forfeit ten pounds and suffer imprisonment at the discretion of the said officers, the said forfeit to be levied by the Vice-Chancellor or whom he shall appoint.
- That upon the day when the King cometh, all graduates shall be ready at the ringing of St Mary's bell to come in their habits and hoods according to their degrees, and all scholars in their gowns and caps shall stand quietly in such orders as shall be appointed, until his majesty be passed into Christ Church, and the train being passed, every one may report to his own college.
- That all scholars, bachelors, and masters do diligently frequent the ordinary lectures during the time of his majesty's abode.
- That no scholar of what degree soever presume to come upon the state in St Mary's, upon pain of one month's imprisonment and forty pounds fine, and that no master of arts presume to come within the compass of the rail or stage below, where the disputers sit, but with his hood turned according to his degree, and none but masters of arts and bachelors of law shall presume to come into that place.
- That the scholars which cannot be admitted to see the plays do not make any outcries or indecent noise about the hall, stairs, or within the quadrangle of Christ Church, upon pain of present imprisonment and any other punishment according to the direction of the Vice-Chancellor and protectors.
- That they warn their companies to provide verses to be disposed and set upon St Mary's, or to other places convenient, and that those verses be corrected by the deans or some others appointed by the head.

- That a short oration be provided at every house to entertain his majesty if his pleasure be to visit the same, and verses set up.
- That University College, All Souls, and Magdalen Hall do set up verses at his majesty's departure, upon such places so as they may be seen as he passeth by.
- That the fellows and scholars of the body of each house be called home and not permitted to go abroad till after his majesty be gone home from the University, and that they may be at home from the first of August.

The Vice-Chancellor in charge of all this was Dr George Abbot. He had a month to prepare for the royal visit, and many of the Oxford translators, who would otherwise have spent the summer months for study of the Bible texts must have helped him.

The paved streets of Oxford were swept for the King's visit, and fresh paint applied to all railings, posts, bars of window, casements, and water pumps. On August 27 the King came riding on horseback, accompanied by Queen Anne and Prince Henry. The Vice-Chancellor and translator, George Abbot made his speech on his knee.

The following day, August 28, for three hours at Christ Church, the royal party watched one of the frivolous plays of the day. Then the King listened with rapt attention to the various sermons, lectures, disputes, and speeches of the translators and others, together with the Latin verses by the students, to which the King from time to time would give a few words of praise in Latin.

The previous year, the King had given the royal patent to the new Oxford library, the Bodleian, named after its founder, Sir Thomas Bodley who had given much encouragement to the exiles in Geneva during Mary's bloody reign. Now the first catalogue of the Bodleian was issued listing thousands of books in its 655 pages. Some of the translators gave books to the King on this royal visit, which were to find their place on the shelves of the Bodleian where the books were chained to the shelves. It was within its walls that King James declared, "I would wish, if ever it be not my lot to be carried captive, to be shut up in this prison, to be bound with these chains, and to spend my life with these fellow captives which stand here chained."

For a man like Reynolds, the royal visit must have been an ordeal. No doubt he was more courteous to the King, than the King had been to him at Hampton Court. Reynolds did lecture before the King, and was present in full academic attire at all the sycophantic amusements, but as soon as the day's fooleries were at an end, we see this champion of the Puritans going back to his Corpus Christi study, and painstakingly poring over the Bible texts. Each week the translators met in his quarters to discuss the translation work, which sadly had been interrupted by the King's vainglorious visit. On 30 August the King left behind the cheers of Oxford.

On the same day Father Garnet was leading a pilgrimage of thirty people to Holywell in North Wales to visit the shrine of St Winifred. Ann Vaux was in that group of Romanists, seeking a cure for some female disorder. The shrine of St Winifred, with its supposed well of healing waters, dates back to the seventh-century when Gwenfrewi's head was struck from her body by a suitor, Caradoc. Where her decapitated head hit the ground, a spring of water welled up, and her uncle Beuno reunited the severed head with the body, leaving only a white mark around her head! The female pilgrims made the last part of the journey barefoot. But the King's men at Oxford, impatient that their labours had been interrupted by his Majesty's egotistical appearance in the city, were at their work that would deliver England from these fantastic superstitions of Popery. They devoted themselves arfesh to the immense and glorious majesty of their translation:

> *And he will lift up an ensign to the nations from far, and will hiss unto them from the end of the earth: and, behold, they shall come with speed swiftly:*
> *None shall be weary nor stumble among them; none shall slumber nor sleep; neither shall the girdle of their loins be loosed, nor the latchet of their shoes be broken:*
> *Whose arrows are sharp, and all their bows bent, their horses' hoofs shall be counted like flint, and their wheels like a whirlwind:*
> *Their roaring shall be like a lion, they shall roar like young lions: yea, they shall roar, and lay hold of the prey, and shall carry it away safe, and none shall deliver it.*
> *And in that day they shall roar against them like the roaring of the sea: and if one look unto the land, behold darkness and sorrow, and the light is darkened in the heavens thereof.* – Isaiah 5.26-30.

SECOND OXFORD COMPANY:—
THE FOUR GOSPELS, ACTS OF THE APOSTLES, AND REVELATION.

They met at the oldest of Oxford's Colleges, Merton.

Dr Thomas Ravis	Dean of Christ Church
George Abbot	Dean of Winchester
Richard Edes	Dean of Worcester
Giles Thompson	Dean of Windsor
John Aglionby	Principal of Edmund Hall
Mr. Savile	Provost of Eton
Dr Perne	Regius Professor of Greek
Leonard Hutten	Of Christ Church
Mr. Harmer	Fellow of New College

This very distinguished Second Oxford Company of translators, with its four deans, and three future bishops, one of them an archbishop, all experts in Greek, worked on an equally distinguished portion of Scripture, a part so well known that only a heavyweight committee could command acceptance. These distinguished and powerful men gathered together to translate these wonderful passages of the New Testament in the rooms at Merton of one of the most flamboyant of the translators, Sir Henry Savile, scholar, courtier, politician, educationalist, mathematician and astronomer. The college register records that their first meeting was on 13 February 1606.

THOMAS RAVIS was Dean of Christ Church the largest and most imposing of colleges. Ravis, the Director of the Second Oxford Company, was born at Old Malden, Surrey, in 1560, and was educated at Westminster School. In 1575, at fifteen years of age, he went up to Christ Church where he studied for twenty years, obtaining his Doctor of Divinity in 1595. In 1591, he had been appointed Rector of All Hallows, Barking, London. The next year, he became Canon of Westminster. Two years later, he was chosen Dean of Christ's Church College. He "always continued both by his counsel and countenance a most especial encourager of the studies of all deserving scholars belonging to that foundation". He was also, in 1596 elected Vice-Chancellor of the University. In 1598, he exchanged his benefice at All Hallows Church for the rectory of Islip. He also held the Wittenham Abbey Church, in Berkshire. All these preferments and profitable livings mark him as a rising man. His holding a plurality of churches for the sake of their revenues, in neither of which he could perform the duties of the pastoral office, was one of the cases that justified the complaint of the Lord Chancellor at the Conference in Hampton Court. The Chancellor said that many learned men at the universities pined for want of places, while others had more than they could fill, "I wish, therefore, that some might have single coats, or one living, before others have doublets, or pluralities." To this, the frugal Bancroft, then Bishop of London, made the thrifty reply, "But a doublet is necessary in cold weather!" This custom of pluralities, whereby a man receives tithes for the care of souls of which he takes no care, fleecing the flock he neither watches nor feeds, was one of the pernicious customs of the age.

He was one of six deans invited to the Hampton Court Conference to humiliate the Puritans for presenting their 'Millenary Petition' of grievances, his role being to suppress the arguments of the Puritans! Following the commencement of the translation work, he was appointed Bishop of Gloucester in October 1604, and then the Bishop of London in 1607. He was a man of great learning, gravity and prudence, but had a reputation for harshness, both as Dean of Christ Church and as Bishop of London. London was awash with those of nonconformist sentiments, both Presbyterians, who wanted to remain part of the Church but could not accept that everything in the Book of Common Prayer was sanctioned by Scripture; and the most deeply entrenched separatists, who could not accept the authority of the Church at all. Ravis stretched forth his hand against the non-conforming Puritans and separatists. As chaplain to Archbishop Whitgift, he dealt sharply with the great Puritan leader, Thomas Cartwright. Among others, he cited before him that godly and blessed saint, Richard Rogers, who for fifty years had been the faithful minister of Weathersfield. Ravis declared, "By the help of Jesus I will not leave in my diocese one preacher that doth not conform." The political prelate was to be disappointed, because he died on the 14 December 1609 before the translation work was complete.

In contrast was **GEORGE ABBOT**, a man renowned for his sincerity and godliness and brought up by staunch Protestant parents in Guildford, Surrey, his sympathies lying with the Reformed and Puritan position. He was born on 29 October 1562. His parents had experienced persecution in the days of Queen Mary, but remained unflinching as Mr. and Mrs. Valiant for Truth until their deaths in 1606. George, their second son, went up to Balliol College at the age of fourteen, obtaining his BA in 1582, his MA in 1585, his BD in 1593, and his DD in 1597. He was a famed lecturer and preacher, and in this latter role his preaching at St Mary's, Oxford, drew vast crowds. His brother Robert was to become Bishop of Salisbury, and his other brother became the Lord Mayor of London.

His published lectures on theology clearly reveal that he had inherited from his parents a strong affection for the Protestant and Reformed faith. He was in the Puritan mould, and organised the market place burning of artefacts of idolatry. Furthermore, he had taken up cudgels with Laud, Canterbury's pope, in 1602 and openly reproved the latter's Romanism, declaring himself on the side of Waldo, Wyclif, Huss, and Luther.

Dr Abbot went to Scotland in 1608 as chaplain to the Earl of Dunbar. While there, by his prudent and temperate measures, he succeeded in establishing a moderate episcopacy in that kingdom. For this, King James ever after held Dr Abbot in great favour and rapidly hurried him into the highest ecclesiastical dignities and preferments. Though an excellent preacher, he had never exercised himself in the pastoral office, rising at once from university lecturer to the highest ecclesiastical position in the church. In 1609 he was appointed Bishop of Lichfield and Coventry, though he regarded bishops as no more than superintending pastors, in the eyes of God indistinguishable from any other minister. Thus he was "made a shepherd of shepherds, before he had been a shepherd of sheep". Upon the death of the Bishop of London, and fellow translator, Ravis, he was appointed at the age of forty-nine, to succeed him as the Bishop of London in St Paul's in February 1610, in which role he continued to repress Romanism throughout his diocese. He had religious pictures burned in the marketplace at Oxford, and a stained glass window in Balliol College, which showed a crucifix, was pulled down and destroyed. In November 1610, Archbishop Bancroft died, and on 25 February 1611 King James chose Abbot to be the new Archbishop. He was duly installed in April 1611. Where Bancroft had been the instrument of clerical repression, Abbot used his position to press for reform both at home and abroad, persuading King James to remove the Arminian Conrad Vortser from the Chair of Theology at Leyden! He raised funds for French and Dutch persecuted Protestants, and at his own expense paid for the Oxford education of several 'strangers' from abroad. He was held in the highest esteem both by the King and the people. In all great transactions, whether in Church or State, Abbot bore a principal part.

In matters of conscience, he was not afraid to be independent of the royal will, feeling he ought to obey God rather than man, even if that man was the king! The King, under the pretence that the strict observance of the Sabbath was an obstacle to Romanists coming to the Protestant faith, issued his infamous *Book of Sports.* The King sought to encourage, at the close of public worship, various recreations, such as "promiscuous dancing, archery, leaping, vaulting, May-games, morrice-dancing, May-poles, and many other sports". This royal edict was to be read by all ministers in their parish-churches, many of whom were fearful of the consequences of refusing to obey the King's orders. But Archbishop Abbot vehemently opposed the royal edict, and forbade it to be read in the church at Croydon, where he was at the time of its publication. The King was forced by Abbot to give up his attempt to secularise the Lord's Day. It is therefore surprising that he was responsible in 1615 for issuing the statute directing that the Apocrypha be included in every copy of the King James Bible! How could a Puritan so offend the Puritans and please the Papists at the stroke of a pen. What a solemn warning to those who hold 'high office'.

There is, however, a sad incident which the opponents of the King James Bible latch on to, and to which we must now turn. In 1621, Abbot had been invited to Bramshall Park in Hampshire to 'consecrate' a chapel. Whilst staying at the home of the Earl of Ashby de la Zouch, he joined a hunting party and, whilst attempting to shoot a stag with his crossbow, his shot went astray and killed a gamekeeper by the name of Peter Hawkins who had strayed into the path of the hunt. Both the Coroner and the King declared the shooting to be an unfortunate accident, but Archbishop Abbot had many enemies, both then and now, accusing him of manslaughter and therefore deserving to be 'unfrocked'. The newly appointed Bishop of Lincoln, John

Williams, protested to the King that he did not want to be consecrated by bloodstained hands. Thereafter, an independent enquiry of bishops, judges and lawyers examined the incident and exonerated George Abbot of all blame. For the rest of his life Abbot fasted and prayed every Tuesday, the day of the accident. He also settled a liberal annuity upon the poor gamekeeper's widow. But for the Primate, there was no alleviation of his grief, and for the rest of his life the incident cast a dark shadow over his tender heart.

Dr Abbot opposed the proposed marriage between Charles, Prince of Wales, and the Infanta, or Princess Royal, of Spain. Whilst he continued to enjoy the confidence of King James, when Charles succeeded James in 1625, the Archbishop's royal favour began to wane, and that of his inveterate foe, Dr Laud, began to wax. He was ushered into premature retirement, and in 1627 suspended from the exercise of his archiepiscopal functions. King Charles I did, however, in 1628 restore him to a degree of favour and bade him attend the Council-table twice a week, and he was permitted to resume some of his spiritual functions until his death five years later. This move by Charles was purely political, as the King sought to ameliorate growing opposition within Parliament to his royal prerogative. Abbot had publicly maintained the divine right of kings, 'that the King's royal will and command, in imposing laws, taxes, and other aids, upon his people, without common consent in parliament, did so far bind the consciences of the subjects of this kingdom, that they could not refuse the same without peril of eternal damnation.'

He died a broken man on the Lord's Day, 4 August 1633, at the age of seventy-one, and was buried in Trinity Church, Guildford.

He was a grave, fatherly figure of unimpeachable character. He was a decided Protestant, a firm Calvinist, and a thorough Churchman. He bore an active part in the translation of the King James Bible, an honour far beyond the chief ecclesiastical dignity in the land, or his outstanding literary work, his *Commentary on the Book of Jonah.*

RICHARD EDES was a native of Bedfordshire, being born at Sewell in 1555, the very year that marked the beginning of Mary's campaign of slaughter of the Lord's finest and best. Edes attended Westminster School and, at sixteen, in 1571, went up to Christ Church, Oxford, obtaining his MA in 1578. In 1584 he was elected University Proctor and obtained his BD. He proceeded to his DD in 1596, and in the same year was made Dean of Worcester and chaplain to the Queen, and, upon James' accession to the throne, he continued in that royal role. He was greatly admired both by Elizabeth and James as an accomplished pulpit orator. He was considered by all to be a most pious and grave minister, an ornament to his calling, and full of grace in the pulpit. He was chosen by James in 1604 to suppress the four Puritans at the Hampton Court Conference. Unfortunately, Edes was unable to complete the task of translation, dying at Worcester in November 1604 shortly after the work of translating the Gospels had begun. Nevertheless, he had been counted worthy of being joined with that able band of scholars and ministers, united in a common cause.

John Aglionby took the place of Richard Edes. Born in Cumberland in 1566 and educated at Queen's College, Oxford, obtaining his DD in 1600. Though he has left no publications to his name, he was regarded as a man of great learning, and also a gifted and most eloquent preacher being appointed chaplain in ordinary both to Queen Elizabeth and King James. In 1601, he was made Rector of Blechindon. In the same year, he was chosen Principal of St Edmund's Hall, in the University of Oxford, and Rector of Islip.

Dr Aglionby was deeply read in the Fathers and the Schoolmen, "an excellent linguist," and an elegant and instructive preacher. He played a prominent part in the translation work of the Second Oxford Company, but died at his rectory on the 6 February 1611, aged forty-three, before the fruits of his expertise had left the press. In the chancel of his church at Islip is a tablet erected to his memory by his widow.

Giles Thomson was a native of London Town and studied at Merchant Taylor's School alongside Lancelot Andrewes, in 1571 entering University College, Oxford. In 1580, he was elected a Fellow of All Souls, chaplain to Queen Elizabeth, and Registrar of the Most Noble Order of the Garter. He was made divinity lecturer in Magdalen Hall. He was appointed Canon in residence of Hereford and Rector of Pembridge in Herefordshire. He was a most eminent preacher. Thomson obtained his DD in 1602, and in that year, appointed Dean of Windsor. A learned and skilled debater, in 1605 he was chosen to debate in the presence of the King the "extent of the knowledge of this world in heaven". He succeeded Ravis as Bishop of Gloucester in 1611, but died on the 14 June 1612, at the age of fifty-nine, "to the great grief of all who knew the piety and learning of the man."

SIR HENRY SAVILE was born on 30 November 1549 at Over Bradley, near Halifax, to parents who belonged to the landed gentry, and began his university career at the age of twelve at Brasenose College. His cousins owned the land outside London on which Savile Row was built. Henry was a brilliant academic with a capacious intellect. At the age of sixteen he was elected a Fellow of Merton College, and by the age of twenty-one was regarded as one of the foremost scholars in Greek and Mathematics. In 1570, he had read his ordinaries on the *Almagest of Ptolemy*, a collection of the geometrical observations and problems of the ancients. He was the most handsome and glamorous of the translators, tall and fair, with a clear, rosy complexion as fine as any lady's.

He became the patron of John Bois in the publishing of the works of Chrysostom, the fourth century patriarch of Constantinople and greatest exegete of the Greek Fathers, whose dramatic style is reminiscent of the early Jacobean period. This massive work was published in eight volumes in 1613, and cost some eight thousand pounds to produce, tasking fifty years to sell the one thousand copies produced. Nevertheless, it has been called "the great work of Renaissance scholarship carried out in England". As Royal Envoy in the Low Countries, he made the acquaintance of the most eminent European scholars of his day and obtained a number of rare Greek manuscripts. He had employed a professional researcher from Chania in Crete to search for the oldest and purest of the Chrysostom manuscripts, particularly on the isle of Patmos. To copy, analyse and translate, Savile hired some of the best scholars in England, including John Bois and Andrew Downes. He returned from Europe highly accomplished in learning, languages, and knowledge of the world and men.

He returned to Oxford and became Tutor in Greek and mathematics to the Queen. The Queen liked him very much. He was elected Warden of Merton College in 1585, a post he was to hold for thirty-six years; then Dean of Carlisle and, in 1595, despite the fact that he never took 'holy orders' and amidst much opposition, he was appointed the Provost of Eton, which was but a mile from Windsor. When the Court came to Windsor, they could visit and discourse with all the learned men that Sir Henry assembled there from his college at Merton. It was at Eton that he assembled all the Greek documents for his monumental work of Chrysostom.

He was a keen gardener, and Fuller writes of him, "This skilful gardener had, at the same time, a nursery of young plants, and an orchard of grown trees, both flourishing under his careful inspection." Savile argued that the study of mathematics turns a man into an educated, civilised human being. In 1591 he published his translation of the four books of Tacitus, and this work sealed his reputation as a man of great learning. He was regarded by many as the most learned Englishman in secular literature. He translated the history of Cornelius Tacitus and gave learned lectures on Euclid. As Provost of Eton he sought to cultivate scholars who were plodders. "Give me," he used to says, "the plodding student. If I would look for wits, I would go to Newgate; there be the wits!" The King knighted him at Eton on the 21 September 1604; thereafter he refused all preferments in either State or Church. In 1618, at the request of Archbishop Abbot, he published Bradwardine's *De Causa Dei Contra Pelagiu,* a medieval defence against the errors of Pelagius. He encouraged and assisted Thomas Bodley in establishing the Bodleian Library, and presented it with an early edition of the Gospels in Russian. Also he founded two professorships in mathematics and astronomy. He was such a man of books that his wife once petulantly said to him, "Sir Henry, I would that I were a book, and then you would a little more respect me." A little before the publication of the works of Chrysostom, when Sir Henry lay sick, Lady Savile said, that if Sir Henry died, she would burn Chrysostom for killing her husband.

He died and was buried at Eton in February 1621, in his seventy-second year. He was styled "that magazine of learning, whose memory shall be honoured among the learned and the righteous for ever." Sir Henry Savile was one of the most precise and critical scholars of his age, and a choice vessel to undertake the work of producing the King James Bible. Through his travels in Europe, he brought the influence of the great European scholars to bear upon the new translation.

JOHN PERRIN was a Fellow of St John's and Regius Professor of Greek in the University of Oxford. He it was who pronounced an oration in Greek, welcoming King James I to Oxford in 1605. He became Canon of Christ's Church, Oxford. Though very little is known about John Perrin (Peryn or Perne), he was undoubtedly one of the workhorses of the Second Oxford Company. He was appointed as Vicar of Wafting in Sussex by Bishop Andrewes, but in 1605 he resigned his post as Regius Professor of Greek to devote himself unhindered to the work on the King James Bible. He died on the 9 May 1615.

LEONARD HUTTEN was born in 1557 and educated at Westminster School and Christ Church, Oxford, from where he received his Doctor of Divinity in 1599. He became the Vicar of Long Preston in Yorkshire in 1587, and then Rampsham in Dorset, and finally Floore in Northamptonshire, before becoming Canon of Christ's Church. He was well known as an excellent Grecian, and was well versed in the Fathers, the Schoolmen, and the learned languages, which were the favourite studies of his day. When the Queen visited Oxford in 1592, it was Hutten who produced a Latin play, "The War of Grammar," between King 'Noun' and King 'Verb'. Hutten was both a learned theologian and a lover of poetry. He officiated at the opening of the Bodleian Library in 1602. Once more, he was present when King James visited the University in 1605 and contributed to a collection of adulatory poems presented to the monarch. Upon completing his part of the translation, he became Prebend of St Paul's Cathedral. He died on the 17 May 1633 at the age of seventy-five. His published works included the *Antiquities of Oxford*, and *A Latin History of Christ Church*.

JOHN HARMER was one of four known members of the General Committee who revised the King James text during 1609. He was born at Newbury in that year of fiery persecution 1555, when, at the height of the Marian persecution, English exiles had formed a church at Geneva. He was educated in William de Wykeham's School at Winchester. He was a brilliant academic in his youth and secured the patronage of the Earl of Leicester, whose father and brother were martyred under Mary. Elizabeth had bestowed upon Robert Dudley, Earl of Leicester, the Chancellorship of Oxford University. The Earl used this position to help brilliant young men such as Harmer—

first of all at St Mary's College, Winchester, on a scholarship in 1569 at the age of fourteen, and then at New College, Oxford, from where he graduated with MA in 1582.

Following graduation he travelled throughout Europe and engaged in debate with the learned popish Doctors of the Sorbonne. Upon his return to Oxford he was appointed Regius Professor of Greek in 1585, but returned to Winchester in 1588 and continued there as first Head, and then Warden.

He published several learned works: among them, Latin translations of several of Chrysostom's writings, also an excellent translation of several of Beza's French sermons into English by which he shows himself to have been a Calvinist. It was Harmer who first translated Calvin's three volumes of sermons on the book of Genesis in 1577, and was decribed as "the master of an excellent English style, and adept in the difficult art of translating." He was a most noted Latinist, Grecian and minister of the Word of God, well read in the Fathers and the Schoolmen. He had a principal part in giving the Scriptures of our beloved Authorised Version to untold millions, and was one of the six translators who met at Stationers' Hall to revise the first draft of the Bible as it came from the six Companies.

He is mentioned twice in the notes of Bois, first at 1 Peter 2:24, where Harmer had suggested *carried up our sins to the tree,* and then again at Revelation 13:5 where Bois' note reads, "In another manuscript *nonemesei.*" The word suggested by Harmer means to "make war" and was included in the marginal reference. Bois refers to Harmer as D. Harmer, which would indicate that he had been awarded a Doctor of Divinity.[34]

TRANSLATION NOTES: There are two extant manuscripts which throw light upon the work of the Second Oxford Company's work, the first in MS 98, which is in Lambeth palace, and the second, the last edition of the Bishops' Bible of 1602, preserved in the Bodleian Library, which contains many pages in the Four Gospels annotated by the Second Oxford Company.

> Let us turn to Luke 1 verse 57. There the Bishops' Bible reads: "Elizabeth's time came that she should be delivered and she brought forth a sonne." At two places in the verse the translator

> inserted a small Greek character to mark places that needed revision, a 'ê' before the first word 'Elizabeth', and a 'ë' between 'time came'. These are repeated in the margin of the page, each with a suggested change. The 'ê' indicates 'Now', and the 'ë' indicated 'was fulfilled'. But then the reviser changed his mind, crossed out 'was fulfilled', wrote 'full time came', instead, while crossing out 'time came' in the text, thus arriving at the verse as it is in the Authorised Version, "Now Elizabeth's full time came, that she should bee delivered and she brought forth a sonne."[35]

Another revision appears in Luke 1 verse 63. The verse reads thus in the Bishops' Bible:

> And <u>when he had asked for writing tables</u>, he wrote saying, his name is John: and they marvelled all". Then the reviser wrote in the margin his alternative to the underlined phrase, 'demanding a writing table'. Then he crossed out 'when' and 'had,' wrote in the margin the word 'and,' and finally crossing out the second 'he' in the verse, arrived at the AV text: "And he asked for a writing table, and wrote, saying, His name is John. And they marvelled all."[36]

FINAL COMMENTS ON THE TRANSLATORS

There was a great variety among the translators: some such as Reynolds were Puritans; the men of Emmanuel College were all of Evangelical and Calvinistic persuasion; some were deans and bishops such as Andrewes; some were outstanding scholars and linguists such as Chaderton, Bois, Downes, Lively, and Miles Smith. But there is nothing to suggest that the King James Version was moulded by them. The majesty of the King James Version is not indebted to individual talent, but to the Divine Author of the original Scriptures, which the translators sought faithfully and accurately to translate into the English tongue.

The King James Bible was the work of six committees, working on a translation that was collaborative and consultative at every stage, whereas Tyndale had worked in isolation and produced a version which bore all the hallmarks of a single genius. Our translators were engaged on a task by royal command, using all the facilities which the State could provide; whereas Tyndale went into exile to escape the wrath of the authorities and was hunted by the King's command, and had to make do with whatever resources he could lay his hands on. Many of our translators were rewarded with bishoprics, whereas Tyndale and his work were publicly burnt.

So far, we have met with forty-seven translators out of the King's original fifty-four. To these should be added the name of **William Thorne**. In 1606, fourteen bishops, including Bilson of Winchester and Ravis of Gloucester, both translators, signed a formal plea at the request of Dr Thorne, his majesty's chaplain,

> We whose names are hereunto subscribed have thought it equal and just to make known unto all, whom it appertaineth, that he for many years read the public Hebrew lecture with very good recommendation in the University of Oxford, *that he is now likewise very necessarily employed in the translation of that part of the Old Testament which is remitted to that University*, that he doth govern the church of Chichester where he is dean with judgment and discretion, and that in the one and other place he hath ever been and now is of very good and honest reputation. In regard whereof our opinion and hope is that he will approve himself worthy of further promotion in the church.[37] [Italics mine]

Whilst the letter failed to secure further promotion within the Church, it nevertheless identifies him as a translator working under Dr John Harding on the Minor Prophets and Lamentations.

It is also highly probable that **Bishop Thomas Bilson** was also involved in translation, but we shall consider him and Arcbishop Bancroft in their labours as reviewers at the Stationer's Hall.

Additional names were Arthur Lake, James Montague (who became Bishop of Bath and Wells), Thomas Sparke (who had been at Hampton Court) and William Eyre. The surmise that many aided in the translation unofficially seems justified. Many must have offered advice on verses, helped solve hard problems, and queried readings on which the chosen learned men agreed.

There is, however, one further name that we must consider, that of the irascible **Hugh Broughton**. This famous Hebrew Scholar had called for a new Bible, but was not selected as part of the Old Testament translation companies. He was a zealous and often hot-headed Puritan with a maverick tendency. His book *A Consent of Scripture,* published in 1588, was a kind of Scripture chronology and genealogy designed to show the chronological order of events from Adam to Christ, and harmonise the apparently jarring passages. It was the fruit of immense labour and study. He personally presented a copy to Queen Elizabeth in 1589 saying,

> The whole book of God, most gracious sovereign, is so harmonious in itself, that every part may be seen to breathe the same spirit. The prophecies briefly told, the events fully recorded, the temple, the altar, the sacrifices, all pointing to one centre, shows, that by Christ, the great propitiatory, the Son eternal, we are made heirs of the heavenly inheritance.[38]

The book, however, was opposed by Archbishop Whitgift, Dr Reynolds of Oxford and Mr. Lively of Cambridge.

Broughton was always firm and a determined defender of what he considered the truth, openly exposing the errors of popery. Such was his proficiency in Hebrew that he had a public disputation with Rabbi Elias, a learned Jew, in the synagogue in Frankfurt. At the conclusion Rabbi Elias departed, defeated by the profundity of Broughton's Hebrew scholarship! Indeed, he was so celebrated for his knowledge of Hebrew learning that he was invited to Constantinople to instruct the Jews in the Christian religion.

In 1591 Hugh Broughton returned to England for the purpose of settling the controversy between himself and Dr Rainolds, but soon found himself embroiled in another controversy, that over the article concerning our Saviour's descent into hell. Broughton attacked both Bishop Bilson and Archbishop Bancroft for the former's thesis on that phrase in the Apostles' Creed, "he descended into hell." Bilson had argued for a literal understanding of the phrase that the soul of Jesus actually went to hell for a short time. In this he had the full support of Bancroft (not then Archbishop), and Queen Elizabeth I. Broughton said that the Archbishop, "is a deadly enemy to both Testaments and unallowable in this course to be a teacher or to rule in learning." Broughton maintained that the word 'Hades', as used by the Fathers for the place where Christ went after his crucifixion, did not mean hell as the place of the damned, but the state of the dead, or invisible world.

Broughton had made his own partial version of the Bible from which the King James' men appear to have been influenced as, for example, in speaking of wild horses, Broughton said of the horse, in Job 39:19, *Canst thou clothe his neck with thundering?* The Authorised Bible asks, *Hast thou given the horse strength? Hast thou clothed his neck with thunder?* Whereas the Bishops' Bible has, *Hast thou given the horse his strength or learned him to neigh courageously?* We can thank Hugh Broughton for this most excellent rendering, *clothed his neck with thunder.* Almost all Hugh Broughton's translations of parts of the Bible were posthumously published in 1662 under the title, *The Works of the Great Albinonian Divine Mr. Hugh Broughton.*

During the course of the translation work there are indications that Broughton mellowed, for in 1609 he wrote,

> None should bear sway in translating but the able ... The care to have the law and gospel learnedly translated hath stirred much study and expectation of good, and all true hearted subjects will be ready for forbearance.[39]

But when at last it was published he wrote,

> The late Bible was sent to me to censure: which bred in me a sadness that will grieve me while I breathe, it is ill done. Tell his Majesty ... that I had rather be rent to pieces with wild horses than any such translation by my consent should be urged upon poor churches ... The new edition crosseth me. I require it to be burnt.[40]

Broughton was undoubtedly one of the greatest Hebraists of the day, and he was extremely critical of the Old Testament scholars who, in his opinion, when they came up with something worthwhile, relegated it to the margin. Hebraist he most certainly was, passionate without question, zealous Puritan unquestionably; but he was an individualist unfitted and unable to work in a company of translators that included men wedded to the established order of episcopalianism. His omission from the list of translators was on the one hand sad, but on the other hand both wise and necessary.

When J.C. Philpot, 1802-1869, was asked to recommend men to undertake a revision of the King James Version, he replied,

> Of course they must be learned men, great critics, scholars, and divines. But these are notoriously either tainted with popery or infidelity. Who are the men, learned, yet sound in Truth, not to say alive unto God, who possess the necessary qualifications for so important work? And can erroneous men, dead in trespasses and sins, carnal, worldly, ungodly persons, spiritually translate a Book written by the blessed Spirit? We have not the slightest ground for hope that they would be godly men, such as we have reason to believe translated the Scriptures into our present version.[41]

In a review of Adam Nicolson's book, *God's Secretaries,* the reviewer in the Daily Telegraph wrote:

> The King James Bible is … the richest, most passionate (and most bought) of all works of English prose. It is full of grandeur and a vivid, heart gripping immediacy. The language of the King James is that of majesty, grace, stateliness, scale, and power. … Never had so many scholars been used for a Bible translation. The pivot was Lancelot Andrewes, Dean of Westminster Abbey, court preacher and scholar, fluent in fifteen modern languages and six ancient, gifted with a musical understanding of English which is responsible for much of the final effect of translation. He was a man with an extraordinary tender relationship with his God, praying five hours every morning, and was said to have been in tears for most of them. … There is no desire to please here; only a belief in the overwhelming divine authority. The translators of the Bible clearly believed that, and the majesty of their translation stems from its belief in that divine authority. The diversity of the enormous committee is all, in the end, subservient to that idea. Yawning between now and then is the great invention of liberalism, the importance of individual freedom. Nothing like the King James Bible could ever be made again.[42]

Merton College, Oxford

The chief conspirators of the Gunpowder Plot

The cellar beneath the House of Lords

CHAPTER 6

Powder Treason

WHILST our translators worked diligently at their royal task, Thomas Percy, a devout Roman Catholic, and his two brothers-in-law, John (Jack) and Christopher (Kit) Wright were spoiling for action. Jack Wright, along with Robert Catesby, had formed part of the 'Court' of the Earl of Essex and had been involved in the Essex uprising, for which Jack Wright had spent a time in solitary confinement.

Both the Wrights were natives of Yorkshire and had attended the same school as Guy Fawkes, St Peter's in York. Fawkes, the Wrights, and Robert Catesby were in their early thirties when James ascended the English throne. Others included Catesby's cousin, Francis Tresham, was in his mid-thirties, and the brothers Robert and Thomas Wintour, who had Vaux blood coursing through their veins. These young men were determined to act to rid the land of the penal statutes against Roman Catholics.

The chief conspirator was not Guy Fawkes, but Robert Catesby. There is no doubt that Fawkes was deeply involved in the plot, but the plot owes its origin and development to the magnetism of Catesby, so adored by Roman Catholic priests. His first cousin was Elizabeth Tresham who was married to Lord Monteagle, the man who would eventually betray the plot. His father had suffered long imprisonment for his recusancy. Catesby had been educated at the new Jesuit College for young Catholic men, Douai, in the Netherlands. He had married a wealthy Protestant girl and had two sons, one of which died in infancy. But, in 1598, both his father and his young wife died, and these two events triggered his return to the historic Roman Catholic Church. From this time forth he was marked by a zealot-like fanaticism and dedication to eradicate the Protestant cause from the land. He was associated with the Essex conspiracy for which he was fined four thousand marks. By April 1604 he was more than prepared to take the sword and to die for the cause he espoused.

In mid-July 1603, Guy Fawkes set out from Flanders for Spain. He had enlisted as a mercenary in the Spanish army in the Low Countries, but now his mission was to enlist Spain's armies in the invasion of his native land. Though his father was a Protestant, his mother's family, the Jacksons, were listed among the Yorkshire recusants. His father died when he was eight, and three years later his mother remarried a recusant, Denis Bainbridge. Their removal from York to Scotton brought the adolescent Guy Fawkes within distinctly Roman Catholic circles. He attended 'Little Rome', that is, St Peter's School in York, and among his contemporaries were Jack and Kit Wright and Oswald Tesimond, later Father Tesimond. The previous headmaster had spent twenty years in prison for being a recusant. The current headmaster, John Pulleine, was a Church Papist. Guy Fawkes was a devout Catholic and had enlisted in the Spanish army where he could practise his faith freely.

Whilst Fawkes was engaged upon his 'ambassadorial' mission to Spain, Roman Catholics in his homeland were eagerly awaiting the toleration they believed had been promised to them by their new king. But Fawkes claimed that James was

> ...a heretic who intended "in a short time to have all the Papist sect driven out of England". His table-talk was equally crude: "Many have heard him say at table that the Pope is Anti-Christ which he wished to prove to anyone who believed the opposite." Any overtures to Spain for peace, Fawkes declared, were to be treated as royal subterfuges of the basest sort. The King's true intention was to enrich himself with the property of Catholics and, once grown powerful as a result, join with the Protestants "to wage war on the rest of Christian princes' who were not heretics".[1]

Fawkes mission, however, was doomed to failure, but he did leave Spain with the name Guido instead of Guy! In Rome, the Pope was advocating that his loyal subjects in England should adopt a passive role, at least in his public pronouncements. Through his envoy, Claudio Aquaviva, General of the Jesuits, he had warned Father Garnet, "I implore you, by the unfathomable mercy of Christ, be prudent." Thus

Fawkes and his fellow activists were cruelly disappointed by both Spain and Rome, both of whom were publicly advocating passivity.

In September 1603 the leading conspirators had already met to determine the ruthless measures to be adopted. Robert Catesby, a gentleman of an ancient family, began by recounting the grievances under which the Roman Catholics of England groaned. His words kindled the anger of Percy, a descendant of the House of Northumberland, who observed that nothing was left them but to kill the King. "That," said Catesby, "is to run a great risk, and accomplish little." He then proceeded to unfold to Percy a much greater design that could be executed with greater safety and would be followed by far greater consequences.

> You have taken off the King; but his children remain, who will succeed to his throne. Suppose you destroy the whole royal family, there will still remain the nobility, the gentry, the Parliament. All these we must sweep away with one stroke; and when our enemies have sunk in a common ruin, then may we restore the Church of Rome in England.[2]

Catesby was alarmed by the strength of an hereditary monarchy. The prospect of an endless line of Protestant Stuart monarchs could not be tolerated by these young men who were ready to resort to violence to achieve their goals. In short, he proposed to blow up the Houses of Parliament with gunpowder when the King and the Estates of the Realm should be assembled there. Parliament was regarded by the plotters as the true source and security of the Protestant regime. It had been responsible for anti-Catholic legislation and hence it was a legitimate choice for the site of the explosion. It was there that the heads of the Protestant party survived, and therefore by destroying the assembled Parliament it would take away at a stroke the King and his princely offspring, his lords and his bishops. In the ensuing mayhem of the plot's success, the Papists would rebel and seize the land and bring this most heretical of nations back under the dominion of Rome.

On the Lord's Day, 20 May 1604, a meeting was held between the chief conspirators (Catesby, Tom Wintour, Jack Wright, Thomas Percy and Guido Fawkes) at the Duck and Drake in the Strand. For Catesby, "the nature of the disease required so sharp a remedy." In the mind-set of the conspirators, theirs was the violence of last resort.

The contemplated destruction was on so great a scale that some of the conspirators shrank back from the perpetration of such aweful wickedness. They therefore consulted their 'spiritual' advisers. "Is it lawful," they asked of Garnet, Tesimond, and Gerard, "to do this thing?" These emissaries of Rome assured them that they might go on with a good conscience and do the deed, seeing that those upon whom the destruction would fall were heretics and excommunicated persons. The conspirators were not acting wrongly by serving as an instrument of justice! "But," it was replied, "some Catholics will perish with the Protestants; is it lawful to destroy the righteous with the wicked?" Was the devout young Lord Montague to die? Montague, who had spoken bravely on behalf of 'the religion of our fathers' in the House of Lords and had been imprisoned for four days in the Fleet prison for his bitter attack on the Act against recusants. Was he to die? And what about Lord Monteagle and the Earl of Northumberland? It was answered, "Yes, for it is expedient that the few should die for the good of the many."

The point of conscience having been resolved, and the way made clear, the next step was an oath of secrecy to inspire them with mutual confidence. The conspirators therefore swore to one another by the Blessed Trinity and by the Sacraments not to disclose the matter, directly or indirectly, and never to desist from the execution of it, unless released by mutual consent. To add to the solemnity of the oath, they retired to an inner chamber, where they heard Mass and received the Sacrament from Gerard. They had thus sanctified themselves as the executioners of the vengeance of Heaven upon an apostate nation. This evil quintet ordered swords of Spanish steel, their blades richly engraved with scenes from the life of Jesus Christ; the swords would bear the legend, "The Passion of Christ."

On 9 June, Thomas Percy was appointed a Gentleman Pensioner —one of fifty special bodyguards—by his kinsman the Earl of Northumberland, though he did so without imposing the oath of supremacy upon Percy. Thus Percy was able to secure a London base in Westminster without arousing any suspicion. Guido Fawkes was installed under the alias of John Johnson, a servant to Thomas Percy.

Parliament was adjourned on 7 July 1604 and set to meet again on 7 February 1605. Meanwhile, King James continued to act against Jesuits, priests and "divers other corrupt persons employed under the colour of religion," and recusancy fines were re-imposed. Such

'Draconian' measures hardened the conspirators' resolve to eradicate the King and all his Protestant progeny.

In October 1604, the number of conspirators was increased to six with the addition of Robert Keyes. Keyes' cousin, Elizabeth Tyrrwhitt, was married to Ambrose Rookwood of Coldham Hall, Suffolk. He was a wealthy Catholic who could provide horses for the conspirators' escape from London. Rookwood would also purchase gunpowder to be used in the plot.

By December the six men became seven when Thomas Bates joined their ranks. Shortly after, the men began to excavate a tunnel from a neighbouring cellar to the wall of Parliament House, only to learn by accident that they might achieve their purpose with less effort. The vault under the House of Lords, commonly used as a coal-cellar, was to be let. They hired it on Lady's Day 1605: it lay at right angles to the House of Lords, parallel to a short passageway known as Parliament Place. This led on to Parliament Stairs, which gave access to the river some forty yards away. The cellar was directly below the House of Lords, and this was to become Guy Fawkes' cellar. It was more of a storehouse than a cellar, and was already cluttered with an accumulation of masonry and timber. Using the access from the river (with ready access to Lambeth and Catesby's lodging on the south bank of the Thames) some thirty-six barrels of gunpowder were smuggled into Fawkes' cellar, covered with logs, stones, and iron bars. They then threw open the doors that all might see how harmless and innocuous were the materials with which the vault was stored.

The New Year began on Lady Day, 25 March 1605, by which date the conspirators had enlarged their numbers by the addition of Robert Wintour, John Grant and Kit Wright. They would meet at the Mermaid Tavern and were lavishly entertained by William Shakespeare's dearest friend, William Johnson. The Treason Plot had been brewing for a year and a half. It had been entrusted to some twenty persons, and not a whisper had been uttered to divulge the terrible secret. One aspect of the plot, not yet considered, was the abduction of the nine-year-old Princess Elizabeth. It was hoped that Princes Henry and Charles would attend Parliament and would therefore be assassinated with their father. Catesby's plan was to have the young princess kidnapped, bring her up as a Catholic, and marry her to a Catholic bridegroom whilst having her proclaimed as Queen. Little did they know that Princess Elizabeth had renounced the Romanism of her mother and espoused the cause of her Protestant father.

When the plot approached maturity, Father Garnett talked much of bulls and mandates from the Pope to charge all the priests and their flocks in England to conduct themselves with profound peace and quiet. Roman Catholics in England had reached a stage of desperation that made them deeply resentful of holding back from violence. Garnet sent Guido Fawkes to Rome with a letter to Clement VIII, supplicating that, "commandment might come from his Holiness, or else Aquaviva, the General of the Jesuits, for staying of all commotions of the Catholics in England"—so anxious were they not to hurt a Protestant, or disturb the peace of the kingdom, or shake his Majesty's throne. Many Protestants were deceived by these conciliatory acts. They didn't know that the men from whom those loud protestations of loyalty and brotherly concord came were all the while storing gunpowder in the vault underneath the House of Lords, counting the hours when they should fire it and shake down the pillars of the State, dissolving the whole fabric of the nation.

A week before the Feast of Corpus Christi (the Blessed Sacrament held in 1605 on the 16 June), Father Tesimond had a conversation with Robert Catesby. In the course of the conversation, Catesby enquired about the morality of killing innocents. Tesimond gave the stereotyped Roman Catholic response, that it was a case of double-effect: the killing of innocents could be justified if the greater cause was achieved. Tesimond in turn, under the seal of the confessional, sought out his Superior, and spilled the beans to Father Garnet. Under Catholic canon law, all information received under the confessional seal was privileged and could not be divulged under any circumstances. But that did not prevent Garnet sending a letter to his own general, Aquaviva in Rome, on 24 July 1605, indicating that there was a risk that some private endeavour may commit treason or use force against the King.

Meanwhile Pope Clement VIII died in the spring and was succeeded by Paul V. There is much evidence for believing that the projected plot had been sanctioned by papal authority. Pope Paul V appointed a jubilee for the year 1605, for the purpose of "praying for help in emergent necessities". Among the reasons assigned by the Pontiff for fixing on the year 1605 was that it was to witness "the rooting out of all the impious errors of the heretics".[3] Two of the Jesuit conspirators who made their escape to Rome were rewarded; one being made penitentiary to the Pope, and the other a confessor in St Peter's. Garnet, who was executed as a traitor, is styled by the Jesuit College at Rome as a martyr!

On July 28 Parliament was dissolved and would not meet again on 3 October as previously announced because some dregs of the plague remained in London, but would reconvene on Tuesday, 5 November. In the interlude, the King resorted to his favourite pastime of hunting, but on Tuesday, 5 August, he celebrated the anniversary of the failed Gowrie conspiracy and heard a passionate anti-Papist sermon preached at St Paul's Cross by the Bishop of London, Dr Bancroft. He declared that the King was determined to sustain the Protestant religion and that he was quite prepared to pour out the last drop of blood in his body.

Back in Guido's cellar, however, the gunpowder had decayed, the elements had separated, and it was now useless, so the conspirators transported more gunpowder and firewood. Then, in late September, Catesby enlisted three more conspirators. The first was a member of the aristocratic Catholic family, the Rookwoods of Euston Hall, Norfolk. Ambrose Rookwood had made his house, Coldham Hall near St Edmundsbury in Suffolk, a sanctuary for priests. His fine stable of horses was to be used by the conspirators to aid their escape. The second man to be recruited was Francis Tresham, his first cousin, and perhaps the man who betrayed his knowledge of the plot to the authorities. Then on the Feast of St Luke (Monday 21 October), a day when Jesuits gathered together to renew their vows, the third man was recruited, Sir Everard Digby, bringing the total number of conspirators to thirteen. Digby would be entrusted with securing the abduction of the Princess Elizabeth.

In mid October the final details of the dastardly plot were ironed out in various hostelries in London and the Midlands. Guido Fawkes would light the fuse in the cellar, before making his rapid escape across the Thames, first to Lambeth and then to the continent to inform the Catholic powers that it had been a holy duty to blow up the King, the Royal Family and the entire English government. At the same time as Fawkes lit the fuse, there would be a Catholic uprising in the Midlands. Princess Elizabeth, having been abducted, would then be installed as a puppet queen.

The hideous crime, which would have removed not only the Royal household but also many of the Bible translators, was prevented by a letter addressed to Lord Monteagle by one of the conspirators. This individual's heart would seem to have failed him at the last moment. The letter lead to a search below the House of Lords leading to the discovery of the astounding plot. The letter was dated Saturday, 26 October:

> My Lord, out of the love I bear to some of your friends, I have a care of your preservation. Therefore I would advise you, as you tender your life, to devise some excuse to shift your attendance at this Parliament; for God and man hath concurred to punish the wickedness of this time. And think not slightly of this advertisement, but retire yourself into your country [county] where you may expect the event in safety. For though there be no appearance of any stir, yet I say they shall receive a terrible blow this Parliament; and yet they shall not see who hurts them. This counsel is not to be condemned because it may do you good and can do you no harm; for the danger is passed as soon as you have burnt the letter. And I hope God will give you the grace to make good use of it, to whose holy protection I commend you.[4]

Immediately, though late at night, Monteagle took the letter to Lord Salisbury. Monteagle was amply rewarded for the part he played in averting the dark treason. There has been endless speculation as to who wrote the letter. Francis Tresham, the brother-in-law of Lord Monteagle, was the chief suspect. Some even suggest that Monteagle, upon being informed of the plot by Tresham, had the letter written to himself! Salisbury was not the least alarmed by the letter; it merely confirmed what he had discovered from other sources. He therefore allowed the Plot to ripen for ten more days before informing the King.

And the Plot did ripen. On Wednesday 30 October, Guido Fawkes inspected the cellar and was satisfied that everything was in place. Then, on Thursday, 31 October, Ambrose Rookwood and other conspirators moved to London. Yet other conspirators and recusants gathered at Coughton Court, Warwickshire, for the Feast of All Saints. High Mass was celebrated by Father Garnet who preached a sermon on the theme of a Latin hymn from the Office of Lauds: "Take away the perfidious people from the territory of the Faithful."

On the Lord's Day evening, 3 November, Thomas Percy met with Catesby and Wintour in London. Meanwhile, Sir Everard Digby and other recusants, including the requisite priest Father Hammond, moved to the Red Lion in Dunchurch, south of Rugby, ready to abduct the young Princess Elizabeth who was staying at Coombe Abbey, some eight miles away. On Monday, 4 November, Father Hammond said Mass for the 'hunting party' at Dunchurch!

When at last Monteagle placed the letter before the King, it was James who deciphered the full extent of the plot. The words, "the danger is past as soon as you have burnt the letter," were the key. James clearly saw in these words a catastrophic explosion involving gunpowder! On Saturday, 2 November, the Privy Councillors had an audience with the King in his palace at Whitehall at which they told him that Lord Suffolk should examine the Houses of Parliament on Monday, 4 November.

Late in the morning of Monday, Thomas Percy moved to the home of the Earl of Northumberland, Syon House, to the west of London. Then, late that night, Robert Catesby, Jack Wright and Thomas Bates travelled to the Midlands so that they could instigate the Catholic uprising that would form the second stage of the plot. Back in London, Guido Fawkes met with Robert Keyes at 10.00 p.m.

At midnight the search of the Houses of Parliament began. Lord Suffolk observed an enormous amount of firewood heaped up in a cellar. Another search party, headed by Sir Thomas Knevett, returned to the cellar and, in the early hours of Tuesday, 5 November, they discovered a figure in a cloak and dark hat, booted and spurred as though for flight. He was apprehended and bound, giving his name as John Johnson, servant to Thomas Percy. The conspiracy thwarted, the conspirators, with the exception of Tom Wintour, fled north to break the news to Catesby.

News of the plot's discovery spread like wildfire throughout London and was greeted with great rejoicing and the lighting of bonfires. Parliament met in the afternoon. The entry in the Commons' Journal for 5 November records:

> This last night the Upper House of Parliament was searched by Sir Thomas Knevett; and one Johnson, Servant to Mr. Thomas Percy was there apprehended; who had placed 36 Barrels of Gunpowder in the Vault under the House with a Purpose to blow the King, and the whole company, when they should there assemble.

Afterwards divers other Gentlemen were discovered to be of the Plot.

Fawkes was defiant under interrogation, maintaining that a "desperate disease required a desperate remedy", and that his one regret was that the plot had not succeeded, for his intention was to blow the Scots back into Scotland. Had the plot succeeded, the King, his male offspring, his parliament, ten of his bishops (including some of the Bible translators) and forty of his peers would have been assassinated, and the 'Jewel in the King's crown', would never have adorned the English language.

CHAPTER 7

Le Roy S'avisera
"The king will take thought of it"

WHILST Robert Catesby, Guido Fawkes, and their fellow conspirators were spoiling for action to overthrow the Protestant cause, others were actively involved in the translation of the Bible that was to firmly establish Protestantism in the hearts and minds of the English speaking people.

Bishop Bancroft was a stalwart defender of the Church of England and had harried and pursued the Puritan extremists with ferocity and vigour. It was he who had opposed the very idea of a new translation of the Bible at the Hampton Court Conference but, once the King had responded with such enthusiasm to the proposal of a new translation of the Bible, the Bishop felt it was his responsibility to take the initiative and mould the new Bible for the Church.

Throughout the spring and early summer of 1604 he was filled with indefatigable energy. He had a commission from the King himself, and so he wrote to the Vice-Chancellor at Cambridge, declaring that it was "his Majesties pleasure" that the most learned men should be drawn into the translation project. He also wrote to his bishops on the King's behalf. He had identified a set of translators, but they would need to have secure 'livings', so that they might devote themselves to the task of translation. Bancroft, therefore, asked the bishops to find suitable livings which would yield the translators an income in excess of £20 a year. Bishop Andrewes placed several of the translators either in parishes in his diocese or as prebendaries in his cathedral.

Bancroft recognised from the start that the translation had to be a truly joint effort. The Geneva Bible had been produced by a handful of Marian exiles; the Bishops' Bible had been translated by a team of sixteen high ranking clerics, working in isolation from each other; but the King James Bible would involve a large number of learned men working together on the project. A committee would produce a work of genius, the greatest literary work of the seventeenth century, a shrine built in words!

The forty-seven translators would be divided into six companies. The very name 'company' serves to emphasis the magnitude of the project in the King's eyes. The closing years of Elizabeth's reign had seen formation of powerful trading companies, such as the East India Company in 1600. The very word suggested power, advancement, and success; and so each of the six 'committees' was to be known as a company, and each company would be led by a 'Director'.

THE KING'S RULES

Meanwhile, the King himself was busy drawing up the rules that he expected the translators to follow. Bancroft tells us that these were the King's own rules. This Bible was to play a major part in defining Jacobean England, and in healing the divisions of the Church. This Bible was to be undertaken with painstaking precision to detail and the King's rules would form the skeletal framework of the finished work.

1. The ordinary Bible read in the Church, commonly called the Bishops' Bible, to be followed, and as little altered as the truth of the original will permit.
2. The names of the prophets, and the holy writers, with the other names of the text, to be retained, as nigh as may be, accordingly as they are vulgarly used.
3. The old ecclesiastical words to be kept, viz. the word *Church* not to be translated *Congregation* &c.
4. When a word hath diverse significations, that to be kept which hath been most commonly used by the most of the ancient Fathers, being agreeable to the propriety of the place, and the analogy of the faith.
5. The divisions of the chapters to be altered, either not at all, or as little as may be, if necessity so require.

The first five rules link the King James Bible with the Tudor Bibles. But, whilst the first instruction directed the translators to revise the Bishops' Bible, that elevated and Latinised translation contributed no more than 8 per cent of its phraseology to the King James Bible. Whilst Tyndale had translated *ekklesia* not as 'church' but 'congregation,' and *presbyteros* not as 'priest' but as 'elder', the Bishops' Bible had reverted back to the ecclesiastical terms, and these were to be retained. Neither James nor Bancroft were prepared to give an inch to either Presbyterians or Puritans on this matter. Further, Rule 4 links the King James Bible with the early Fathers of the Church, to Jerome, Augustine, and Chrysostom. The King James Bible was not to be seen as new and innovative, but rather the full fruition of past labours.

6. No marginal notes at all to be affixed, but only for the explanation of the Hebrew or Greek words, which cannot, without some circumlocution, so briefly and fitly be expressed in the text.
7. Such quotations of places to be marginally set down, as shall serve for the fit reference of one Scripture to another.

James so disliked the Genevan notes that he insisted there be "no marginal notes at all". There were to be no doctrinal notes in the King James Bible. The doctrinal notes in Geneva in the sixth, seventh, and eight chapters of Romans "are so explicit that the most careless of readers is put on his guard against heresies". However, the King did allow "some circumlocation", that is, a more extensive explanation of the meaning or nuances of a Hebrew or Greek word, where a single text carried a variety of meanings. An example of this is found in the Song of Songs chapter 5 where the bride describes her Beloved as *the chiefest among ten thousand,* and the marginal note adds *chiefest: Heb. A standard-bearer.* Such 'circumlocations', is one of the outstanding features of the Authorised Version, for they bring out the richness of the original languages.

The seventh rule served to emphasise the continuity of the Old and New Testaments. They form an organic whole, as Christ Himself taught, *Search the scriptures; for in them ye think ye have eternal life: and they are they which testify of me.* (John 5:39)

Indeed James had taught his son Prince Henry:

> The whole Scripture is dyted [dictated] by God's Spirit ... to instruct and rule the whole Church militant to the end of the

world: It is composed of two parts, the Olde and New Testament: The ground of the former is the Law, which sheweth our sinne, and containeth justice: the ground of the other is Christ, who pardoning sinne containeth grace.[1]

8. Every particular man of each company, to take the same chapter or chapters, and having translated or amended them severally by himself, where he thinketh good, all to meet together, confer what they have done, and agree for their parts what shall stand.
9. As any one company hath dispatched any one book in this manner, they shall send it to the rest, to be considered of seriously and judiciously, for his majesty is very careful in this point.
10. If any company, upon the review of the book so sent, doubt or differ upon any place, to send them word thereof; note the place, and withal send the reasons; to which if they consent not, the difference to be compounded at the general meeting, which is to be of the chief persons of each company at the end of the work.

Rules 8-10 show how the work progressed. Each member of each company worked alone, "severally by himself," translating all the chapters allotted unto him. Then, the company met together and discussed the text, the individual contributions sifted into one common text, individuality moulded into a collegiate and majestic oneness. Bancroft tells us that "his majesty is very careful upon this point", these were clearly the King's own rules. The work of each company was to be refined by each of the other companies. By this process, Puritan and Churchman were to counterbalance each other. Like the refining of the purest gold, it was to be repeatedly exposed to the crucible of the finest linguistic learning ever assembled. Therefore, every part of the Bible would be fully considered, first, separately, by each member of the company to which it was originally assigned; secondly, by the whole company in concert; thirdly, by the other five companies severally; and fourthly, by the general committee of revision. By this judicious plan, each part must have been closely scrutinised at least fourteen times. Nothing quite like the King James Bible could ever be produced again.

11. When any place of special obscurity is doubted of, letters to be directed, by authority, to send to any learned man in the land, for his judgment of such a place.
12. Letters to be sent from every bishop, to the rest of his clergy, admonishing them of this translation in hand; and to move and charge as many as being skilful in the tongues; and having taken pains in that kind, to send his particular observations to the company, either at Westminster, Cambridge, or Oxford.
13. The Directors in each company, to be the Deans of Westminster and Chester for that place; and the King's Professors in the Hebrew or Greek in either University.
14. These translations to be used, when they agree better with the Text than the Bishops' Bible: Tindall's, Matthew's, Coverdale's, Whitchurch's, Geneva.

This rule provided a loophole, which enabled the translators to move away from their primary task which was to revise the Bishops' Bible (Rule 1). The object of this regulation was to avoid the suspicion of novelty on the one hand, and also of implying to Romanists that the previous translations were full of error. Eighty years of scholarship was to produce a Bible which has lasted for four hundred years!

15. Besides the said directors before mentioned, three or four of the most ancient and grave divines, in either of the Universities, not employed in translating, to be assigned by the Vice-chancellor, upon conference with the rest of the Heads, to be overseers of the translation, as well Hebrew as Greek; for the better observation of the fourth rule above specified.

When the translators met to compare what they had done, each of them held in his hand a Greek New Testament or Hebrew Old Testament.

THE TEXTS

The Greek New Testament used by the translators had been firmly established by Erasmus. Erasmus is dismissed by critics of the Textus Receptus as a Roman Catholic scholar who used only seven manuscripts to compile his Greek New Testament. They do not tell us that he died in 1536 in Basel, surrounded by his Protestant friends, and that his Roman Catholic relatives refused to be in attendance. They do not tell us that he defied the Pope in publishing the Greek New Testament in 1516. In 1514, Martin Dorp had written to him asking him not to publish his forthcoming Greek New Testament, because it would cast doubt upon the Latin Vulgate of Jerome that Rome claimed was alone inspired. And, when it was published in 1516, a Spanish scholar, Stunica, accused it of being an open condemnation of the Latin Vulgate.

The teaching of Erasmus was revolutionary. There was no man in the whole of Europe better prepared than Erasmus for the work of editing the first printed Greek New Testament text. He contended that men should study the Fathers of the Church, and above all the New Testament. He showed that the Latin Vulgate swarmed with

Desiderius Erasmus (1466-1536)

faults, and rendered an immense service to the truth, by publishing his edition of the Greek text with a new Latin translation. The first published Greek New Testament reached England from Basel in 1516, and this was revised in 1519 and 1522. It was this Traditional Text, preserved by what Hills describes as "the universal priesthood of believers", which Erasmus used. Between 1516 and 1535 he published five editions. He used five manuscripts in particular, but it is evident that he widely consulted many others. He had made his own Latin translation of the New Testament whilst at Oxford in 1505-06. He travelled widely, and had taken notes from other manuscripts, and no doubt he used these, together with the five manuscripts consulted at Basel.

He was aware of all the variant readings thrown up by textual critics of today, and these are discussed in notes which he placed after the text in his editions of the Greek New Testament. Here, for example, Erasmus dealt with such problem passages as the conclusion of the Lord's Prayer (Matt. 6:13), the interview of the rich young man (Matt. 19:17-22), the ending of Mark (16:9-20), the angelic song (Luke 2:14), the angel, agony, and sweat of blood (Luke 22:43-44), the woman taken in adultery (John 7:53-8:11), and the mystery of godliness (1 Tim. 3:16). In his first two editions he had omitted 1 John 5:7, but then included it in his third edition of 1522. True, Erasmus was not an outstanding man of faith, but in his editorial labours with the Greek Text of the New Testament he was providentially influenced and guided by the faith of others. He was not a humanist when it came to handling the sacred text of the Word of God! Without doubt it was this work of Erasmus that first suggested to William Tyndale his noble design of translating the Word of God into the language of his countrymen.

After the death of Erasmus, Robert Stephanus (1503-59) produced four editions of the Greek New Testament (1546,1549,1550, and 1551 respectively), which aroused the hostility of the Roman Church so much that he left Paris in 1550 and settled in Geneva. His third and fourth editions follow closely the fifth edition of Erasmus. Theodore Beza (1519-1605), produced ten editions of the Greek New Testament, and although he lists the textual materials that he consulted, including the infamous Bezae manuscript, he follows the fourth edition of Stephanus. In his notes he upholds the genuineness of Mark 16:9-20, defends the reading of 1 Timothy 3:16, *God was manifest in the flesh*, and concerning 1 John 5:7 Beza says, "It seems to me that this clause ought by all means to be retained."

The Elzevirs were a family of Dutch printers. Bonaventure Elzevir published his first edition of the New Testament in 1624 and his second in 1633. He follows the text of Beza and Erasmus, and in the preface states, "You have therefore the text now received by all *(textum ab omnibus receptum)* in which we give nothing changed or corrupt." So that the phrase Textus Receptus dates from the Elzevirs' second edition of 1633. The Textus Receptus really was the text received by all. In England, Stephanus' third edition was the form of the Textus Receptus generally preferred. In Europe it was the Elzevirs' second edition.

The King James Vesion is based on the Textus Receptus of which there are the five editions produced by Erasmus (1516, 1519, 1522,1527, and 1535); the four editions by Robert Stephanus (1546, 1549, 1550, 1551) that were largely based upon the fifth edition of Erasmus; Theodore Beza's ten editions between 1556 and 1598, for which Beza followed the fourth edition of Stephanus; and the Elzevirs' two editions in 1624 and 1633. The Elzevir brothers followed the fourth edition of Beza.

It was that found in the Complutensian Polyglot of 1520; Luther's New Testament of 1522 (which also formed the basis of the Flemish 1526, the Zurich of 1529); Tyndale's New Testament of 1525; the Olivetan French Bible of 1535; the Geneva Bible of 1560; the Spanish Bible (1602) of Cipriano de Valera; the Diodati Italian Bible of 1607; the Dutch Bible of 1637; and the King James Bible of 1611.

The translators of the King James Bible relied mainly on the later editions of Beza's Greek New Testament, especially his fourth edition of 1588/89, but also they consulted the editions of Erasmus and Stephanus.

> According to Scrivener (1884), out of the 252 passages in which these sources differ sufficiently to affect the English rendering, the King James Version agrees with Beza against Stephanus 113 times; with Stephanus against Beza 59 times; and 80 times with Erasmus ...against Beza and Stephanus. Hence the King James Version ought to be regarded not merely as a translation of the Textus Receptus but also an independent variety of the Textus Receptus.[2]

This text was reconstructed by Scrivener and is now published by the Trinitarian Bible Society in London.

The Process

Robert Barker, the king's printer, printed forty folio-sized Bishops' Bibles of his latest 1602 edition for the six companies of translators. These were delivered unbound in quires, that is to say in sections of twenty-four folio sheets folded once, each containing four pages of type. Therefore, when a translator was at work, his basic tool was one of these folio sheets on which alterations were made. On the table were copies of the Bibles specified by King James, that is, Tyndale's Bible, Matthew's Bible, Coverdale's Bible, and Whitchurch's Bible, plus the Rheims. Also available were other Bible translations and exegetical works.

Work on the translation progressed in three stages:

First, each company prepared its preliminary translation.

Second, from these preliminary translations, the committee of review prepared a final version at Stationer's Hall in London, situated in Ave Maria Lane, off Paternoster Row. The General Committee met for some nine months during 1610.

Third, Thomas Bilson, Bishop of Winchester, and Dr Miles Smith, Prebendary of Hereford and Exeter Cathedrals and later Bishop of Gloucester, provided the finishing touches.

The chief requirement was accuracy. Ninety per cent of the English text was already satisfactorily established in the earlier Bibles. Each scholar worked alone, using the pages from the Bishops' Bible supplied by Robert Barker. In the alternate blank columns, each man would make notes, which he then compared with his brethren's comments at the weekly discussion.

The translators of the King James Bible worked on that part of the sacred Scriptures assigned to him; then the company of men would meet together and one read his translation, the rest holding in their hands some Bible, either of the learned tongues, the Bishops', Tyndale, Coverdale, Geneva. If they found any fault in the translation they spoke, if not he read on. Thus the Authorised Version took shape as spoken language and not as silent text on a page, being prepared for public reading.

> In an age when excellence in rhetoric was highly prized, the text had to satisfy the company in style as well as accuracy. ...This well-trained feeling for style, disciplined by the grammatical structure

> of the originals, was placed at the service of dignified ritual, and produced the special qualities of Authorised Version that we recognize. That the solemnity did not descend into dullness or turgidity is due partly to the ear of the revisers, and partly to the underlying strength of the original work of Tyndale and Coverdale.[3]

Though their base was supposedly the Bishops' Bible, the truth is that the ultimate base was Tyndale. The estimates of Tyndale's influence on the King James Bible ranges from 83-90% for the New Testament, and 76% for the Old Testament. The King James Bible's rhythm, vocabulary and cadence, has a root in the English language shaped by Tyndale's translation.

We cannot assume that each company completed its work at the same time. Indeed, there is evidence to suggest that Bois's company at Cambridge finished its translation of the Apocrypha so early that Bois was able to assist another company in its work. As soon as a book was completed, copies were submitted to the other groups for their comments, and then to outside scholars for their suggestions, but not in either case for alterations. In the case of the First Oxford Company, who had finished in May 1607, this further process went on until December 1608. King James then called all copies for final revision by the General Committee of twelve translators, who met in London from January 1609, to make the final revisions. This important task took some nine months. Only the General Committee was permitted to make alterations. John Bois was also a member of the final revision committee in Westminster. He took notes of that committee's work, which remained undiscovered until 1959 but have now been made available by Ward Allen in his work on Bois, *Translating for King James.* (See example of Bois's notes and comments in Appendix 6.)

Finally, Bishop Bilson of Winchester, together with Dr Smith, Bishop of Gloucester, put the finishing touches to this version after all things had been maturely weighed and examined. According to Anthony Wood, Bishop Bilson of Winchester was

> As learned a Prelate as England ever afforded, a deep and profound scholar, exactly read in ecclesiastical authors. ... In his younger years he was infinitely studious in poetry, philosophy, physics and divinity, especially the last. His genius inciting him,

> he became so well skilled that at length he was no longer a common soldier but a Commander-in-Chief of spiritual warfare.[4]

This latter description is no doubt based upon his defence in 1585 against Papal censures, Jesuit sophisms, and the Rhemish Testament.

Bilson wrote the fulsome Dedication:

> To the most high and mighty Prince, James by the grace of God... And now at last, by the mercy of God and our labours, it is brought to such a conclusion that the Church of England shall reap good fruit thereby, we hold it our duty to offer it to your Majesty, as principal Author of the Work: Hoping that since things of this quality have ever been subject to the censures of ill meaning and discontented persons, your allowance shall more encourage us than all the calumniations of other men shall dismay us. So that if on one side we be traduced by many popish persons, or if on the other side we be maligned by self-conceited brethren, we may rest secure, supported by a good conscience and by the powerful protection of your Majesty.[5]

And to Miles Smith, the long and very learned preface, "The Translators to the Reader," in which he assures us that he admired earlier English translators,

> We are so far off from condemning any of their labours that travailed before us in this kind, either in this land or beyond sea, either in King Henry's, or King Edward's, or Queen Elizabeth's of ever renowned memory, that we acknowledge them to have been raised up of God for the building and furnishing of his Church, and that they deserve to be had of us and of posterity in everlasting remembrance. ...Therefore, blessed be they, and most honoured be their name, that break the ice and give the onset upon that which helpeth forward to the saving of souls.

Then he states that it was never the purpose to make a new English Bible,

> We never thought to make a new translation, nor yet of a bad one to make a good one, but to make a good one better; or out of many good ones, one principal good one. ...The work hath not been huddled up in 72 days, but hath cost the workmen the pains of twice seven times seventy-two days and more. Neither did we

> think it too much to consult the Translators or Commentators, Chaldee, Hebrew, Syrian, Greek or Latin, no nor Spanish, French, Italian, or Dutch. Neither did we disdain to revise that which we had done, and bring back to the anvil that which we had hammered. But, using as great helps as were needful, fearing no reproach for slowness, no praise for expedition, we have at length, through the good hand of the Lord upon us, brought the work to that pass which you see.

According to Miles Smith, the translation took twice seven times seventy-two days, that is, 1008 days; or two years and nine months! Between June 1604 and 1610, the translators with painstaking diligence devoted over half of their working days to the task of translation, not neglecting their other duties of preaching each Lord's Day and the pastoral care of their flocks.

Significantly, Smith goes on to explain the need for marginal readings, and variety of expression:

> Variety of translations is profitable for finding out the sense of Scripture; so diversity of signification and sense in the margin where the text is not clear, must do good, yea is necessary. ...We have not tied ourselves to an uniformity of phrasing, or to identical words, as some peradventure would wish, because they see some learned men have been as exact as they could that way. Truly, we were especially careful and made conscience of our duty that we did not vary the sense of what we had translated before if the same word signified the same thing in both places, but that we should express the same notion in the same particular word, as for example to say 'purpose' and never 'intent', or 'journeying' and never 'travelling', or 'think' and never 'suppose', or 'pain' and never 'ache', or 'joy' and never 'gladness', that would savour more of curiosity than wisdom.

However, neither Bilson nor Smith had the final say, because Archbishop Bancroft claimed his rights as Archbishop to have the last word. It was Bancroft who at first had opposed the idea of a new translation, "If every man's humour should be followed there would be no end to translating," but who then became its chief promoter, and diligently provided the rules for translation. He was no lover of the Puritans, and initiated a great drive against Puritan ministers, silencing and banishing many of them. Lord Clarendon claimed that if Bancroft had lived he would have "quickly extinguished the flames kindled at Geneva". Mercifully, Bancroft was removed from this earthly scene in November 1610, and his death brought to an end the confrontation, aggravation, suppression and persecutions. Bancroft is reported to have made some fourteen changes, including his insistence that the word "bishoprick" be inserted at Acts 1:20 *For it is written in the book of the Psalms, Let his habitation be desolate, and let no man dwell therein: and his bishoprick let another take.* The word 'Bishoprick' was used in Psalm 109 by Miles Coverdale and the Great Bible, but not in the Geneva, which says, 'charge,' or in the Bishops', which says 'office,' nor in the King James, which says 'office,' with 'charge,' in a marginal note. The word 'Bishoprick' was quoted uniformly at Acts 1:20 by all versions but Geneva, leaving this the only place in the new Bible where it survived.

Dr William Gouge, Puritan author of that remarkable commentary on the Epistle to the Hebrews, father of the London ministers, Rector of St Anne's, Blackfriars, and member of the Westminster Assembly of Divines, penned a Preface to the first complete Concordance of the King James Bible in 1650.

> "[T]he translation allowed by his late Majesty of Great Britain ... the last and best translation of the English Bible which is now in use". This comment written forty years after the first edition of the King James Bible shows us steady progress during a period of increasing conflict with some two editions a year. No special proclamation, Act of Parliament or Royal Injunction marked its advent. No record of intervention by James. No forced sale, as there was with the Great Bible and Bishops', when parishes were instructed to buy copies.[6]

Style, scholarship, faith, prayer, and humility all contributed to make the King James Bible

> a wonderful 'glove' for Holy Scripture. ... But this is a princely glove, an embroidered gauntlet, so apt, so true, so pure, so strong and beautiful, that surely we may call it the World's gem! Yet after all it is not the glove so much as the Divine 'HAND' within the glove who matters most. "Not unto us, O LORD, not unto us, but unto thy name give glory."[7]

CHAPTER 8

The King's Printers

AFTER Guttenberg, printing developed more rapidly in Europe than in England, so much so that in 1500 there were over one thousand printers in Europe and only two in England: Wynkyn De Worde (former partner of William Caxton) and Richard Pynson! By the late 1530's, two London merchants, Richard Grafton and Edward Whitchurch, had arranged, under licence, the printing of the Matthew's Bible in Antwerp in 1537. Then in 1539 they took over and finished in London the printing of the Great Bible. After 1538 Tyndale's New Testament and the Taverner Bible were all printed in London. Richard Jugge first printed Tyndale's New Testament in 1548. Jugge was to hold the monopoly as the Royal Printer throughout the middle years of Elizabeth's reign. On Jugge's death in 1577, the office of Royal Printer was granted to Sir Thomas Wilkes, who transferred a portion to Christopher Barker. In 1589, Barker and his son Robert obtained the exclusive patent as Royal Printer. Christopher Barker died in 1599, and therefore, at the accession of James I in 1603, Robert Barker held the office of King's Printer, which in time passed to his elder son Christopher, and second son, Robert. King James I confirmed the royal patronage at an annual salary of six pounds, thirteen shillings and four pence (£6.66) for printing all Statutes and Bibles, with reversion to Robert's eldest son, Christopher, who was then eight years old.

Once work had commenced upon the King James Bible one might have expected that there would be no further editions of either the Bishops' or the Geneva Bible by Robert Barker. However, this was not the case. The last folio edition of the Bishops' Bible was the Black Letter volume of 1602, but there did follow a further three printings of the Bishops' New Testament in 1605[1], and then another in 1606[2], and the last printing of the Bishops' was that of 1608[3] with its title in black and red. The Geneva Bible continued to be printed by Robert Barker in great profusion: folio editions were printed in 1607 and 1608[4]; some twelve quarto editions were printed between 1604 and 1611, with three of them in 1611; there were four octavio editions; and at least two other Geneva printings from Barker's press. Barker's last edition of the Geneva Bible was the folio edition of 1616[5], and the Octavio New Testament[6].

Barker's premises were then in Northumberland House, Aldersgate. A Bible offered a printer unique opportunities. The length of the text at 774,746 words was precisely known, which means that costings could be accurately assessed; moreover, there was ready demand for it in many sizes and formats. It was then, as now, a lucrative market for the printer! It was to the Aldersgate premises that the finished manuscripts of the King James Bible were delivered in 1610. There is evidence[7] that Robert Barker paid £3,500 for the right to print the new Bible.

> Printing was highly competitive, revolving round the Stationers Company, its Masters and its Wardens. In the 1580's Whitgift authorised an Inquisition showing that Christopher Barker had five presses, more than all other printers save one. At that time there were 23 licensed printers working fifty-three presses. All along the Barkers shared their work with journeymen printers, ever eager for copy. ... Much the most important and demanding job in the printing trade was the making of a new folio Bible. And the most essential process was of course setting of the type, each pair of facing pages locked in a wooden frame which printed one side of thick strong folio paper, three folios, each carrying six pages, made up into a quire. This Bible occupied 366 folios containing four pages each, a total of 1464, unnumbered in the original editions.[8]

The first edition of the Authorised Version is the Black Letter folio edition of 1611[9]. The general title page is a fine copper-plate engraving, inscribed "C. Boel fecit in Richmont", with representations of the sacred name of Jehovah, the Holy Dove, the Agnes Dei, and a group of Apostles with St Matthew seated on the extreme left and St Mark on the extreme right. In the middle on the left side there is Moses, whilst on the right is Aaron. Below these are St Luke on the left and St John on the right whilst in the centre at the bottom is the pelican in her piety. The New Testament title-border is a wood-engraving with representations of the Sacred Name, the Agnes Dei, the Holy Dove, and Matthew and Mark. In the centre on the left side are the tents of the ten tribes, and on the right side the twelve Apostles. Below these are the Lamb slain, and Luke and John whilst at the bottom is a tablet bearing the words "Cum Privilego".

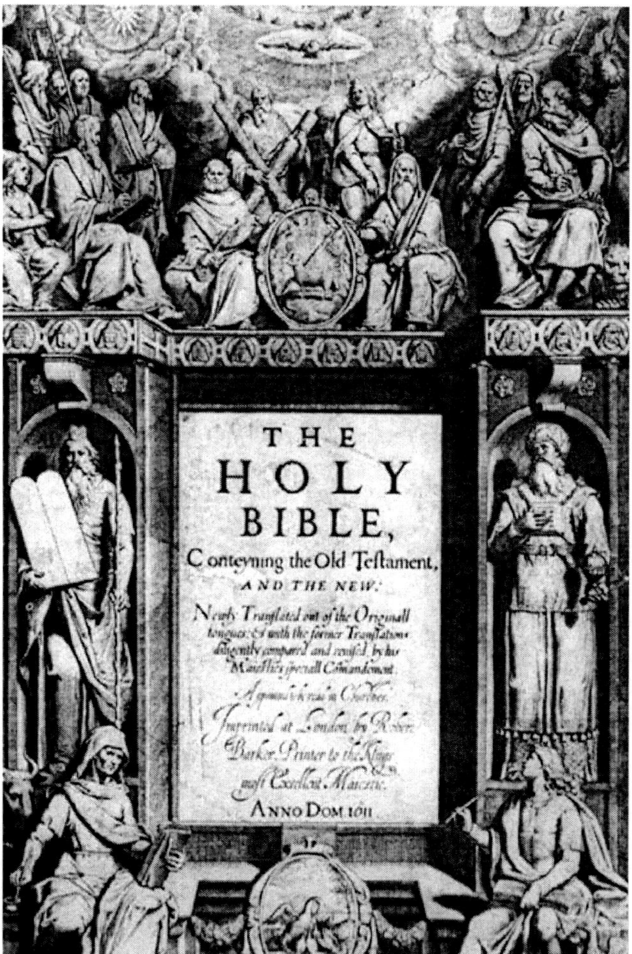

This first folio edition is known as the "great HE Bible," because of a printer's mistake at Ruth 3:15, which reads, *he went into the city*, instead of *she went into the city.* It is recognized that from 1611 to 1614 there are two distinct series of editions in various sizes, which differ throughout in many minor points of typography, and are generally distinguished by the names "He" Bibles and "She" Bibles, from their respective readings in Ruth 3:15. The suggested explanation of this dualism is that the printing was at first carried on in two separate offices in order to facilitate rapid production, and that two standard copies were used, one of which had received a certain amount of additional correction from the press editors. 'She' later became the accepted wording.

There were other printer's errors which marred the first edition: at Genesis 10:16 it reads *Emorite* for *Amorite;* at Exodus 14:10, three lines were repeated; then at Exodus 38:11 it had *hoops,* instead of *hooks;* at Leviticus 13:56 it has *plaine* for *plague;* and in Psalm 69:32 it reads *seek good*, instead of *seek God.*

Later editions of the King James Bible resulted in some infamous printers' errors, the most notable of which were the so called 'Wicked Bible' of 1631[10] from the error in Exodus 20:14 where the Seventh Commandment reads, *Thou shalt commit adultery!* The printers Barker and Bill were fined £300 for the offence. Another infamous printing error was printed in the 1717, 'Vinegar Bible', printed by J. Baskett of Oxford[11], so named because the parable of the vineyard in Luke 20 is referred to as the "parable of the vinegar"!

A copy of the first folio edition of 1611 was purchased for West Rudham at Lynn Mart, 6 February 1611, for 53 shillings and 4 pence (£2.66), and in 1611 the Dean and Chapter of Worcester bought one for 58 shillings (£2.90).

There was a Black Letter New Testament produced also in 1611[12], and the first quarto edition was printed in Roman type in 1612. This follows closely the text of the folio Bible of 1611, but corrected some of the printers' errors. The quarto editions have thirty-nine pages of *Speed's Genealogies* showing "the line of Jesus Christ from Adam to the Blessed Virgin Mary". This ends with a very fine engraving of "Canaan and the bordering Countries". John Speed had been granted a Royal Privilege to insert these genealogies after the Dedication and Preface.

In 1629 Thomas and John Buck produced the first folio edition printed at Cambridge. This in reality is the first revision of the King James Bible. Cambridge had begun to print the Bible in the Geneva version in 1588 under a charter granted by Henry VIII in 1534. The charter was ratified by Charles in 1628 and this edition[13] was the first production under the new charter. Dr Goad of Hadleigh, Dr Joseph Meade, Dr Bois, and Dr Samuel Ward—the last two of whom had been part of the original company of translators some twenty years before—revised this edition. They corrected many of the printers' errors of the earlier editions, and took considerable care to the words printed in italics and to punctuation. Robert Barker then printed a special folio edition, and a thousand quarto copies, which he sold at five shillings (25p) in order to overthrow the competition from Cambridge.

Buck and Roger Daniel at Cambridge issued a second revision of the King James Bible in 1638[14]. Again, it was Drs Ward, Goad, Bois and Mead who completed the work of correction that they had commenced in 1629.

J. Bentham of Cambridge published a third revision in 1762[15]. This was the standard edition prepared by Dr F. S. Paris, of Sidney Sussex College, Cambridge, and H. Therold, Fellow of Magdalene. In this Bible a serious attempt was made to correct the text of the King James' version by amending the spelling and punctuation, unifying and extending the use of italics, and removing printers' errors. Marginal annotations, which had been growing in some Bibles since 1660 although excluded from others, were finally received into the place they have occupied ever since.

The final revision of the King James Bible was that printed by Wright and Gill of Oxford in 1769[16]. This is the Oxford 'standard' edition, carefully revised by Dr Benjamin Blayney of Hertford College, following the lines of Dr Paris' Cambridge edition of 1762. It is this edition which has remained the standard edition ever since.

CHAPTER 9

The Crown Jewel of England, and of the English Speaking Peoples

THE publication in 1611 of the Authorised Version marked an epoch, in the proper sense of that term, in the history of the English Bible. It was a point at which one period ended and another began. It marked the culmination of a long series of attempts to produce an accurate and reliable translation of the Scriptures in English. It began a period of supremacy, unassailed after the first thirty years of its existence, and unquestioned for two hundred years thereafter. It gave to the English nation, and eventually to all the English-speaking peoples throughout the world, a most faithful and accurate version of the Scriptures, and expressed in prose so stately and splendid as to make it the greatest classic of the English tongue. For the English language, for English literature, for true Christianity, the publication of 1611 was in the fullest sense epoch-making. Geographically, its spread has been global and its influence incalculable.

The language of the King James Bible shaped the speech of England. The language of the Authorised Version became Bunyan's breath, so that in reading through *Pilgrim's Progress*, the reader becomes thoroughly acquainted with the Scriptures!

> The language of the Authorised version has been called 'the noblest monument of English prose', the 'pure well of English undefiled'. It has the virtues of clarity, simplicity, and intelligibility that have characterised the mainline of English versions of the Bible since Tyndale. Its desire was that 'the Scriptures may speak like itself, as in the language of Canaan, that it may be understood even by the very vulgar'. But in

> addition the Authorised Version has a remarkable sense of appropriateness, felicity, and effective expression. It had the instinct of genius for music and rhythm. It could discover the 'inevitable' word or phrase for a given context. Its style admirably reflected the dignity, majesty and sublimity of the original. The men who prepared the English Revised Version commended the stylistic excellence of the Authorised Version, 'we have learned to admire its simplicity, its dignity, its power, its happy turns of expression, its general accuracy, and we must not fail to add, the music of its cadences, and the felicities of its rhythm'. Isaacs has said: 'The Authorised Version is a miracle and a landmark. Its felicities are manifold, its music has entered into the very blood and marrow of English thought and speech... there is no corner of English life, no conversation... it has not adorned'. ...The Authorised Version ... was a revision prepared by gifted men in a golden age of English literature, ...when the English language had reached its vigorous maturity ... the literary gifts which made the King James Version a truly distinguished work belonged to no one man or no one decade, but were those of an exceptional era united to produce a version of unique excellence.[1]

The Authorised Version is the greatest of our national treasures, the crown jewel of the last four hundred years! The sheer longevity of this version is a phenomenon. It has served as the standard English translation for almost 400 years throughout the English speaking world. It still reads with clarity and authority and is much in demand throughout the English speaking developing world. No other version has taken its place in this respect.

THE MAJESTY OF ITS LANGUAGE

The translators gave the King James Version a majestic quality that raises it high above all other translations. They recognised God to be God! A God of majesty, and a God of glory. Consider the grandeur of the following:

> *The LORD is my strength and my song, and he is become my salvation: he is my God, and I will prepare him an habitation; my father's God, and I will exalt him.*
> *The LORD is a man of war: the LORD is his name.*

> *Pharaoh's chariots and his host hath he cast into the sea: his chosen captains also drowned in the Red sea.*
> *The depths have covered them: they sank into the bottom as a stone.*
> *Thy right hand, O LORD, is become glorious in power: thy right hand, O LORD, hath dashed in pieces the enemy.*
> *And in the greatness of thine excellency thou hast overthrown them that rose up against thee: thou hast sent forth thy wrath, which consumed them as stubble.*
>
> Exodus 15.2-7

> *Thou didst blow with thy wind, the sea covered them: they sank as lead in the mighty waters.*
> *Who is like unto thee, O LORD, among the gods? Who is like thee, glorious in holiness, fearful in praises, doing wonders?*
>
> Exodus 15.10-11.

The words and phrases of the Authorised Version have become part of our very language. Consider the following: *Am I my brothers' keeper?* (Genesis 4); *Escaped with the skin of my teeth* (Job 19); *They have sown the wind, and they shall reap the whirlwind* (Hosea 8); and *Let brotherly love continue* (Hebrews 13).

As the Bible is the Word of God, it should be read both in public and in private, and it should be remembered. A translation therefore needs to be in a form of English suitable for public and private reading, and easy to learn by heart. The rhythm of the Authorised Version, its reverent and dignified style, and the very high proportion of simple short words of Anglo-Saxon origin that have continued to provide the 'basic' vocabulary of our language in everyday use, all combine to make this version the most suitable in all these respects. *The Son of man is come to seek and to save that which was lost ... he that hath the Son hath life; he that hath not the Son of God hath not life.* These great statements are given to us in simple words all of one syllable, and much of the Authorised Version is in simple 'timeless' English that a child can read, learn, and understand.[2]

Dr Andrew Edgar quotes F. W. Faber, a Roman Catholic priest, who declared,

> It lives on the ear like a music that can never be forgotten, like the sound of church bells which the convert scarcely knows how

he can forego. Its felicities often seem to be things rather than words. It is part of the national mind, and the anchor of the national seriousness. Nay, it is worshipped with a positive idolatry, in extenuation of whose fanaticism its intrinsic beauty pleads availingly with the scholar. The memory of the dead passes into it. The potent traditions of childhood are stereotyped in its verses. It is the representative of a man's best moments; all that there has been about him of soft and gentle and pure and penitent and good, speaks to him for ever out of his English Bible. It is his sacred thing which doubt never dimmed and controversy never soiled; and in the length and breadth of the land there is not a Protestant with one spark of religiousness about him whose spiritual biography is not in his Saxon Bible.[3]

Lord Thomas Babington Macaulay, First Baron Macaulay (25 October 1800 – 28 December 1859), was a nineteenth-century British poet, historian and Whig politician and one of the two Members of Parliament for Edinburgh. He wrote extensively as an essayist and reviewer, and on British history.

The English Bible – a book which, if everything else in our language should perish, would alone suffice to show the whole extent of its beauty and power.[4]

Some thirty years or so ago, the Banner of Truth magazine had articles supporting the retention of the Authorised Version, in which it was argued that,

The purpose of Scripture is to reveal God to us in His fulness and grace. ... In the past so great an accent fell upon the

> memorisation of Scriptures. It is not for nothing that on the title page of the Authorised Version the words appear: "appointed to be read in churches." To be sure, the words mean that the translation had a very high, authoritative status. One notices, however, that the familiar version reads much better out loud than any other. Why? Because attention clearly was paid to this very matter. The translators were concerned with the oral effect of their work, with the ease with which it could be used in public and private worship, still more, with the facility with which men could commit verses and whole passages to memory, thus helping them to hide it in their hearts. Everyone knows and has been struck by the grandeur and beauty of the cadences in the common version; not everyone has realised what an enormous aid these are to getting of the Scriptures by heart, the memorising of them. It does seem to me incontrovertible, however, that there are great advantages in the use of a single, great translation of the Word of God. I refer to the devotional reading of Scripture, its memorisation, its use in worship: in a word, to the reading of Scripture. ... When and while one reads, he ought to be getting the Word by heart, allowing his whole being to be saturated with what he reads, permitting it to effect him intellectually, emotionally, spiritually. And if he changes his version by the day or week, or even year. .... The end result will be that he knows no version thoroughly, that his mind is quite confused as to the wording of Scriptures, that, in short, he memorises and gets by heart nothing at all. ... My own view is that people ought to choose a great, churchly, version of the Scriptures—not one produced privately, or by a group of men working on their own—and stick to it, getting it by heart, learning it, mulling over it, loving it, letting it penetrate them altogether, so that its language becomes their own. Leave the litter of modern translations or paraphrases to one side. ... My view continues to be that ... the King James Version remains unequalled in the splendour of its language, its devoutness, its dignity, and its sheer memorizableness. ... Have it always with you, read it, and get it by heart. [5]

The multiplication of modern speech versions has had the unintended consequence of discouraging memorisation of the

Scriptures. Why memorise something that will be out of date in less than a decade? And which of the plethora of versions on the market are you to memorise? A generation of Christians are growing up ignorant of the Holy Bible, because they are not encouraged, nor are they able, to hide its life-giving words in their hearts. Constantly the proponents of the modern translations of the Bible argue that the King James Version is archaic. No one speaks like that now as they did in 1611! No one uses those incomprehensible pronouns and verbal forms like these:

> *For he that speaketh in an unknown tongue speaketh not unto men, but unto God: for no man understandeth him; howbeit in the spirit he speaketh mysteries. But he that prophesieth speaketh unto men to edification, and exhortation, and comfort.* (1 Corinthians 14.2-3)

Now whilst it is true that no one uses verbal endings like these, it does not mean that they cannot now be understood. Are the verbs 'speaketh', 'understandeth,' and 'prophesieth' so dreadfully difficult to understand? There is a sense in which the King James Bible was archaic in 1611, because those 'incomprehensible' pronouns: thee, thou, thy, and thine, were not the speech of 1611. Read the preface of the King James Bible and you will soon discover that in 1611 the common second person pronoun usage was you, ye and your.

THE TREASURE OF THE CHURCH

The Authorised Version is suitable for public as well as private reading and admirable for memorisation. The language sends forth the message of the Bible with clarity, music and power. For the sick, the depressed, the doubting, the dying, for the lonely, the fearful, the tempted, and the wanderer, its majestic and familiar phrases can come as a balm from Gilead. The translators deliberately chose words and phrases that were no longer used in general conversation even in their day in order that they might set this book apart from all others. F. F. Bruce in his book, *The English Bible*, tells the story of a pastoral call that a young minister in Scotland made to an elderly woman. The minister read to her a chapter from Moffatt's translation of the Bible. She listened to him and said, "Well, that was very nice; but now, won't you just read a wee bittie of the Word of God before you go."[6]

Dr William Lyon Phelps, Professor of English Literature at Yale, writes:

> Priests, atheists sceptics, devotees, agnostics, and evangelists, are generally agreed that the Authorised Version of the English Bible is the best example of English literature that the world has ever seen. ... Every one who has a thorough knowledge of the Bible may truly be called educated; and no other learning or culture, no matter how extensive or elegant, can, among Europeans and Americans, form a proper substitute. Western civilisation is founded upon the Bible. ... I thoroughly believe in a university education for both men and women; but I believe a knowledge of the Bible without a college course is more valuable than a college course without the Bible. ... The Elizabethan period—a term loosely applied to the years between 1558-1642—is generally regarded as the most important era in English literature. ... But the crowning achievement of those spacious days was the Authorised Translation of the Bible, which appeared in 1611. ... Three centuries of English composition followed; but the art of English composition reached its climax in the pages of the Bible. ... Now, as the English-speaking people have the best Bible in the world, and as it is the most beautiful monument erected with the English alphabet, we ought to make the most of it, for it is an incomparably rich inheritance, free to all who can read. This means that we ought invariably in the church, and on all public occasions to use the Authorized Version; all others are inferior.[7]

Queen Victoria recognised the importance of the English Bible when she was asked by an African Prince what was the secret of England's greatness and Britain's glory.

> It was a noble and beautiful answer of our Queen ...to an African Prince. Our beloved Queen told him, not of the number of her fleet, nor the number of her armies; not the account of her boundless merchandise. Nor the details of her inexhaustible wealth. She did not, like Hezekiah, in an evil hour, show the ambassador her diamonds, and her jewels, and her rich ornaments, but handing him a beautifully bound copy of the Bible, she said, " ... ... this is the secret of England's greatness."[8]

Thomas James Barker, The Secret of England's Greatness, c.1863. Queen Victoria, flanked by Prince Albert is presenting to a 'native' chief a copy of the Bible.

Charlton Heston said:

> The King James translation has been described as "the greatest monument of English prose", as well as "the only great work of art ever created by a committee". Both statements are true. Fifty four scholars worked seven years to produce the work from its extant texts in Aramaic, Hebrew, Greek, Latin, English. Such an undertaking can be expected to produce great scholarship, but hardly writing as sublime as the King James ... The authors of several boring translations that have followed over the last fifty years mumble that the KJV is 'difficult' filled with long words. Have a look at the difficult long words that begin the Old Testament, and end the Gospels: *In the beginning God created the heaven and the earth. And the earth was without form, and void; and darkness was upon the face of the deep.* And *there are also*

> *many other things which Jesus did, the which, if they should be written every one, I suppose that even the world itself could not contain the books that should be written.* ... there's no comparable writing in the language. Over the past several centuries it's been the single book in most households, an enormous force in shaping the development of the English language. Carried around the world by missionaries, it provided the base by which English is about to become the lingua franca of the world in the next century. Exploring it during this shoot [Ten Commandments] was one of the most rewarding creative experiences in my life.[9]

George Bernard Shaw wrote:

> The translation was extraordinarily well done because to the translators what they were translating was not merely a curious collection of ancient books written by different authors in different stages of culture, but the word of God divinely revealed through His chosen and expressly inspired scribes. In this conviction they carried out their work with boundless reverence and care and achieved a beautiful artistic result ... they made a translation so magnificent that to this day the common human Britisher or citizen of the United States of North America accepts and worships it as a single book by a single author, the book being the Book of Books and the author being God.[10]

Sir Winston Churchill wrote:

> At this time [early 17th century] a splendid and lasting monument was created to the genius of the English-speaking people. The scholars who produced this masterpiece [the Authorised Version] are mostly unknown and unremembered. But they forged an enduring link, literary and religious, between the English-speaking people of the world.[11]

Professor Mark A. Knoll (Professor of History at the University of Notre Dame) wrote:

> In 1911 the English-speaking world paused to mark the 300th anniversary of the King James Version of the Bible, with American political leaders foremost in the chorus of exaltation. To former president Theodore Roosevelt, the Bible translation was "the Magna Carta of the poor and the oppressed ... the most democratic book in the world". Soon-to-be president Woodrow Wilson said much the same thing: "The Bible (with its individual value of the human soul) is undoubtedly the book that has made democracy and been the source of all progress."
>
> Americans at the time mostly agreed with these sentiments, because the impact of the King James Version was everywhere so obvious, ... with no occasion more memorable than March 4, 1865, when four quotations from the King James Bible framed Abraham Lincoln's incomparable Second Inaugural Address: Genesis 3:19; Matthew 18:7; Matthew 7:1; and Psalm 19:9.
>
> Because the King James Bible was so widely read for religious purposes, it had also become a source of public ideals. Because it was so central in the churches, and because the churches were so central to culture, the King James Bible functioned also as a common reservoir for the language. Hundreds of phrases ... and thousands of words ... were in the common speech because they had first been in this translation.
>
> ...Today the legacy of the King James Bible remains fixed in the common speech, even if awareness of the language's debt to this translation is fading. Whether any modern translation of the Scriptures ... can anchor the culture as the King James Bible once did, is a question worth serious consideration in the run-up to 2011 and the four hundredth anniversary of this unsurpassed cultural force.[12]

Dean Frederic William Farrar (1831 - 1903), often known as Dean Farrar, was a theological writer born in Bombay, India, and educated at King William's College on the Isle of Man. He then went to King's College London and the University of Cambridge and was for some years a master at Harrow, before becoming Master (headmaster) of Marlborough College from 1871-76 . He became successively Canon of Westminster and Rector of St Margaret's, Archdeacon of

Westminster, and Dean of Canterbury. He was an eloquent preacher and a voluminous author. His writings included stories of school life, such as *Eric, or, Little by Little* and *St Winifred's;* a *Life of Christ* (1874), which had great popularity, a *Life of St Paul* (1879) and two historical romances. His works were translated into many languages, especially his *Life of Christ.* He says,

> It was the Bible which created the prose literature of England, of which the Authorised Version was the noblest monument; it was the Bible which gave fire and nobleness to her language; it was the Bible which turned a dead oppression into a living Church; it was the Bible which put to flight the nightmare of ignorance before the rosy dawn of progress; it was the Bible which made each free Christian man feel some grandeur in the beatings of his own heart, as of a being who stood face to face with God, responsible to Him alone, having "the dignity of God's image upon him, and the sign of His redemption marked visibly upon his forehead". It was the Bible which saved England from sinking into a tenth-rate power as a vassal of cruel, ignorant, superstitious Spain, whose Dominicans and tyrants would have turned her fields into slaughterhouses as they turned those of the Netherlands, and would have made her cities reek as she made Seville reek with the bale-fires of her Inquisition.

> ... But this is certain: so far as, and so long as, England remains true to that simple, unadulterated Word of God, which has been purchased for us by the misery of exiles and the blood of martyrs; so far and so long as she stands fast in the freedom wherewith God has made her free, and is not again entangled with the yoke of bondage—so far and so long as she refuses to be either driven into indifference by disgust, or seduced into delusion by false religion; so far and so long will she maintain the honours of this great people ... Let England cling to her open Bible; let her learn from it the broad truths of primitive Christianity, and be faithful to them; let her teach it to her children, and her children to their children, and their children to generations yet unborn, and then no wind that blows, no storm that beats, will shake her invincible foundations, for she will be founded upon a rock! But let her apostatise from its pure lessons into humanly invented falsities, and I would not give fifty years' purchase either for her greatness or for the stability of her Church. The world has no other trumpet of peace save Holy Scripture for souls at war; no other weapon to slay terrible passions; no other teaching to quench the heart's raging fires. This book alone makes mortals immortal, makes immortals gods.[13]

The Authorized Version is the greatest of our national treasures. It has served as the standard English translation for almost 400 years throughout the English speaking world. It reads with clarity and authority. No other version has taken its place in this respect. The greatest evangelists and missionaries have used this version for their ministry, and God has blessed millions of people with the light and truth of the Gospel of Christ.

The Authorised Version has remained the acknowledged Bible of the English speaking nations throughout the world simply because it is the best. A work that embodied the ripe fruits of nearly a century of labour, gained by its own internal character, a vital authority that could never have been secured by any mere edicts of sovereign rulers. It is an inestimable part of our Protestant heritage, has been the means of spiritual enrichment to millions of readers for almost 400 years, and remains peerless among the English translations of the Bible.

> He removeth the scales from our eyes, the veil from our hearts, opening our wits that we may understand His Word, enlarging

> our hearts, yea, correcting our affections, that we may love it above gold and silver, yea, that we may love it to the end. Ye are brought unto fountains of living water which ye digged not; do not cast earth into them, with the Philistines, neither prefer broken pits before them, with the wicked Jews. Others have laboured, and you may enter into their labours. O receive not so great things in vain; O despise not so great salvation! Be not like swine to tread under foot so precious things, neither yet like dogs to tear and abuse holy things. Say not to our Saviour with the Gergesites, Depart out of our coasts; neither yet with Esau sell your birthright for a mess of pottage. If light be come into the world, love not darkness more than light; if food, if clothing, be offered, go not naked, starve not yourselves.[14]

The King James Version, which we have today, is basically the same as that published in 1611. It is still the choice of God's people. It is the most accurate and reliable of all the English translations and ought to be the choice, the only choice, of lovers of the Truth.

Which Bible? That which was the result of the Protestant Reformation, headed up by the Authorised Version; or that of the influence of Darwinism, higher criticism, incipient modern religious liberalism, and a reversion to Rome, as headed up by Westcott and Hort's Greek text.

> The present English Bible (Authorised Version) has been blessed to thousands of saints of God; and not only so, it has become part of our national inheritance which we have received unimpaired from our fathers, and are bound to hand down unimpaired to our children. It is, we believe, the grand bulwark of Protestantism; the safeguard of the Gospel, and the treasure of the Church; and we should be traitors in every sense of the word if we consented to give it up ...[15]

John Skilton quoting Isaacs writes,

> The Authorised Version is a miracle and a landmark. Its felicities are manifold, its music has entered into the very blood and marrow of English thought and speech ... there is no corner of English life, no conversation ... it has not adorned. The Authorised Version ... was a revision prepared by gifted men in a golden age of English literature, ... when the English language had reached its vigorous

> maturity … the literary gifts which made the King James Version a truly distinguished work belonged to no one man or no one decade, but were those of an exceptional era united to produce a version of unique excellence.[16]

It was translated by men who will never be surpassed in their knowledge of the biblical languages. The translators were men who were whole heartedly committed to the plenary and verbal inspiration of the Scriptures. Their work was based upon the Greek text of the New Testament used by the Reformers. It is a word for word translation which faithfully and accurately reflects the original Hebrew and Greek. Its language is one of reverence and respect which gives honour and glory to its Divine Author.

The Puritan John Owen wrote:

> We went from Rome under the conduct of the purity of the originals; I wish none have a mind to return thither again under the pretence of their corruption.[18]

Using the King James Version is a clear statement of where we stand. *Thus saith the LORD, Stand ye in the ways, and see, and ask for the old paths, where is the good way, and walk therein, and ye shall find rest for your souls* (Jer. 6:16). In choosing the Authorised Version we choose to stand where our forefathers stood; we stand with all that is best in the great tradition of historic Christianity.

Even in 1611, the King James Bible sounded old-fashioned, archaic, like a voice from the past. This was to command a reverent hearing, and to suggest the timeless and eternal character of the Word of God. Could it be, that a return to the Authorised Version, a version so uniquely and singularly blessed by God to His English-speaking Church for four hundred years, may yet lead to that blessing which that church so desperately needs. David said of the sword of Goliath, "There is none like that; give it me." Now, why did David say that? Was it, because it had been laid up in the sanctuary? Never. There was none like it, because it had slain the enemy. It had the blood of Goliath upon it. And truly, we can say of the Authorised Version, "There is none like that; give it me." It was, and still is, the Jewel in the King's crown.

Appendices

APPENDIX I [1]

The Popish Doctrine of the Sacrament Confuted More Largely

First, where they allege the Catholic Church to have taught concerning the supper the doctrine of transubstantiation, of Christ's real and carnal presence, dearly beloved, know that this is a manifest lie. For as the Catholic Church never knew of it for nine hundred years at the least after Christ's ascension; so after that time no other church did obstinately defend, cruelly maintain, and wilfully wrest the Scriptures and doctors for the establishing of it, save only the popish church, and their own doctors do teach.

Whereas they say, that Christ in his supper by taking bread and speaking words of consecration did make it his flesh, according to his promise in John, when he saith, "And the bread which I will give is my flesh, &c."—The sentence is this: "And the bread that I will give is my flesh, which I will give for the life of the world." First mark that he saith, "The bread is my flesh." He saith not, "shall be my flesh," but it "is my flesh." This, I trow maketh against them; for the sacrament a year after at the least was not instituted. Again he saith, that the bread is his flesh, which he will give for the life of the world. Here would I ask them, whether Christ's death was for the life of the world, or vain. If they say it was for the life of the world, then why do they apply and give it to the sacrament? Was it crucified? Or of it be the same sacrifice (for so they say,) either it was effectual or not. If it was effectual, then Christ's death needed not. If it was not effectual, then Christ was not God, and could not do what he would. Thus ye may see their ungodly foolishness, or foolish ungodliness, I cannot tell which to call it well. Whereas they require the intent of the priest to consecrate Christ's body; ... I pray you, in what a doubtfulness are we brought whether it be a sacrament or not! In what peril are we of worshipping a piece of bread for our Christ! Is not this, trow you, sweet and comfortable gear, that a man shall always stand in doubt whether he have received the sacrament or not? Whereas they will have it bread to the eye, and not to the mouth, judge then, whether a dog may not eat Christ's body; judge whether the devil, if he would come in the likeness of a priest, might not swallow up Christ, and so bring him to hell, from whence, because there is no redemption there, Christ's body should never come, but be damned. Judge, whether the taste of thy mouth is not as much to be credited as the sight of the eye; specially in that the Scripture so often calleth it bread after the consecration, as before I have shewed. Judge, whether Christ's body be not very petty, that it can be in so little a room. Judge, whether Christ hath more bodies than one, when perchance the priest hath twenty or a hundred before him. Judge, whether the priest brake not Christ's body in breaking of it. Judge, whether it be seemly to chew Christ's body with the teeth. Judge, whether Christ did eat his own body: yea, or no? Christ did eat the sacrament with his disciples. Judge, whether it be seemly that Christ should be kept in prison, as they keep him. Judge, whether it be seemly that Christ's body should be so dindle-dandled and used, as they use it. Judge, whether the people, knocking and kneeling at the elevation of that they see (for they see but the forms of bread and wine, and not Christ's body, if it be as the papists feign); judge, I say, whether the people by the papists' own doctrine be not made idolaters.

Many more absurdities there be, which I purposely omit. This little is enough hereby to give you occasion to know the more. Where they say that the bread is made Christ's body, flesh, blood, &c., that is, that Christ's body is made of the bread; as the Bishop of Winchester in his book for this matter of the *Devil's Sophistry* and elsewhere doth affirm; you may see how shamelessly, yea, blasphemously they speak. For Christ's body crucified was born of the virgin Mary, even of her substance; but they say the supper is that body which is crucified. Now, I trow, bread is one thing, and the virgin's flesh another thing: therefore indeed they deny Christ in the flesh, that they may establish their Christ in the bread; which is the very root of the antichrist. Last of all, whereas they say they receive the sacrament to damnation, which do not believe their transubstantiation; if with Paul their words were conferred, you should see otherwise. For he saith, they receive this bread (for so he calleth it after the words of consecration) unworthily, which do not esteem Christ's body: as indeed the papists do not, which would bring Christ down out of heaven for thieves and whores to chew and eat, for moths to corrupt, and to be in danger of moulding; as if they kept their hosts long, indeed they will mould, and then will they burn them. Do these men, trow you, esteem Christ's body? Paul plainly sheweth in the same place, that the wicked man receiveth the sacrament unworthily, eateth not Christ's body, but his own damnation, which I trow be not Christ's body. And this shall serve for the time to shew you, how shameless, filthy, and abominable this their doctrine of transubstantiation is. If in so short a sum of their doctrine there be so many abominations, I pray you, how much is in the whole sum of the same? Now for the sacrifice.

THE POPISH DOCTRINE OF THE SACRIFICE CONFUTED

First, in that they grant Christ's sacrifice on the cross done by himself to be full and perfect enough, we may well see that we need not this which they have found out, indeed to make the other imperfect; for else it needed no reiteration. But seeing they reiterate it by this, and make it needful even as baptism, easily may all men know, that though they speak one thing, they mean another, and so are dissemblers and destroyers of Christ's sacrifice, little considering the great pain that Christ suffered, seeing they weigh it no better.

Whereas they say, that it is the same sacrifice which Christ offered on the cross, but unbloodily (wherein they seem to deny transubstantiation; for else I trow it must needs be bloody), I would thus reason with them. Inasmuch as Christ's sacrifice on the cross was the only perfect and all-sufficient propitiatory sacrifice for the sins of the world, as they confess; this could not be the same, because it was done before that upon the cross. Or else the full perfect sacrifice was then in the supper finished, and so Christ's death is in vain, and a foolish thing. If Christ's death be not foolish, but indeed, as it is, the full and perfect sacrifice for the sins of the world; then this, which they feign he offered in his last supper, is not the same, prate what pleaseth them; or else it is not of value, take whether they will. Whereas they prate of Christ's will, that it was accepted before his Father for the deed; as they shall never be able to shew one word to prove that Christ would in his supper sacrifice himself to his Father for the sins of the world (for there is not one word throughout the whole Bible), so do they belie God the Father, which would indeed have his Son to drink the cup he prayed to be taken from him, or else make Christ's death frustrate and more than need; which is the only thing that all their doctrine tendeth unto. For if the Father alloweth his will for the deed, I pray you, who seeth not now the deed to be more than needeth?

Where they say, that Christ commanded his church to offer this sacrifice to his Father in remembrance of his bloody sacrifice; I would pray them to shew me, where he commanded it, and then good enough. But, dearly beloved, they can never shew it. If they will say, *hoc facite,* to take *facere* for *to sacrifice,* as some teach it; then will I say, that a boy of twelve years old can tell they lie. For *hoc facite, do you this,* pertaineth to the whole action of Christ's supper, of taking, eating, drinking of the sacrament, &c., and as well spoken to the laymen as to the priests: but I trow they will not suffer the laymen to say mass another while for them. No, this were too much against their honour and gain also.

But if one would ask them, what they offer to the Father, then a man should see their abominations. For if they should say nothing, then men would take them as they be, liars. If they say, bread and wine, as indeed they do in their mass horribly; then in that they say they offer the same thing which Christ offered on the cross, and he offered his body, bread must needs be Christ's body, and so Christ's body is bread and wine. If they say, that they offer up Christ, in that the offerer must needs be as good at the least, yea, a better than the thing offered, then must they needs shew themselves open antichrists. For they make themselves equal with Christ, yea better than he: which thing indeed their holy father and grandsire the pope doth. For where Christ would take upon him nothing, but that he had received of his Father, and therefore willed men to search the Scriptures, as all his apostles did, whether their doctrine was not according thereunto; the pope and his prelates will be bold to teach what please them more than God biddeth, yea, contrary to that which God biddeth; as it is plain by all these four points, transubstantiation, sacrifice, praying for the dead, and to the dead. But see, I pray you, these abominations. The sacrifice of Christ for the redemption of the world was not simply his body and blood, but his body broken and his blood shed, that is, all his passion and suffering in his body and flesh. In that therefore they offer , as they say, the same sacrifice which Christ offered, dearly beloved, do they not, as much as in them is, kill, slay, whip, and crucify Christ again with wretches and antichrists? Who would not desire to die for his Master Christ's cause against this their heinous and stinking abominations?

Whereas they call this sacrifice of the mass the principal mean to apply the benefit of Christ's death to the quick and dead, I would gladly have them to shew, where and of whom they learned it. Sure I am they learned it not from Christ. For when he sent his disciples abroad to apply unto men the benefit of his death, he bade them not mass it, but preach the gospel, as the mean by which God had appointed believers to be saved. The which thing Peter told Cornelius plainly; as Paul also teacheth almost everywhere in his epistles. But indeed preaching they may not away with, as well for that it is too painful, as for that it is nothing so gainful, nor of authority and estimation in the world. Nothing so displeaseth the devil as preaching the gospel, as in all ages easily we may well see, if we will mark to our comfort in this age. And therefore by giving his daughter idolatry, with her dowry of worldly wealth, riches and honour, to the pope and his shaven shorelings, they have by this means in many years been begetting a daughter, which at length was delivered to destroy preaching, even the minion *Missa;* mistress Missa, who danced daintily before the Herods of the world, and is the cause even why John the Baptist and the preachers be put into prison and lose their heads. This dancing damsel, the darling of her mother, the fair garland of her fathers (for she hath many fathers), the gaudy gallant of her grandsire, is trimmed and tricked in the best and most holy manner or wise that can be, even with the word of God, the epistle and the gospel, with the sacrament of Christ's body and blood, with the pomander and perfumes of prayer, and all goodly things that can be; but blasphemously and horribly abused to be a mermaid to amuse and bewitch men, sailing in the seas of this life to be enamoured by her. And therefore besides her aforesaid goodly apparel, she hath all kinds of sweet tunes, ditties, melodies, singing, playing, ringing, knocking, kneeling, standing, lifting, crossing, blessing, blowing, mouthing, incensing, &c. Moreover she wanteth no gold, silver, precious stones, jewels, and costly silks, velvets, satins, dumasties, &c., and all kind of things which are gorgeous in the sight of men; as, if you call to mind the chalices, copes, vestments, crucifixes, &c, you cannot but see. And hereto is she beautified yet more, to be shewed and set forth in lying words and titles given to her; that she hath all power in heaven, earth, and hell, that she hath all things for soul and body, for quick and dead, for man and beast. And lest men should think her too coy a dame, lo, sir, she offereth herself most gently to all that will come, be they never so poor and stinking and foul, to have their pleasure on her. Come who will, she is "Hail, good fellow;" and that not only to make herself common to them that will, but also to ply them plentifully with the most pleasant promises falsely, and giving most licentious liberties to all her lovers, and great fees and wages to her diligent servants and ministers; so that there needeth no preaching of the gospel. She hath all things, she will give all things; the death of Christ she will apply and can to whom she will, and when she will. For this daughter the mothers, the fathers, the grandfathers watch night and day, as the only mean whereby Herod and Herodias may live as they lust … . But, dearly beloved, as from the devil's darling indeed, fly from her; and know that the true and only way to apply the benefit of Christ's death and sacrifice, is in the minister's behalf by preaching, and in your behalf by believing.

This is a sacrament, and not a sacrifice; for in this, using it as we should, we receive of God obsignation and full certificate of Christ's body broken for our sins, and his blood shed for our iniquities. As in baptism we are confirmed, and settle ourselves in possession of the promise of salvation to appertain unto us, God to be our God, Christ to be our Christ, and we to be God's people; the promise of the word of God giveth and offereth, faith in us applieth and receiveth the same, and the sacraments do confirm and (as it were) seal up: baptism, that we are regenerated with the Spirit of God, made his children, brethren to Christ, and engrafted into him; the supper, that we are fed with Christ spiritually, with his body and blood, yea, that we be incorporated into Christ, to be flesh of his flesh and bone of his bones, as he by being born of the virgin Mary was flesh of our flesh and bone of our bones. Away therefore with their abominable doctrine, that the sacrifice of the mass is the principal means to apply Christ's death to the quick and dead; wherein all men may see that they lie boldly. For as the word of God in the ministry pertaineth not to the dead, (for who will be so mad as to go and preach on dead men's graves, that the dead men may hear?) so likewise do not the sacraments. Little beholden were men to Christ and to the apostles, if this were the principal mean to apply salvation, that they would use it so little, and preach so much. Paul, having respect to the chiefest end wherefore he was sent, said, that he was not sent to baptize, but to preach. And often saith he, that he was an apostle segregate of God to preach the gospel. And the bishop Timothy did he warn to preach in season and out of season, speaking never a word of this massing or sacrificing Christ's body.

Last of all, where they make a similitude, that as by baptism the minister applieth to the child regeneration, so in this, &c. O that this similitude were well looked on! Then would it make them to bluster; for they are no more like than an apple like an oyster. In baptism the child is alive, but here the man is dead: in baptism the child is present, but here the man is perchance forty miles off, if he sacrifice for the quick, yea, hundred miles from him: in baptism the child receiveth the sacrament, but here you must look and gape; but beware you take not; for ye may receive but once a year, but then also you must receive but the one half, the cup he will keep from you. In baptism is required God's election, if he be an infant; or faith, if he be of age; and therefore he reciteth the promise, that it may be heard: but here is no faith required; for how can men believe, when they are dead? No promise is then preached or heard. So that even this their similitude maketh the matter plain enough: for baptism all men know to be no sacrifice. But of this I have spoken a little before, that if applying come by the priest's massing, then were preaching in vain, believing in vain, godly life in vain; the priest were God's fellow, yea Christ's superior, as is aforesaid.

APPENDIX 2 [1]

The History of Dr Rowland Taylor,

who suffered for the Truth of God's Word,
under the tyranny of the Roman Bishop, the 9th of February, 1555.

THE town of Hadley was one of the first that received the Word of God in all England, at the preaching of Mr. Thomas Bilney; by whose industry the gospel of Christ had such gracious success, and took such root there, that a great number in that parish became exceedingly well learned in Holy Scriptures, as well women as men, so that a man might have found among them many who had often read the whole Bible through, and that could have said a great deal of St Paul's Epistles by heart, and very well and readily have given a godly learned opinion in any matter of controversy. Their children and servants were also brought up and trained so diligently in the right knowledge of God's Word, that the whole town seemed rather a university of the learned, than a town of cloth-making or labouring people. And what most is to be commended, they were for the most part faithful followers of God's Word in their living.

In this town was DR ROWLAND TAYLOR, doctor in both civil and canon laws, and a right perfect divine and parson; who, at his first entering into his benefice, did not (as the common sort of beneficed men do) let out his benefice to a farmer, that shall gather up the profits, and set in an ignorant and unlearned priest to serve the cure, and so they having the fleece, little or nothing care for feeding the flock; but contrarily, he forsook the Archbishop of Canterbury, Thomas Cranmer, with whom he before was in household, and made his personal abode and dwelling in Hadley, among the people committed to his charge. Where he, as a good shepherd abiding and dwelling among his sheep, gave himself wholly to the study of the Holy Scriptures, most faithfully endeavouring himself to fulfil that charge which the Lord gave unto Peter, saying, "Simon, son of Jonas, lovest thou me?" Feed my lambs, feed my sheep, feed my sheep." This love of Christ so wrought in him, that no Sunday, nor holiday passed, nor other time when he might get the people together, but he preached to them the Word of God, the doctrine of their salvation.

Not only was his word a preaching unto them, but all his life and conversation was an example of unfeigned Christian life and true holiness. He was void of all pride; humble, and meek as any child; so that none were so poor but they might boldly, as unto their father, resort unto him; neither was his lowliness childish or fearful, but as occasion, time, and place required, he would be stout in rebuking the sinful, so that none were so rich but he would plainly tell him his fault, with such earnest and grave rebukes as became a good curate and pastor.

To the poor that were blind, lame, sick, bed-rid, or that had many children, he was a very father, a careful patron, and a diligent provider, insomuch that he caused the parishioners to make a general provision for them; and he himself (beside the continual relief that they always found at his house) gave an honest portion yearly to the common almsbox. His wife also was an honest, discreet, and sober matron, and his children well nurtured, brought up in the fear of God and good learning.

To conclude: he was a right and lively image or pattern of all those virtuous qualities described by St Paul in a true bishop; a salt of the earth savourly biting the corrupt manners of evil men; a light in God's house, set upon a candlestick for all good men to imitate and follow.

Thus continued the good shepherd among his flock, governing and leading them through the wilderness of this wicked world, all the days of the most innocent and holy king of blessed memory, Edward VI. But after it pleased God to take King Edward from this vale of misery unto his most blessed rest, the Papists (who ever sembled and dissembled both with King Henry VIII and King Edward his son) now seeing the time convenient for their purpose, uttered their hypocrisy, openly refusing all reformation made by the said kings: and, contrary to what they had all these kings' days preached, taught, written, and sworn, they violently overthrew the true doctrine of the gospel, and persecuted with fire and sword all those that would not agree to receive again the Roman bishop as supreme head of the universal church, and allow all the errors, superstitions, and idolatries, that before God's Word were disproved and justly condemned, as though now they were good doctrine, virtuous, and true religion.

In the beginning of this rage of Antichrist, a certain pretty gentleman after a sort of a lawyer, called Foster, being a steward and keeper of courts, a man of no great skill, but a bitter persecutor in those days, with one John Clerk, of Hadley, (which Foster had ever been a secret favourer of all Romish idolatry,) conspired with the said Clerk to bring in the pope and his image worship again into Hadley church. For as yet Dr Taylor, as a good shepherd, had retained and kept in his church the godly church service and reformation made by King Edward, and most faithfully and earnestly preached against the popish corruptions, which had infected the whole country.

Therefore the aforesaid Foster and Clerk hired one John Averth, parson of Aldam, (a very mammonist, a blind leader of the blind, a popish idolater, and an open adulterer and whoremonger,) a very fit minister for their purpose, to come to Hadley, and there to give the onset to begin again the popish mass.

To this purpose they builded up with all haste possible the altar, intending to bring in their mass again, about the Palm Monday. But this their device took none effect: for in the night the altar was beaten down. Wherefore they built it up again the second time, and laid diligent watch, lest any should again break it down.

On the day following came Foster and John Clerk, bringing with them their popish sacrifice, who brought with him all his implements and garments to play his popish pageant; whom they and their men guarded with swords and bucklers, lest any man should disturb him in his missal sacrifice.

When Dr Taylor, who according to his custom sat at his book, studying the Word of God, heard the bells ring, he arose and went into the church, supposing something had been there to be done, according to his pastoral office; and coming to the church, he found the church doors shut and fast barred, saving the chancel door, which was only latched. Where he entered in, and coming into the chancel, saw a popish sacrificer in his robes, with a broad new shaven crown, ready to begin his popish sacrifice, beset round about with a swords and bucklers, lest any man should approach to disturb him.

Then said Dr Taylor, "Thou devil, who made thee so bold to enter into this church of Christ, to profane and defile it with this abominable idolatry?"

With that started up Foster, and with an ireful and furious countenance said to Dr Taylor, "Thou traitor, what doest thou here, to let and disturb the Queen's proceedings?"

Dr Taylor answered, "I am no traitor, but I am the shepherd that God my Lord Christ hath appointed to feed this his flock; wherefore I have good authority to be here: and I command thee, thou popish wolf, in the name of God, to avoid hence, and not to presume here with such popish idolatry to poison Christ's flock."

Then said Foster, "Wilt thou traitorously, heretic, make a commotion, and resist violently the Queen's proceedings?" Dr Taylor answered, "I make no commotion, but it is you Papists that make commotions and tumults. I resist only with God's Word against your popish idolatries, which are against God's Word, the Queen's honour, and tend to the utter subversion of this realm of England: and further, thou dost against the law, which commandeth that no mass be said but at a consecrated altar."

When the parson of Aldam heard that, he began to shrink back, and would have left his saying mass; then started up John Clerk, and said, "Mr. Averth, be not afraid, you have a *superaltare;* go forth with your business, man."

Then Foster, with his armed men, took Dr Taylor, and led him with a strong hand out of the church, and the popish prelate proceeded in his Romish idolatry. Dr Taylor's wife, who had followed her husband into the church, when she saw her husband thus violently thrust out of his church, she kneeled down, and held up her hands, and with a loud voice said, "I beseech God, the righteous Judge, to avenge this injury that this popish idolater to this day doth to the blood of Christ." Then they thrust her out of the church also, and shut the doors; for they feared that the people would have rent their sacrifice in pieces.

Thus you see, how, without consent of the people, the popish mass was again set up, with battle array, with sword and buckler, with violence and tyranny; which practice the Papists have ever yet used: as for reason, law, or Scripture, they have none on their part.

Within a day or two after, with all haste possible, this Foster and Clerk made a complaint of Dr Taylor, by a letter written to S.

Gardiner, Bishop of Winchester, and Lord Chancellor. When the Bishop heard this, he sent a letter missive to Dr Taylor, commanding him within certain days to come and appear before him, upon his allegiance, to answer such complaints as were made against him.

When Dr Taylor's friends heard of this, they were exceedingly sorry and grieved in mind; which when foreseeing to what end the same matter would come, seeing also all truth and justice were trodden under foot, and falsehood with cruel tyranny were set aloft, and ruled all the whole rout; his friends, I say, came to him, and earnestly counselled him to depart and fly, alleging and declaring to him, that he could neither be indifferently heard to speak his conscience and mind, nor yet look for justice and favour at the said Chancellor's hands, who, as it was well known, was most fierce and cruel; but must needs, if he went up to him, wait for imprisonment and cruel death at his hands.

Then said Dr Taylor to his friends, "Dear friends, I most heartily thank you, for that you have so tender a care over me: and although I know that there is neither justice nor truth to be looked for at my adversary's hands, but rather imprisonment and cruel death; yet know I my cause to be so good and righteous, and truth so strong upon my side, that I will by God's grace go and appear before them, and to their beards resist their false doing."

Then said his friends, "Master doctor, we think it not best so to do: you have sufficiently done your duty, and testified the truth both by your godly sermons and also in resisting the parson of Aldam, with other that came hither to bring again their popish mass. And forasmuch as our Saviour Christ willeth and biddeth us, that when they persecute us in one city, we should fly into another; we think in flying at this time ye should do best, keeping yourself against another time, when the church shall have great need of such diligent teachers and godly pastors." "O," quoth Dr Taylor, "what will ye have me to do? I am old, and have already lived too long, to see these terrible and most wicked days. Fly you, and do as your conscience leadeth you: I am fully determined, with God's grace, to go to the Bishop, and to his beard to tell him that he doth naught. God shall well hereafter raise up teachers of His people, which shall with much more diligence and fruit teach them than I have done; for God will not forsake His church, though now for a time He trieth and correcteth us, and not without a just cause."

" As for me, I believe before God I shall never be able to do God so good a service as I may do now; nor shall I have so glorious a calling as I now have, nor so great mercy of God proffered me, as is now at this present. For what Christian man would not gladly die against the pope and his adherents? I know that the Papacy is the kingdom of Antichrist, altogether full of lies, altogether full of falsehood, so that all their doctrine, even from Christ's cross be my speed, and St Nicholas, unto the end of the Apocalypse, is nothing but idolatry, superstition, errors, hypocrisy, and lies. Wherefore I beseech you, and all my other friends, to pray for me, and I doubt not but God will give me strength and His Holy Spirit, that all mine adversaries shall have shame of their doings."

When his friends saw him so constant, and fully determined to go, they with weeping eyes commended him to God; and he within a day or two prepared himself to his journey, leaving his cure with a godly old priest, named Richard Yeoman, who afterwards for God's truth was burnt at Norwich.

Dr Taylor, being accompanied by a servant of his own, named John Hull, took his journey towards London, and presented himself to the Bishop of Winchester, Stephen Gardiner, then Lord Chancellor of England. Now when Gardiner saw Dr Taylor, he according to his common custom, reviled him, calling him knave, traitor, heretic, with many other villainous reproaches; all of which Dr Taylor heard patiently, and at the last said unto him:

"My Lord, I am neither traitor nor heretic, but a true subject, and a faithful Christian man, and am come, according to your commandment, to know what is the cause that your Lordship hath sent for me." Then said the Bishop, "Art thou come, thou villain! How darest thou look me in the face for shame! Knowest thou not what I am?"

"Yes, (quoth Dr Taylor,) I know who you are: ye are Dr Stephen Gardiner, Bishop of Winchester, and Lord Chancellor; and yet but a mortal man, I trow. But if I should be afraid of your lordly looks, why fear you not God, the Lord of us all? How dare you for shame look any Christian man in the face, seeing ye have forsaken the truth, denied our Saviour Christ, and His Word, and done contrary to your own oath and writing? With what countenance will ye appear before the judgment-seat of Christ, and answer to your oath made first unto King Henry VIII of famous memory, and afterwards unto blessed King Edward VI his son?"

The Bishop answered, "Tush, tush, that was Herod's oath, unlawful; and therefore worthy to be broken: I have done well in breaking it; and I thank God I am come home again to our mother the Catholic Church of Rome; and so I would thou shouldest do."

Dr Taylor answered, "Should I forsake the church of Christ, which is founded upon the foundation of the apostles and prophets, to prove those lies, errors, superstition, and idolatries, that the popes and their company at this day so blasphemously do approve? Nay, God forbid. Let the pope and his return to our Saviour Christ and His Word, and thrust out of the church such abominable idolatry as he maintaineth, and then will Christian men turn unto him."

The Bishop answered, "Ye are false, and the whole family of you are liars ... Thou hast resisted the Queen's proceedings, and wouldest not suffer the parson of Aldam, a very virtuous and devout priest, to say mass in Hadley."

Dr Taylor answered, "My Lord, I am parson of Hadley; and it is against all right, conscience, and laws, that any man should come into my charge, and presume to infect the flock committed unto me, with the venom of the popish idolatrous mass."

With that the Bishop waxed very angry, and said, "Thou art a blasphemous heretic indeed, that blasphemest the blessed sacrament, and speakest against the holy mass, which is made a sacrifice for the quick and the dead."

Dr Taylor answered, "Nay, I blaspheme not the blessed sacrament which Christ insitituted, but I reverence it as a true Christian man ought to do, and confess that Christ ordained the holy communion in the remembrance of His death and passion, which when we keep according to His ordinance, we through faith eat the body of Christ and drink His blood, giving thanks for our redemption; and this is our sacrifice for the quick and the dead, to give thanks for His merciful goodness shewed to us, in that He gave His Son Christ unto death for us."

"Thou sayest well, (quoth the Bishop;) it is all that thou hast said, and more too: for it is a propitiatory sacrifice for the quick and the dead."

Then answered Dr Taylor, "Christ gave Himself to die for our redemption upon the cross, whose body there offered was the propitiatory sacrifice, full, perfect, and sufficient unto salvation for all them that believe in Him. And this sacrifice did our Saviour Christ offer in His own person Himself once for all, neither can any priest any more offer Him, nor we need any more propitiatory sacrifice; and therefore I say with Chrysostom, and all the doctors, Our sacrifice is only memorative, in remembrance of Christ's death and passion, a sacrifice of thanksgiving; and therefore by the Fathers called *eucharistia:* and other sacrifice hath the church of God none."

"It is true, (quoth the Bishop,) the sacrament is called *eucharistia,* a thanksgiving, because we there give thanks for our redemption, and it is also a sacrifice propitiatory for the quick and the dead, which thou shalt confess ere thou and I have done."—Then called the Bishop his men, and said, Have this fellow hence, and carry him to the King's Bench, and charge the keeper he be straitly kept.

Then kneeled Dr Taylor down, and held up both his hands, and said, "Good Lord, I thank Thee: and from the tyranny of the Bishop of Rome, and all his detestable errors, idolatries, and abominations, good Lord deliver us; and God be praised for good King Edward."

So they carried him to prison to the King's Bench, where he lay prisoner for almost two years. Being in prison, Dr Taylor spent all his time in prayer, reading the Holy Scriptures, and writing and preaching, and exhorting the prisoners, and such as resorted to him, to repentance and amendment of life. After that, Dr Taylor was cited to appear in the arches at Bow church; to answer unto such matter as there should be objected against him. Where when he came, he stoutly and strongly defended his marriage, affirming by the Scriptures of God, by the doctors of the primitive church, by both laws civil and canon, that it is lawful for priests to marry. The judge gave sentence that he should be deprived of his benefice, because he was married. He was carried into prison, and his livings taken away, and given to others.

After a year and three-quarters, in the which time the Papists got certain old tyrannous laws (which were put down by King Henry VIII, and by King Edward) to be again revived by parliament; so that now they might, *ex office,* cite whom they would upon their own suspicion, and charge him with what articles they listed, and, except they in all things agreed to their purpose, burn them. When these laws were once established, they sent for Dr Taylor, with certain other prisoners, which were again cited before the Chancellor and other commissioners about the 22 of January. He, was charged with heresy and schism and required to submit himself to the Roman Bishop or else proceed to his condemnation. He declared that he would not depart from the truth nor submit himself to the Romish Antichrist, but thanked God that he counted him worthy to suffer for His Word and truth. And when condemned to death, declared, "I doubt not but God, the righteous Judge, will require our blood at your hands, and the proudest of you all shall repent this receiving again of Antichrist, and your tyranny that ye now shew against the flock of Christ."

On the 4 February 1555, Edmund Bonner, Bishop of London, came to the prison cell to degrade him, bringing with him such ornaments as do appertain to their massing mummery! The Bishop said, Mr. Doctor, "I would you would remember yourself, and turn to your mother holy church." Whereunto Mr. Taylor answered, "I would you and your fellows would turn to Christ: as for me, I will not turn to Antichrist." "Well", quoth the Bishop, "I am come to degrade you: wherefore put on these vestures." "No (quoth Dr Taylor,) I will not." "Wilt thou not?" Said the Bishop; "I shall make thee ere I go." Quoth Dr Taylor, "You shall not, by the grace of God."

So the Bishop willed another to put them upon his back; and when he was thoroughly furnished therewith, Dr Taylor walked up and down and said, "How say you, my Lord, am not I a goodly fool? If I were in Cheapside, should I not have boys enough to laugh at these apish toys, and toying trumpery?" So the Bishop scraped his fingers, thumbs, and the crown of his head, and did the rest of such like devilish observances. So the Bishop laid his curse upon him. Then Dr Taylor said, "Though you do curse me, yet God doth bless me. I have the witness of my conscience, that ye have done me wrong and violence; and yet I pray God, if it be His will, forgive you: but from the tyranny of the Bishop of Rome, and his detestable enormities, good Lord deliver us."

The night after that he was degraded, his wife and his son Thomas, resorted unto him, and were by the gentleness of the keepers permitted to sup with him. After supper, and turning to his son Thomas, he said: "My dear son, Almighty God bless thee, and give thee His Holy Spirit, to be a true servant of Christ, to learn His Word, and constantly to stand by His truth all thy life long. And, my son, see that thou fear God always. Flee from all sin and wicked living; be virtuous, serve God with daily prayer, and apply to thy book. In any wise see thou be obedient to thy mother, love her and serve her; be ruled by her now in thy youth, and follow her good counsel in all things. Beware of lewd company, of young men that fear not God. Fly from whoredom, and hate all filthy living, remembering that I thy father do die in the defence of holy marriage. Another day, when God shall bless thee, love and cherish the poor people, and count that thy chief riches is to be rich in alms; and when thy mother is waxed old, forsake her not; but provide for her of thy power, and see that she lack nothing. For so will God bless thee, and give thee long life on earth, and prosperity; which I pray God to grant thee."

Then turning to his wife, "My dear wife," (quoth he,) "continue steadfast in the fear and love of God; keep yourself undefiled from their popish idolatries and superstitions. I have been unto you a faithful yoke-fellow, and so have you been unto me; for which I pray God to reward you, and doubt not, dear wife, but God will reward it. Now the time is come that I shall be taken from you, and you discharged of the wedlock-bond toward me: therefore I will give you my counsel what I think most expedient for you: you are yet a child-bearing woman, and therefore it will be most convenient for you to marry. For doubtless you shall never be at a convenient stay for yourself and our poor children, nor out of trouble, till you be married. Therefore, as soon as God will provide it, marry with some honest faithful man that feareth God. Doubt you not, God will provide an honest husband for you, and he will be a merciful father to you and to my children; whom I pray you to bring up in the fear of God, and in learning, to the uttermost of your power, and keep them from this Romish idolatry." He gave unto his son, Thomas, a Latin book, containing the notable sayings of old martyrs; and in the end of that book he wrote his last will and testament:

> I say unto my wife, and to my children, The Lord gave you unto me, and the Lord hath taken me from you, and you from me: blessed be the name of the Lord. I believe that they are blessed which die in the Lord. God careth for sparrows, and for the hairs of our heads: I have ever found him more faithful and favourable than is any father or husband. Trust ye, therefore, in Him, by the means of our dear Saviour Christ's merit: believe, love, fear, and obey Him. Pray to Him, for He hath promised to help. Count me not dead, for I shall certainly live, and never die. I go before, and you shall follow after, to our long home. I have bequeathed you to the only Omnipotent.

I say to my dear friends of Hadley, and to all others which have heard me preach, that I depart hence with a quiet conscience, as touching my doctrine, for the which I pray you thank God with me. For I have after my little talent declared to others those lessons that I gathered out of God's book, the blessed Bible. Therefore if I or an angel from heaven should preach to you any other gospel than ye have received, God's great curse upon that preacher.

But for God's sake, that ye deny not God, neither decline from the word of faith, lest God decline from you, and so do everlastingly perish. For God's sake, beware of Popery, for though it appear to have in it unity, yet the same is vanity and antichristianity, and not in Christ's faith and verity.

The Lord grant all men His good and Holy Spirit, increase of His wisdom, contemning the wicked world, hearty desire to be with God and the heavenly company, through Jesus Christ our only mediator, advocate, righteousness, life, sanctification, and hope, Amen, Amen. Pray, pray, pray.

Departing hence in sure hope, without any doubt of eternal salvation, I thank God my heavenly Father, through Jesus Christ my certain Saviour. Amen."

February 5, 1555

Shortly afterwards, he was delivered into the hands of the Sheriff of Essex, and was set on horseback. As he came out of the gates, John Hull stood at the rails with Taylor's son, Thomas. When Dr Taylor saw them, he called them, saying, "Come hither, my son Thomas." And John Hull lifted the child up, and set him on horse before his father; and Dr Taylor put off his hat, and said to the people that stood there looking on him, "Good people, this is mine own son, begotten of my body in lawful matrimony; and God be blessed for lawful matrimony." Then lifted he up his eyes towards heaven, and prayed for his son, laid his hat upon the child's head, and blessed him; and so delivered the child to John Hull, whom he took by the hand, and said, "Farewell, John Hull, the faithfullest servant that ever man had." And so they rode forth, the Sheriff of Essex, with four yeomen of the guard, and the sheriff's men leading him.

All the way Dr Taylor, now with a closed hood, with two holes for his eyes to look out at, and a slit for his mouth to breathe at, was joyful and merry as one that accounted himself going to a most pleasant banquet. He spoke many notable things to the sheriff and the yeomen of the guard, and often moved them to weep through his much earnest calling upon them to repent, and to amend their evil and wicked living. Oftentimes also he caused them to wonder and rejoice to see him so constant and steadfast, void of all fear, joyful in heart, and glad to die. At Chelmsford met them the Sheriff of Suffolk, there to receive him, and to carry him forth into Suffolk, and to Hadley where he suffered. Coming within two miles of Hadley, he desired to alight off his horse. Which done, he leaped for joy. "Why, master doctor, (quoth the sheriff,) how does you now?" He answered, "Well, God be praised, good master sheriff; never better, for now I am almost home; I lack not past two stiles to go over, and I am even at my Father's house. But master sheriff, shall we not go through Hadley?" "Yes (said the sheriff,) you shall go through Hadley." Then said he," O good Lord, I thank thee, I shall yet once ere I die see my flock, whom thou, Lord, knowest I have most heartily loved, and truly taught. Good Lord, bless them, and keep them steadfast in Thy word and truth."

When they were now come to Hadley, and came riding over the bridge, at the bridge waited a poor man with five small children; who, when he saw Dr Taylor, he and his children fell down upon their knees, and held up their hands, and cried with a loud voice, and said, "O dear father, and good shepherd, Dr Taylor, God help and succour thee, as thou hast many a time succoured me and my poor children!"

The streets of Hadley were beset on both sides the way with men and women, who waited to see him; whom when they beheld so led to death, with weeping eyes and lamentable voices they cried, saying one to another, "Ah, good Lord! There goeth our good shepherd from us, that so faithfully hath taught us, so fatherly cared for us, and so godly hath governed us. O merciful God! What shall we poor scattered lambs do! What shall come of this most wicked world! Good Lord, strengthen him, and comfort him." Dr Taylor evermore said to the people, "I have preached to you God's Word and truth, and am come this day to seal it with my blood."

Coming against the alms-houses, he cast the poor people money. The money which remained, he put in a glove, and coming to the last of the alms-houses, and not seeing the poor that dwelt ready at their doors, he asked, "Is the blind man and blind woman that dwelt

Dr Roland Taylor praying for his sons.

there alive?" It was answered, "Yea, they are there within." Then threw he glove and all in at the window, and so rode forth. Thus this good father and provider for the poor now took leave of those for whom all his life he had a singular care and study.

At the last coming to Aldham Common, the place assigned where he should suffer, and seeing a great multitude of people gathered together thither, he alighted from his horse, and with his hands tore the hood from his head. When the people saw his reverend and ancient face, with a long white beard, they burst out with weeping tears, and cried, saying, "God save thee, good Dr Taylor! Jesus Christ strengthen thee, and help thee! The Holy Ghost comfort thee!" Then would he have spoken to the people, but the yeomen of the guard thrust a tipstaff into his mouth, and would in no wise permit him to speak.

Dr Taylor perceiving that he could not be suffered to speak, sat down, and seeing one named Soyce, he called him, and said, "Soyce, I pray thee come and pull off my boots, and take them for thy labour." Then rose he up, and put off his clothes unto his shirt, and gave them away. Which when he had done, he said with a loud voice, "Good people, I have taught you nothing but God's Holy Word, and those lessons that I have taken out of God's blessed book, the Holy Bible; and I am come hither this day to seal it with my blood." With that word, the yeoman of the guard, gave him a great stroke upon the head with a waster, and said, 'Thou heretic.' Then he, seeing they would not permit him to speak, kneeled down and prayed, and a poor woman that was among the people stopped him and prayed with him; but her they thrust away, and threatened to tread her down with horses; notwithstanding, she would not remove, but abode and prayed with him. When he had prayed, he went to the stake, and kissed it, and set himself into a pitch barrel, which they had set for him to stand in; and so stood with his back upright against the stake, with his hands folded together, and his eyes towards heaven; and so he continually prayed.

Then they bound him with chains, and the sheriff called one Mulleine, of Carsey to set up the faggots and to make the fire, which he most diligently did. The one, a man called Warwick cruelly cast a faggot at him, which hit him upon his head, and brake his face, that the blood ran down his visage. Then said Dr Taylor, "O friend, I have harm enough: what needed that?" Then, Dr Taylor lifted up both his hands, and called upon God, and said, Merciful Father of heaven, for Jesus Christ my Saviour's sake, receive my soul into Thy hands. So stood he still without either crying or moving, with his hands folded together, till Soyce with a halberd struck him on the head that the brains fell out, and the dead corpse fell down into the fire.

Thus rendered the man of God his blessed soul into the hands of his merciful Father, and to his most dear and certain Saviour Jesus Christ, whom he most earnestly loved, faithfully and earnestly preached, obediently followed in living, and constantly glorified in death.

APPENDIX 3 [1]

Richard Bancroft

RICHARD BANCROFT, 1544-1610. Archbishop of Canterbury, Christ's College, Cambridge. B.A. 1556. Licensed University preacher. D.D. 1585; Bishop of London 1597.

In the latter years of Elizabeth's reign religious feelings were growing impassioned. It was apparent to the ecclesiastical establishment that the Puritan movement was intent upon undermining episcopacy. The Queen herself did not favour the Puritan infiltration of the church, which she equated with a threat to authority, and that, in the end, meant her authority; but as usual, she did not wish to be personally embroiled in the contest. Her method was to appoint Richard Bancroft to the bishopric of London. Bancroft was a strong man with decided views on the issue. In 1588 this future Archbishop of Canterbury had preached a sermon at St Paul's Cross which had spread resentment and consternation in Puritan circles and marked him out as the most formidable enemy of Puritanism.

A WARNING AGAINST PURITANS

A sermon preached at St Paul's Cross on the 9th February 1588

The doctrine of the Church of England, is pure, and holy: the government thereof, both in respect of her Majesty, and of our Bishops is lawfull, and godly: the booke of Common Prayer containeth nothing in it contrary to the Word of God.

All those points have bene notably approoved, and maintained not onely against the Papists, but likewise against some other schismatikes, and you your selves with great joy, and comfort have in time past imbraced them accordingly. If any of you now, my brethren, be otherwise affected, the fault is in your selves: for they remaine (as the nature of truth requireth) to be as they were before: but you through your rashness in following of every spirit, are growen to a wonderfull newfanglenes: and are in deed become mere changelings. *Quemadmodum eadem terra stat recte valentibus, quæ veritigine correptis videtur moveri* : As the same earth appeareth immooveable to those that are in health, which to the giddy doth seeme to turne about; so you, my brethren, by following the perswasions of false Prophets who, as *Irenæus* saith; *De iisdem non simper easdem senentias habent:* Of the selfe same things have not always the same opinions; are drawen to an unjust mislike of the Church; *Et amantes vel non amantes, haud eadem de eisden judicatis:* And according to your love, or hate your judgments upon the selfe same things do vary, and alter.

See, I pray you, what dislike is able to worke; and therefore take heed of those, who shall indevour, through lies, and slanders, to make the truth, and the preachers thereof odious, and hatefull unto you. For as the Apostle writeth; *ümulantu vos non bene, sed excludere vos volunt, ut, illos æmulemini:* They are jealous over amisse, even for their own purpose, and commodity; yea they would exclude you from the Doctrine you have received at our hands, and from the affection, and love, which you once bare unto us, that ye might altogether love them, and follow their devices.

And that is the end of their railings, and libelling. *Mos simper fuit hæretuorum, quorum doctrinam non possunt confutare, illorum vitam in odium adducer:* It hath always bene the manner of heretikes, to bring their lives into hatred, whose Doctrine they cannot confute. Knowing that by the contempt of the one, doth easily ensue the dislike of the other.

Howbeit, they will pretend that the zeale of Gods glory doth move them unto such bitterness, against the present state or Religion, and against the chiefe maintainers of it, and that for conscience sake, and for the glory of Sion they are driven to use such more than tragicall outcries. But *Bernard* will not suffer them to hide their malice under these maskes, who writing against certain schismatikes in his time, saith, *Allii quidem nude atque irreverenter, uti in buccam venerit, virus evomant detractionis:* Some do plainely, and irreverently, even as it comes into their stomacke, spue out the poison of their slanders. Many others there be, who cover their malice more cunningly, nay more hypocritically, as though all they said proceeded of mere love, and Christian charity, of whom it followeth, *Videas alta præmitti suspiria: sicque quadam cum gravitate et tarditate, vultu mæsto, demissis superciliis et voce plangenti egredi maledictionem, et quidem tanto persuasibiliorem, quanto crediur ab his qui audiunt corde invite et magis condolentis affect, quam malitiose proferri.* You shall see some, that after they have set divers great sighes, and groanes, will presently with great gravity, and drawing out of their words, with a heavy countenance, with casting downe their heads, and with a pittifull voyce, breath out malediction, the which men do rather believe, because it seemeth by such their hypocriticall dealing, rather to proceed of a sorrowfull compassion, than of malice, and hatred. But dearly beloved, take heed of these spirits. Where you finde these conditions, beleeve not, I pray you, any such protestations.

Furthermore, you shall have some that will come unto you with a long tale, protesting that they cannot refraine their teares; with the ancient men in Ezra, to see the foundation of our new Temple not to be answerable (as they say) to the beauty of the old. And herein they thinke they should be very acceptable unto you: whereas in truth the crying of these aged men, was a great discouragement to the builders, and one of the principall lets, why the worke went no better forward: and the Prophet *Aggæus* was sent from God to reprove them for it; allowing nay, preferring in some respects, the new building, which then they had in hand, before the other, which some so much affected.

So as, deerely beloved, when you heare the like cries, in any wise believe them not; but rather shout aloud for joy (as there it is likewise noted) in that you have lived to see your Temple purged from the leaven of Popery, and to flourish, as they do, with the sincerity, and truth of Christian Religion.

They will furthermore (the better to creepe into your harts) pretend great humility, and bitterly exclaime against the pride of Bishops as though they affected nothing else by their desired equality, but some great lowliness, and to prostrate themselves at your feete for your service: whereas in deede they shoote at greater superiority, and pre-eminence, than ever your Bishops did use of challenge unto them: and would no doubt tyrannize by their censures over both Prince, and people at their pleasure, in most untollerable, and pope-like manner. As partly you may gather by their premises, and partly furthermore understand in that not onely they do use the very same arguments for the soveraigne authority of their presbyteries (against the Prince) in causes Ecclesiasticall: that the Pope doth for his principality in the same (and none other so far as I can read, or thinke can be shewed by any) but do likewise make to all our arguments for her Majesties supremacy against them, the very same answers, (if not word for word, always in effect) that *Harding, Stapleton, Dorman,* and *Saunder*[2] have made to the same arguments, used by Bishop *Jewell,* Bishop *Horn,* Master *Nowell,* and others to the same purpose, and against the Pope. I cannot stand to enter into any particular examples of this matter, onely I thought it necessary at this time to advertise you of it (take his advantage thereof who list) that you might the better be aware of such kinde of spirits.

You have heard them, I am sure, greatly exclaime against our Bishops livings, as though they had too much, thereby to perswade you with what simple, allowance they could content themselves: and yet (as you have heard) they reckon all the livings of the Church too little for themselves: condemning you of the laity, who eyther have or would have part with them, for cormorants, *Dionysians*[3], and for such wicked traitors against the Church, as *Judas* was against Christ.

They would gladly seeme to be very godly, zealous, and religious: and yet notwithstanding, if you will rely upon Saint *Iames* his opinion, and judge of them by the usage of their tongues, in their immodest speeches, and libelling, you shall finde their profession thereof to be full of so great vanity, as that particularly it may be verified almost of everyone of them: *Huius vana est religio.*

If they set foorth a booke of Common Prayer, then caution is made that nothing be done contrary to any thing set downe in the same. If they decree any thing in their synods (yea though it be in civill matters) against an act of Parleament, that treason is not treason, yet if you withstand them, you are foorwith accursed: or as touching Church causes, except it should so fall out, that they do erre in their determinations, and that in some great matter of faith, all men must stand unto their orders, decrees, laws, and constitutions.

But on the other side, if the Church indeed, upon sufficient grounds, shall eyther publish a booke, or command any thing to be observed, though that which is commanded have been determined of, not onely by provinciall or nationall synods, but by all the general councels in effect, which were held before the tyranny of popery: yet (as Saint *Bernard* saith in the like case) *Hærent ad singular quæ insunguntur, exigent de quibusque rationem, male suspicantur de omni præcepto, nec unquam libenter acquiescent, nisi cum audire contiferit quod forte libuerit:* they sticke at all things which are injoined, they require the reason of every thing, they suspect amisse of every precept, and will never willingly hold themselves contented but when they heare that, which peradventure doth please them.

APPENDIX 4 [1]

William Barlow

WHEN, on Lord's Day, February 8, 1601, Robert Devereux, Earl of Essex, aged thirty-three, rode out of his London house at the head of a party of armed men, made his bid, and failed, to capture the person of the sixty-four-year-old queen and arrest her advisers, it was deemed necessary, on conviction of treason, to exact the death penalty. Even if his intentions had been no more than he averred "to change Her Majesty's counsellors and summon parliament"—alive, he would have remained, as he himself admitted, a resort for discontented men of both extremes, Papists and Puritan. These were the potentially explosive elements which it had always been the Crown's domestic policy to keep dispersed and unled. But Essex personally had been a popular hero to the citizen's of London, and it was judged advisable, that any lingering sympathy might be quenched, to present a persuasively unfavourable account of the Earl's actions to the people without delay. The preacher selected for this commission was William Barlow, a discreet, ambitious, orthodox divine, averse to the Puritan element and approved of by the Queen.

Familiar as Barlow was with the mobility of court intrigue, he felt embarrassment as he mounted the pulpit at St Paul's Cross, a few days after he had attended Essex on the scaffold, because, from that same pulpit, he had on an earlier occasion preached an oration in fulsome praise of the living man whom, in death, he was now come to denounce. But, meticulously briefed by Cecil, he knew his duty and addressed himself to the appointed task.

On the Beheading of the Earl of Essex

A Sermon preached at Paule's Cross on the first Sunday in Lent, 1601

One thing I cannot omit, which much mooved me against him, (though I honoured him as much as any follower of his, who carieth with him a good subjects hart) which perhaps you knowe not, namely his strange Apologie of himself unto Master Deane of Norwiche, sent unto him by the Lordes for his soules good, the next day after his arraignement, who urging him to acknowledge his offences, the late Earle utterly denied, *That in any thing he had done he was guiltie of offending Almighty God.* But because I promised to give you nothing of report, I call to minde the very speech he uttered unto my Lordes Grace of Canterburie in Lambeth house, the night of his apprehension. Oh, my Lord, saith the Archbishop, I am sorie to see thee this day, & that you have so farre forgot your selfe: the Earle replyed smilingly, *that the sinceritie of my conscience and the goodnesse of my cause doth comfort me:* this speech argues he thought himself not guiltie of *offending God.* As if a good intention, we will suppose it so, dooth make the action good. The Canon Lawyers say, that God loves Adverbes better than Adjectives, he cares not how good *quam bonum,* but *quam bene,* how well, and by what good meanes it is done which we intend. The justifying of an ill execution upon a good purpose and meaning, is the utter subversion of all religion and policie: an opinion forged at the fire of hell, and hammered at the Anvile of the Popes' faculties. The same Deane asking him why he refused to come to the Lords, being sent for by the appointment of her Majestie, he answered that, by Scripture, and thus reasoneth, *David refused to come to Saul when he sent for him: Ergo I might lawfully refuse to come to Queen Elizabeth.*

Here a divine cannot be patient, to see Gods word alleadged in despight of Gods ordinance , thus the devil delt with Christ *Math.4,* in quoting a place of scripture to justifie the breaking of his neck. And *Clement* the Frier who killed *Henry* the third the French king, reasoned thus with himself for his bloudy murther out of Gods booke, *Ehud* killed King *Eglon,* therefore I may kill *Henry, Eglon* was a king, so is *Henry.* What then? *Eglon* signifieth a Calve and *Henrie* is a Calvenist, *Ergo* I may kill him by authority of scripture. It is recorded by *Mercurius Gallobelgicus* in his first booke. Let Papists lay these grounds, and make these proofes, I am sory that any, who caries the name of a Protestant, should argue thus. It is the speech of *Salomon, He that wrings his nose, fetcheth out bloud.* Which *Gregory* fitly applies, that he which wresteth the scripture from the true sence, bringeth forth either an heresie or a phrensie, it is that which the learned call *Glossa viperine* which an interpretation like a Viper, eates out the bowels of the text. For, God be thanked, there is no semblance of this example makes for his refusall. Because *Saule* was rejected by God, but Queene *Elizabeth* is the chosen and beloved of God, which from heaven by his providence over her, as in shielding her from many, so from this *Presumptuous* attempt, he hath demonstratively shewed. *David* by a Prophet, at Gods appointment was anointed king, so was not he. But I urge this no further because it is not within his confession verball or written, to which I promised to stand, yet to shew you how farre he was gone that way, the word he used to us of *Leprosie,* makes that good which he spake in a passion to the Deane, *If you knew how many motions have beene made to me to do my best to remoove such evills as the common wealth is burthened with, you would be greatly wounder.* It seems the contagion is spred. To which the Deane replying, that extraordinary attempts must have extraordinary warrants, and willed him to shew his authority, his answer was, that *He was Earle Marshall of England and needed no other warrant.* Yet that was not so, because he was sequestered from it long before. But his conclusion peremptory *what should I* (saith he) *reason with you upon this point, seeing we holde not one principle,* which was, *that hee might remoove evils from the land,* for that was it which from the beginning to the end he held, as by complaint to us of *some things to be reformed,* he insinuated. Indeede the wise man saith *Prov. 25. Remoove the wicked from the King, and his throne shall be established in iudgement:* but who must remoove them, and by what meanes? he there sheweth by similitude, *as the drosse must be taken from the silver:* The Gold finer must do it, by the fire; so just authority and lawfull meanes; the first over Kings in Gods alone, as before I proved, otherwise, as *S. Augustine* speaketh of impatient worldlings, *Nisi homini Deus placuerit Deus non erit,* unless God please men, he shall be no God: so in this case of discontented subjects, except the prince please them, she shall be no prince, and all shall be accompted wicked who satisfie not their humors. Belooved, see here what it is, when it pleaseth God to leave a man to himself; or as the Earle said of himself, *to be carried away and puffed up by vantitie and worldly love,* in his first speech uppon the scaffold.

This stifnesse of his, both at the barre, and with the Deane, my associate and my selfe hearing, not understanding of his repentance, we agreed between us, fearing he would so have dealt with us, to have beate him downe, and to have wounded his hart with the dreadfull judgementes of God: yet afterward to have raysed him agayne with the comfortable promises of the gospel: but when we came unto him, we found him more open to reveale, then became us to inquire, and more resolute himself, then we, upon the suddayne, could have made him, and we more welcome a great deale then we expected: for most hartely desired *God so to blesse us as our coming did comfort him:* and so fell into expressing the memorie of this his purposed mischief, with such detestation and remorse, that I, fearing as the Apostle speaketh of that Corinthian, *2 Cor.2:7* that he should be overcome with overmuch heavinesse, layd before him the comfortable speech of *S. Paul,* that Christ Jesus came into the world to save sinners, though a man were *peccatorum maximus, 1.Tim.1:17* but sayth *Doctor Montford* unto him, who had beene at his arraignement: I wonder your Lordshippe thus guiltie to your selfe, could be so confident at the barre, it offended many of your very good friends: yea, but now saith the late Earle, *I am become another man,* the cause thereof he ascribed *to the worke of Gods spirite within him;* and *the meanes to his chaplain Master Ashton who was there* present with us; for *he,* as he said to the honourable the Lord Keeper and the rest, *hath plowed up my hart,* as he sad to us, *hath brought me down and humbled me.* And then he tolde us he *had satisfied the Councell with his voluntary confession under his owne hand subscribed with his name, wherein though I have, said he, detected many (already apprehended) yet I hold it my duty to God and the Realme to cleare my conscience.* For some three or four days before his execution he made meanes by maister *Warburton* one of her Maisties gentlemen Pencioners, to have some *conference with three or foure of the Lordes of her Maisties Counsell, wishing also if it pleased her Majestie, that master Secretary Cecill might be sent with them: whereuppon the Lord Keeper, Lord Treasurer, & the Lord Admiral, taking Maister Secretary with them, came unto him, to whome he clearly laide open the whole project and purpose, presently confessed it, expressed his harty sorrow for his confidence at his arraignment, asked forgivenes of the Lord Keeper, &, by him, of the rest whome he caused in his house to be imprisoned: partiuculerly and vehemently in Christian charitie desired Maister Secretary to forgue him that great injury which at the Barre in his passion, by unjust calumniation, he had cast upon him, and of them also he requested forgivenes whom he had challenged for his enemies, & had charged with such great, but false imputations.* (All which, in grosse and general, he *confessed to us, forgiving and asking forgivenes)* & so after an entire reconciliation with teares on both sides shed, he moved two requestes, the one very earnest, the other most necessary: the first was, *it would please them to move her majestie that he might die privately within the Tower;* the reason thereof he expressed unto us in the morning of his execution, of which anone. The second was, *that he might have libertie to set downe in writing what in worde he had confessed to them, and other things which either at the barre he had denied, or should then occure to his memory.* The confession it selfe filles foure sheetes of paper, every worde in his owne hand, and his name at the end, which my selfe have seene, and will shew unto you so much as is fit: the preface thereof I have transcribed for your sakes, and this it is, *Since that God of his mercie hath opened mine eyes, and made me see my sinne, my offence, and touched my hart as I hate it both in my selfe and others, I will as God shall inable my memorie, set downe how far we are all guiltie, and where, and by what degrees our sinne, this offence grew.* The chiefe, and the briefe is this, his purpose *of surprising the court with a power;* the places allotted to foure persons, *S. Christopher Blunt* the gate with a company; *S. John Davis* to master the guard by seazing the halberds; *S. Charles Davers* to possesse the privie chamber with another companie; all this confest by himself, and the rest under their hands.

Here now imagine with your selves what affrighting even the rumour thereof had been to a prince of that sex, a Lady Queene, in a time of peace, and the peace so long by her meanes continued; in her owne court and chamber; the proverbe is, *Leves loquntur, ingentes stupent,* that sleight feares make women shrike, but if they be great and sodayne, they cast them into a swoune; and I doubt if in that case she should have swounded, they would have taken it for death, and have bestowed little paynes to fetch her againe. But resistance being made, as it is not possible but there would, there must needs be bloud shed: now thinke you what an horror would this have been to her gratious nature, to have seen bloud running in her chambers?

Then looke to the commanders, two of the principall, stiffe and open Papists, and the fourth, by report, affected that way, what danger to her person, to religion, to the Realme they may gesse, who have reade the libelles of *Bozius, Reynolds, Gifforde* [1], and others of that church, writing slanderously of her Majesties person, blasphemously of our religion; and basely of our Realme and policie. You may remember the state of Israel, when they were forced to sharpen their axes and tooles, and have no weapons but from the *Philistines. 1 Sam.13.* And such a slavery and misery, assure your selves, had ours been for Prince and religion, if we had stoode to the courtesie of armed Papists and their reformation. Perhaps you will say, that this was but like the grouth of a Tadstoole, *Oritur, mritur,* a nights conceit, but vanished in the morning. Yea, but himself voluntary confessed to us, that *it was plotting and devising not long after heel aye in the Lorde Keepers house:* even then when he protested that he had made a divorce between the worlde and himself; But he meant no hurt to the Queenes person, say you. Surely that hee protested both in his confession to the Lords and to us, and writeth it, *that when he sent the Articles to Drury house be considered of, by his complices, he put in caveat still, that as little bloud might be shed as could, and that the Queenes owne person might receive no harme.* And we will beleeve it. Marry the question is first, whether it had beene in his owne power at the time of their rage and in hot bloud to have kept her safe? Certainly, as we objected to him, hee *which could not,* as him selfe, to us confessed, *restraine them from murthering the*

Queenes subjects when he stood upon his defence in his house, they being but a few, must not thinke hee could have stayed them in the Court, the object of their revenge. For being many, and many of them needy, what Rapine would have satisfied them? Being youthful, and lustfull, what Rapes woulde have stanched them? Being discontented and revengefull, what bloud would have glutted them? And the chiefe of them Popish and armed, would they not have said, which comes even now to my minde, as that bloudy *Story* once saide; What doe we pruning the boughs and branches, let us strike at the roote.

For mine owne part, I professe, I would trust never a Papist in the world, if he might have her at that vantage. God be thanked that this is but an imagination, for had it come *ab imagine ad rem,* from a purpose to an effect; *God knows,* saith he himself to us, *what daunger and harme it had wrought to the Realme.*

But in this point of the *Queenes safetie,* what thinke you of summoning a Parlament, which foure of five under their hands, and himself also hath confessed. Who should have called it, she or they? It is a controversie between us and the Papists, whether the Emperor or the Pope, have the absolute authoritie of calling a Councell, but it was never made a question, that I can read, in England who hath authoritie to call a Parliament, either the Prince or the Peers. Among the Spaniards and French they may, saith *Bodin* [3], but *apud Anglos,* in the Realme of England, *nec admitti possunt conuentis, nec dimitti absque Principis edicto,* without the Princes warrant it cannot either be summoned or dissolved. Why, she should have done it; how? Voluntarily or by force? The first we may not imagine that she would so soone yield; if the second, where is the safety of her person? unlesse you count that safety for a Prince to be a prisoner to her subjects. God forbid we should have felt the Issue of this, nay *God be thanked* saith he to us, *that it was prevented.* And withal gave God like thankes *that he made him this example to be justly spewed out of the land.* Which word *Spewed* he inforced with a violence, arguing himself thereby to be, unto this Realme, as a surfeit unto the stomack, both a burthen and a danger. He saw himself a burthen in this charge of souldiers, being a burthen to the Cittie and countrie, which but for him had now been spared: he felt himself a burthen, as it seemed, to us by longing and desiring, which oft he did, that the time of execution were come. A danger he confessed himself to be in these words of his, which I pray you observe, *he knew that the Queene could not be in safetie so long as he lived upon earth.* I will stretch nothing to farre, but yet marke this, if her safety were so uncertain, he being a prisoner in the Tower, what could her safety have beene when he was possessed of her court with an armed power?

But why do I eyther amplifie by circumstance, or inforce by argument the haynousnesse and daunger of this plot? if I had the tongue of men and Angels, I could not better, nor would in more bitter tearmes expresse it, then himself hath done in foure epithets or adjunctes in his prayer to God, or in his speech to the Lordes, or in both upon the Scaffolde: desiring God to forgive him *his great sinne, his crying sinne, his infectious sinne:* why these words, for none of them is, *as Basil* speaketh, αργον ρημα an idle worde. First, *great* in comparison of his other sinnes, which he on the Scaffold laide out in odious termes against himself his *delicta juuentutis,* not that they were little sinnes, for unto us, in his Chamber, he confessed that *sometimes in the Fielde encountering the enemye, being in any danger the weight of his sinnes lying heavie upon his conscience, being not reconciled to God, quelled his spirits, and made him the most timorous and fearefull man that might be.* But this sinne exceeded them all, even that which we objected to him in his chamber, and he acknowledged, which the Schoolemen call *Vactans conscientiam,* so wasting and spoiling his conscience, as that not one good thought was left in his hart. That sinne which *Moses* calleth the sinne with an high hand. *Nomb.33.* himself called it, *a Presumptuous sinne.* Secondly, *great* in it selfe, because as the *Nabis* in *Egipt* [4] is a beast shaped of many beasts; and *Hannibals* armie in *Livie,* was *collunies omnium gentium,* the miscellany of all nations; so this his offence and treason, the compound of all the famous rebellions eyther in Gods booke, or our owne land: (which himself in other words scatteringly expressed:) consisting of *Abners* discontent, of *Corahs* envie, of *Absolons* popularity, of *Sheba,* defection, of *Abimelechs* faction, and banding his familie and allyes, of *Hamans* pride and ambition: in presence small, all one with that of *Henrie,* Duke of Lancaster, against *Richard* the second, *remooving certain which misled the King.* In pretence originall, that of *Kettes* and *Tylers* for the King, as they in your citty cryed in the insurrection *for the Queene, for the Queene.*

The second worde was *his bloudy sinne.* It should have been no *drye rebellion,* for how could it be? in that he who could hardly represse the rage of his own people from murthering the honourable counsellors in his owne house, they being the men not aymed at in show of their *reformation,* should not be able to stay their armed fury in the place designed for the execution of their intent. But here you of the citie will say, it should not have beene bloudy to us, he loved us well: be it so; yet I will tell you his opinion uttered of you the very nyght of his apprehension, and his being in Lambeth house, in the hearing of the Lord Archbishop, of the Lord Admirall, of the Lord of Effingham, and divers other, and my selfe among the rest. *That you were a very base people: that he trampled up and downe your city without any resistance: that he would undertake with foure hundredth men of his choise to have overrunne your citie: that he passed many of your lanes and chaines baraccadoed* (it was his worde) *without one blow offered at him, in his returne from Ludgate at Queenehith.* Againe, what his concept was of your love to him, his own speeches shall testifie, whereby he argued that you were both a daunger to his body and his soule: in the first, I telling him that his relying upon the peoples plausibility spurred him on, but now they had deceived him. *True* (sayth he) *a mans friends will fayle him;* and addes to that a very divine speech, *All popularitie and trust in men is vayne, whereof my selfe have had late experience.* Thus he accompted your love at the best to be but vanitie, or as he sayd in the prophet, an *Aegiptian* reede, which eyher breaketh & fayleth him that leaneth on it or pearceth his hand to his hurt: in-sinuating hereby, that, had he not trusted upon you, he would not have ventured so farre: and thus you seemed by his words to have indaungered his body, as being a remote motive to that his action. Then the request which he so *earnestly made unto the Lordes for his private death within the tower,* was principally because of you: for in the morning he confessed *himself much bound to God, and her majestie that he should die thus privately, because he feared, least if it had beene publike, your acclamations should have hoven him up* (for this he much doubted in himself even in that small companie which was there, and therefore *desired God still to graunt him an humbled spirite: and requested us if we eyther see his countenance, eye, or tongue wander, that we would interrupt him) and so have withdrawn his minde from God, and have beene a temptation unto him: and thus he tooke your love to him, but as a danger to his soule: but thinke you had it had it not been unto you a* bloudy day, if it had beene effected what they purposed: now heare and tremble; being asked what he meant by taking the *tower of London,* sithence his principall project was for the court? he answered, *that he meant it should have beene a bridle, to your citie,* marke that worde, *a bridle* hath raines and a bit: so that if you had made an head for him against the Queene (which I hope you would not) he would have given you the raines, you should have gone on without any restraint to have beene rebels to your prince and country: but if you had united your force against him as good subjects (and as I am fully perswaded you would) they are his owne words, *if happely the Citie should have misliked his other attempt,* then you should taste of the Bit. They call it the playeng of the Bit in the horse mouth: but I beleeve the playing of the Ordinance from the Tower would have fetcht both your houses downe, and your *bloud* out.

The third word, *his crying sinne,* which word is borrowed from *Gen.19* where the sinnes of Sodom are said to cry up to heaven, namely, to fetch down vengeance from God, so intolerable they were, and one of those sinnes was *pride;* which, I was bold to tell him, was the ground of all this action, and he tooke it very well. This also argued, that there was *bloud* in this sinne, for the first crying sinne we read of was *Caines* murther *Gen. 4.* The last word was *his infectious sinne,* the meaning thereof he explaned to us in our conference with him (which I named before) that *it was a leaprosie which had infected far and neare.* Which unfoldeth both the greatnesse of the danger, and argueth that the contagion of the sinne is not gone with him. Doctor *Montford* asked him if there were not an oath taken by them for secrecie and resolution. He utterly denied that: how durst you trust each other being so many said we? His answere was *that they were firmly perswaded each of others faithfulnesses mutually, as any one of them could be of his owne hart to himself.* Now then, the time being more than spent, conferre these points together, all out of his own words, and beginne with the last first, they are thirteen in all.

1. This conspiracie thus banded.
2. The offence *contagiously,* and generally dispersed.
3. His sinne crieng to God for present vengeance.
4. A sinne bloudy in execution, if effected.
5. Great in selfe, the compound and mixture of all rebellions.
6. His life a daunger to that Queene.

marke that

7. Himselfe a surfet to the realme, to be spewed out justly.
8. Articles propounded, disputed, concluded so long together aguynst the state.
9. The court surprised with an armed power, and the Queene mured up with her own vassalles.
10. A parlament to be summoned.
11. The Chiefe places of the court at the command of Papists armed and attended, neyther with the wealthiest, nor the contenedest men.
12. The Command of the tower a bridle to you of this city.
13. His hard opinion and censure of your basenesse and unfaithfulnesse to the Queene.

And then judge you with what safty to the Queene's person; with what peace to the law; with what hope of the Gospels continuance could this man have lived, if he had beene remitted: and thinke with your selves whether you may not justlye conclude that it was the most dangerous plotte that ever was hatched within this land. What now remains—but to conclude with my text, Give unto Caesar the things of Caesar, oure most gracious Soveraigne, I meane, honour her, obey her, feare her, but abouve all pray for her, that she being the light of this land may shine among us as long as the two great lights of heaven, the sonne and the moone endureth. The God grant for his mercie sake. Amen.

APPENDIX 5 [1]

Lancelot Andrewes

ANDREWES' works rank with the finest English prose or their time, of any time. He was a superlative scholastic orator, indeed the most celebrated of his age. But Andrewes never sought to write literature at all. He was a preacher in an intellectual court, presided over by the royal pupil of George Buchanan, where theological and philosophical disputation were favourite pastimes, and nimbleness of wit and ingenuity of arguments were prerequisites. His congregation to which he constantly addressed himself, was a body of men and women whose conversational exercise consisted of fencing with epigram and paradox, and who sought recreation in acrostics, riddles, anagrams, quotation-matching, puns, conundrums and theological disputation, mainly in the Latin tongue.

He was less a man of letters than a man of learning, with a sharpened wit practised in the special skill of contracting, almost to the form of notes, the largest number of ingenious variations upon a given theme, and then expanding and projecting them into an interpretative performance. The process would employ a dramatic pause, variety of inflection, and all the technical resources of rhetoric, in support of the quickening vitality which every orator must be able to call upon.

Andrewes preached an annual sermon on the anniversary of the failed Gunpowder Plot, and it needs to be remembered that had the plot succeeded, then Andrewes himself would have been among the select victims to ascend heavenwards with the explosion.

In the following sermon, we join the King and a most distinguished congregation at Whitehall, a year after the failed plot, and listen with them in rapt attention to the superlative oratory of Bishop Andrewes.

A SERMON PREACHED BEFORE THE KINGS MAJESTIE AT WHITEHALL, ON THE FIFTH OF NOVEMBER ANNO DOM. MDCVI

"This is the Lord's doing, and it is marvellous in our eyes. This is the day which the LORD hath made; let us rejoice and be glad in it."

Psalm CXVIII Ver. XIII. XIV.

To entitle this time to this Text, or to shew it pertinent to the present occasion, will ask no long processe. This Day of ours, this fifth of November, a day of GOD's making; that which was done upon it, was the LORD's doing. Christ's own application (which is the best) may well be applied here: *This day, is this Scripture fulfilled in our eares.* For, if ever there was a deed done, or a day made by God, in our days; this day, and the deed of this day was it: If ever He gave cause of marvelling (as in the first;) of rejoicing (as in the second verse) to any land; to us this day, He gave both: If ever saved, prospered, blessed any; this day, He saved, prospered, and (as we say) fairely blessed us.

The day (we all know) was meant to be the day of all our deaths; and we, and many were appointed as sheepe to the slaughter; nay, worse than so. There was a thing doing on it, if it had been done, we all had been undone. And the very same day we (all know) the day, wherein that appointment was disappointed by God, and we all saved, that we might not die but live, and declare the praise of the Lord: the Lord of whose doing, that marvellous deed was; of whose making, this joyfull day is, that we celebrate.

This mercifull and gracious LORD (saith David, Psalme 111.5) hath so done His marvellous works, that they ought to be had, and kept in remembrance. Of keeping in remembrance, many ways there be: Among the rest, this is one, of making days; set solemn Dayes to preserve memorable Acts, that they be not eaten out, by them, but ever revived, with the returne of the Yeare, and kept still in continuall memory. God Himself taught us this way. In remembrance of the great delivery from the destroying Angell, He himself ordained the day of the Passe-over yearely to be kept. The Church, by Him taught, tooke the same way. In remembrance of the disappointing of Haman's bloudy lots (Esther 9.26), they likewise appointed the days of Purim, yearely to be kept. The like memorable mercy did He vouchsafe us: The destroyer passed over our dwellings, this day: It is our Passe-over. Haman, and his Fellowes had set the dice on us, and we by this time had been all in peeces. It is our Purim day.

We have therefore well done and upon good warrant, to tread the same steps, and by law to provide, that this Day should not die, nor the memorial thereof perish, from our selves or from our seed; but be consecrated to perpetuall memory, by a yearly acknowledgment to be made of it throughout all generations. In accomplishment of which order, we are all now here in the presence of GOD, on this day, that He first, by His Act of doing, hath made; and we, secondly, by our act of decreeing, have made before Him, His holy Angels, and men, to confess this His goodnesse, and our selves eternally bound to Him for it. And, being to confesse it, with what words of Scripture can we better or fitter doe it, than those we have read out of this Psalme? Sure, I could think of none fitter.

The treaty whereof may well be comprised in three points: 1. The Deed; 2. The Day; and 3. The Duty

To proceed orderly, we are to begin with the day. For though (in place) it stand after the deed; yet to us, it is first: our knowledge is *à posterior.* The effect ever first, where it is the ground of the rest. Of the day then first.

This is the day: This? Why, are not all days made by Him? Is there any days not made by Him? Why then say we, *This is the day the Lord hath made?*

And so for days: GOD leaveth a more sensible impression of His favour, upon some one, more than many besides, by doing upon it some marvellous work. And, such a day on which GOD vouchsafeth some speciall *factum est,* some great and publike benefit; notable for the time present, memorable for the time to come, in that case, of that Day (as if GOD had said *Faciamus dieum hunc,* shewed some workmanship, done some speciall cost on it) it may with an accent, with an emphasis be said, *This verily is a day which* GOD *hath made,* in comparison of which, the rest are as if they were not; or at least were not of His making. There are those days made, and crowned with some extraordinary great favour, and thereby get a dignity, and exaltation above the rest: exempted out of the ordinary course of the Calendar. Such, in the Law, was the Day in the Passe-over, made by God, the head of the yeare. Such, in the Gospell, of CHRIST'S resurrection, made by God; and to it, do all the Fathers apply this verse. And we had this day, our Passe-over, and we had a resurrection, as Isaac had (Heb. 11.19).

Every deliverance is from a danger; and, by the danger, we take measure of the deliverance. The greater that, the greater the Delivery from it: and the greater the delivery, the greater the day, and the more likely to be of GOD'S owne manufacture. In David's case, he was in great distresse. Three severall times, with great passion, he repeats it, that his enemies; compassed him round; compassed and kept him in on every side (verse 10,11,12). Were, no swarme of bees so thicke: That they gave a terrible lift or thrust at him, to overthrow him; and very neare it they were. And at last, as if he were newly crept out of his grave, out of the very jawes of death and despaire, he breaks forth and saith, *I was very neare my death;* neare it I was, but die I will not now, for this time, but live a little longer to *declare the works of the Lord.* This, was his danger: from this danger, he was delivered.

This then was not any mans, not any Princes doing, but GOD'S alone, His might, His mercy, that brought it to passé: Not any arme of flesh, but GOD'S might; not of any merit of his, but of His owne mere mercy. This was done by His might: Thrice he tells us of it; *It was the right hand of the Lord, that brought this mighty thing to passe.* This was done by His mercy; His ever-enduring mercy: foure times he tells us, it was that, did it. With that he begins, and makes it the key of the song. The right hand of God, brought this mighty thing to passe.

Will these be found in ours? They will, all of them certainly; and that, in an higher degree, in a greater measure; match David's day, and overmatch it in all. We were delivered, and from a danger that is cleare. How great? Boldly, I dare say, from a greater than Davids. Thus I shew it, and go no further than the Psalme it selfe.

1. David called upon GOD in his danger; he knew of it, therefore. We did not: we imagined no such thing; but that all had been safe, and we might have gone to the Parliament, as secure as ever. The danger never dreamt of, that is the danger.

2. His was, by compassing and hemming in, that is, above ground, and may be descried from a watch-tower. Ours was by undermining, digging deep under ground, that none could discerne.

3. One cannot be beset, but he may have hope to break through, at some part. But here, from this, no way, no meanes, no possibility of escaping. The danger not to be descried, not to be escaped, that is the danger.

4. His were a swarme of bees (He calleth them so) they, buzze and make a noise when they come. Ours, a brood *vipers, mordents in silentio*; still, not so much as a *hisse*, till the deadly blow had been given.

5. His was but himself alone; so he saith *I was in trouble, They came about me, kept me in, thrust fore at me:* But one person, David's alone. Ours of a farre greater extent; David, and his three Estates with him. Now, though David himself were valued by them at ten thousand of themselves (2 Sam. 18.3); yet he and they too, must need be more, than He alone. Not onely King David had gone, but Queen Esther too: and not onely they, but Salomon the young Prince, and Nathan his brother. Nor these were not all. The Scriptures recount, David had Jehosaphat for his Chancellour, Adoram his Treasurer, Seraja his Secretarie, Sadoc and Abiathar, and twenty more, the chief of the Priests, Admo his Judge, Joab his Generall; all had gone (2 Sam. 20.24). His forty eight Worthies or Nobles, all they too. The Principall of all the Tribes in the kingdom: all they too; and many more than these: no man knoweth how many. It is out of the question, it had exceeded this of David's here.

6. One more. His danger (he confesseth) was from man: He goeth no further, *I will not feare what man doeth unto me.* This of ours was not: merely mans, I deny it: it was the devil himself. The instruments (not as his, a swarme of bees, but) a swarme of Locusts, out of the infernal pit. Not men; no not Heathen men; not savage wilde men, noted for inhumanity, never so inhumane. Even among those barbarous people, this would be accounted barbarous. How then? Beasts: There were at Ephesus, beasts in the shape of men. But this is more than brutish; what Tiger, though never so inraged, would have made the like havock? We must not looke to patterne it upon earth, we must go to hell;

thence it was certainly, even from the devil. He was a murderer from the beginning, and will be so to the ending. In every sinne of bloud, as he hath a claw, but, all his clawes, in such an one as this: wherein so much bloud, as would have made it raine bloud; so many baskets of heads, so many peeces of rent bodies cast up and downe, and scattered all over the face of the earth. Never such a day; all Joels signes of a fearfull day, bloud and fire and the vapour of smoake. As he is a murtherer; so we see (in Marke) by his renting and tearing the poore possessed childe, he is cruell; and in this, all his cruelties should have met together. Pharaoh's and Herod's killing innocent and harmless children; yet, they spared the Mother: It yrketh me to stand repeating these; that ever age, or land, but that our age, and this land should foster or breed such monsters!

One more yet: that this abomination of desolation (so calleth Daniel; so calleth our Saviour, the uttermost extremity of all that is bad is: so may we this truly): that this abomination of desolation tooke up his standing in the holy place.

1. An abomination: so it is; abhorred of all flesh, hated and detested of all, that but heare it named: yea, they themselves say, they should have abhorred it, if it had taken effect. It is an abomination.

2. Every abomination doth not forthwith make desolate. This had. If ever a desolate kingdome upon earth, such had this beene, after that terrible blow. Neither root nor branch left, all swept away: Strangers, called in; murtherers exalted; the very dissolution and desolation of all ensued.

3. But this, that this so abominable and desolatory plot, stood in the holy place, this is the pitch of all. For, there it stood, and thence it came abroad. Undertaken with an holy oath; bound with the holy Sacraments (that must needs be in a holy place); warranted for a holy Act, tending to the advancement of a holy Religion, and by holy persons, even the chiefe of all religious persons (the Jesuites) gave not only absolution, but resolution, that all this was well done; that it was by them justified as lawfull, sanctified as meritorious, and should have been glorified (but it wants glorifying, because the event failed), and canonized, as a very good and holy act, and we had had orations out of the Conclave in commendation of it. We see their practice, they begin

with rejecting this Stone, as one that favoured hereticks at least, and therefore excommunicate, and therefore deposed, and therefore exposed, to any that could handle a spade well, to make a mine to blow him up; *Him*, and all his *Estates* with him to attend him: (The corner Stone being gone, the walls must needs follow). But then, this abomination sitting in the holy place, so ougly and odious; making such a treason as this a religious, missall, sacramental treason; hallowing it with orison, oath, and eucharist; this passeth all thes rest.

Tell me now if this were not His doing, and if it should not have beene a day of His making, the Devil's owne making? This should have beene done. All these were undone, and blowen over; all the undermining disappointed; all this murder, and crueltie, and desolation defeated. The mine is discovered, the snare is broken and we are delivered. All these, the King, Queene, Prince, Nobles, Bishops, Iudges, both Houses alive, all: not a haire of any of their heads perished; not so much as the smell of fire on any their garments. Give thanks O Israel, unto the Lord thy God in the congregation, from the bottome of the heart; here is little Benjamin, thy Ruler, the Princes of Juda. That they are here and do see them here, and that the Stone these Builders refused, is still the Head-stone of the corner. That, should have beene done; this, was done: and we all, that are here this day, are witnesses of it.

But by whom, whose doing? Truly, not man's doing this; it was the Lord's. It was the Devil's devising (the plot), this was God's doing (the deliverance). The blow was the Devil's: the ward was God's. Not man, but the Devill, devised it: not man, but God defeated it. He that sate in the heaven all this while, and from thence looked downe and saw all this doing of the devil and his lims, in that mercy of His, which is over all His works, to save the effusion of so much blood, to preserve the soules of so many innocents, to keep this Land from so foule a confusion, to shew still some token, some sensible token upon us for good, that they which hate us may see it, and be ashamed; but especially, that that, was so lately united, might not so soone be dissolved; He tooke the matter into His own hand. And, if ever God shewed, that He had a hooke in Leviathan's nose, that the Devil can go no further than his chaine: if ever that there is in Him more power to help, than in Sathan to hurt; in this, He did it. And, as the devil's claws to be seene in the former; so God's right hand, in this mighty thing (He brought to passé) and all the fingers of it.

1. To shew it was He. He held His peace and kept silence, sat still, and let it go on, till it came neere, even to the very period, to the day of the lot; so neere, that wee may truly say (with King David) as the Lord liveth, there was but a step between death and us. We were on the point of going to the hill, all was prepared, the traine, the match, the fire, wood, and all, and we ready to be the sacrifice, and even then and there, God provide for our safety; even in that very place, where we should have beene the burnt offering; from heaven, stayed the blow. It was the Lord's doing.

2. When treachery hath his course like water, and creepes along like a snail (it is the fiftie eight Psalme) then to make it like the untimely birth of a woman, never to see the sun; ... but ever the thornes gate heat, or the powder, fire; then men shall say, verily, there is a God, and this was His doing.

3. And not only, that it was bewrayed, but that he made them the bewrayers of it themselves; and even according to the place (Eccl. 10.10) made things with feathers to disclose it: When (as in Psalme 64.8) their owne tongues (or, which is all one, their owne pens) make them to fall: all that consider it, shall be amazed; and then all men shall say, *This hath God done; for they shall perceive it plaine, it is His worke.* Was not this God's doing?

4. Yet further, to shew it was so That which was written, was so written, as diverse of profound wisdom, knew not what to make of it. But then cometh God againe (God most certainly) and (as in Prov.16.10) puts a very divination, a very oracle, in the King's lips, and his mouth missed not the matter; made him, as Ioseph, the revealer of secrets, to read the riddle: giving him wisdom to make both explication, what they would doe; and application, where it was they would doe it. This was God certainly.

5. Lastly, as that, when it was come forth they were not reclaimed; not then, when they saw, the hand of God was gone out against them, and that it was even God they strave withal: no, but even then, from hidden treacherie, fell to open rebellion and even perished in it (if God shewed not a miracle of his mercie on them) perished there, and perished eternally. So, that (before they came thither) God cast their owne powder in their faces,

poudered them and disfigured them with it; and that their quarters stand now in peeces, as they meant, ours should: It is the case of the CIX Psalme (Ps. 109.29) *And hereby shall they know, that it is thy hand, and that thou Lord hast done it.* How? In that they are cloathed with their owne shame, and even covered with their owne confusion; that they fall as fast as they rise; are still confounded, and still thy servants rejoice. These five (as prints) shew, it was God's hand. It was the Lord, that made the day; it was the day, that the Lord made. Be Thou exalted Lord in Thine owne strength: It was Thy right hand, that brought this mighty thing to passé.

I conclude: as, that was the Divel's doing, and was monstrous in our eyes; so, this is God's doing, and it is marvellous in our eyes. And againe, upon all these markes, that, as this was a day, the Devill would have marred; so this is a day that the Lord made.

To end then. This Day, which the Lord hath thus made so marvellously; so marvellously and mercifully; let us rejoice in the Maker, for the making of it, by His doing on it that deed, that is so marvellous in our eyese, in all eyes; returning to the beginningof the Psalme, and saying with the Prophet: *O give thankes to the Lord, for he is gracious, &c. Let Israel, let the house of Aaron, yea, let all that feare the Lord, confesse that His mercie endureth for ever.*

Who only doth great wonders.
Who remembred us when we were in danger,
and hath delivered us from our enemies,
with a mightie hand and stretched out arme.
And, as for them, hath turned their device upon their owne head.
And hath made this day, to us a day of joy and gladnesse.
To this God of Gods, the Lord of heaven,
glorious in holinesse, fearfull in Power, doing wonders,
be, &c.

APPENDIX 6

Translating for King James:

Notes made by a translator of King James Bible.[1]

I Corinthians 10 verse 11 where Bois comments, "A.D. (Downes) sharply and violently exerted himself beyond measure for the interpretation of Augustine, that the examples and types were understood as concerning types and figures of the people of old: but the scope of the passage does not seem to admit this interpretation." [2]

I Corinthians 10 verse 30 "[and if I by thanksgiving] This interpretation, rejected by Beza, A.D. deemed worthy of his advocacy." [3]

I Peter I verse 7 "[unto praise] that is to say, praise to God, or your praise. We have not thought that the indefinite sense ought to be defined". In this instance the suggestion in the Notes was adopted in the AV, and a change made at Geneva and retained by the Bishops was abandoned.

I Peter I verse 23 "The participles [living] and [abiding] it seems ought to be referred rather to [word], than to [God], because of that which follows in the last verse".

Revelation I verse 5 "[unto him that loved us] These words are more correctly joined with [to him be glory] v.6. than made continuous with those preceding. See below c.5.13".

Revelation 2 verse 6 "[but this thou hast] supply [worthy of praise]".

Revelation 7 verse 15 "[shall dwell among them] shall stretch his pavilion over them. Italian version. I would prefer, 'shall dwell with them, or, rest upon them.' See below c.21.3".

Revelation 16 verse 8 "[to burn, scorch up] to burn. And in the following verse 'were burned.' Others. 'to scorch: but this is too mild to express the force of the word [to burn]: for, 'to scorch,' is to wound with a flame only so far as the surface of the skin, or to burn as far as the skin." [4]

APPENDIX 7[1]

Special Providential Preservation of the Old and New Testament Scriptures

THE doctrine of the providential preservation of the Word of God was not explicitly stated in any creedal confession until the seventeenth century.

The Westminster Confession of 1646:—The Westminster divines, focussed authority in present, extant copies of the biblical texts *(apographa).* Article VIII states that "The Old Testament in Hebrew and the New Testament in Greek being immediately inspired by God, and by his singular care and providence kept pure in all ages, are therefore authentical". The stress is on the authenticity and purity of the extant manuscripts in Hebrew and Greek, that is the sacred apographa. The ***autographa*** are those original manuscripts written by the hands of those holy men of God who spake as they were moved by the Holy Ghost. The Sacred ***Apographa*** are the faithful copies or transcripts made of the ***autographa***.

Formula Consensus Helvitica of 1675:—"God, the supreme Judge, not only took care to have His Word, which is the 'power of God unto Salvation to everyone that believeth,' committed to writing by Moses, the prophets, and the apostles, but also watched and cherished it with paternal care ever since it was written up to the present time, so that it could not be corrupted by craft of Satan or fraud of man." Therefore, the church justly ascribes it to His singular grace and goodness that she has, and will have to the end of the world, a "sure word of prophecy" and "holy Scripture" from which, though heaven and earth perish, "one jot or one tittle shall in no wise pass." (Matt. 5:18)

The London Baptist Declaration of 1689 states:—"The Old Testament in Hebrew and the New Testament in Greek were immediately inspired by God, and were kept pure through subsequent ages by his singular care and providence".

The great Puritan theologian, Dr John Owen writes,

> The providence of God hath manifested itself as no less concerned in the preservation of the writings than of the doctrine contained in them; the writing itself being the product of His own eternal counsel for the preservation of the doctrine. .... And hence the malice of Satan hath raged no less against the Book than against the truth contained in it. ... It is true, we have not the autographa of Moses and the prophets, of the apostles and the evangelists; but the apographa or "copies" which we have contain every iota that was in them. ... But yet we affirm, that the whole Word of God, in every letter and tittle, as given from him by inspiration, is preserved without corruption. ... In them all, we say, is every letter and tittle of the word. These copies we say, are the rule, standard, and touchstone of all translations, ancient or modern, by which they are in all things to be examined, tried, corrected, amended; and themselves by themselves. Translations contain the word of God, and are the word of God, perfectly or imperfectly, according as they express the words, sense and meaning of those originals.[2]

Protestant theologians throughout Europe held tenaciously to the doctrine of the divine preservation of the Word of God. They, and our translators believed that by a perpetual miracle the Lord preserved His Word in purity in the Hebrew Massoretic Text of the Old Testament, and in what has become known as the Textus Receptus of the Greek New Testament

Bibliography

Allen W. (Editor), *Translating for King James*, Penguin Press, 1970.
Andrewes L., *The Pattern of Catechistical Doctrine (Ten Commandments)*, Norton, 1650.
——— *XCVI Sermons*, London, MDCXLI.
——— *Private Devotions*, Lancelot Andrewes Press, Colorado, 2006.
Bevan B., *King James VI of Scotland & I of England*, Rubicon Press, 1996.
Black J.B., *The Reign of Elizabeth 1558-1603*, Clarendon Press, 1987.
Boys J., *The Works of John Boys*, Soli Deo Gloria Publications, 1997.
Brook B., *The Lives of the Puritans*, Soli Deo Gloria Publications, Vols. I,II,II, 1994.
Bruce F.F., *The English Bible*, Lutterworth, 1961.
——— *The Books and the Parchments*, Pickering & Inglis, 1963.
Cartwright & His Contemporaries, *The English Puritans in the Reign of Elizabeth I*, Thomas Nelson, 1848.
Chandos J., *In God's Name: Examples of Preaching in England, 1534-1662*, Bobbs-Merrill, 1971.
Churchill, Sir Winston, *A History of the English-Speaking Peoples, Vol. II*, Cassell,1956.
Daiches D., *The King James Version of the English Bible*, Archon Books, 1968.
Daniell D., *William Tyndale*, Yale University Press, 1994.
——— *The Bible in English*, Yale, 2003.
Darlow T.H. & Moule H.F., *Historical Catalogue of the Printed Editions of Holy Scripture, Volume 1, English.*
Davies G., *The Early Stuarts 1603-1660*, Clarendon Press, 1938.
Dore J.R., *Old Bibles*, Eyre & Spottiswoode, 1888.
Eadie J., *The English Bible*, Macmillan, 1876.
Edgar A., *The Bibles of England*, Alexander Gardner, 1889.
Fraser A., *Mary Queen of Scots*, Weidenfold & Nicolson, 1970.
——— *King James VI of Scotland, I of England*, Weidenfold & Nicolson, 1974.
——— *The Gunpowder Plot*, Weidenfold & Nicolson, 1996.
Frere W.H., *A History of the English Church, Vol. V*, Macmillan, 1911.

Fuller T., *Church History of Britain,* Thomas Tegg, 1837.

Grierson, Sir Herbert, *The English Bible,* Collins, 1947.

Herbert A.S., *Historical Catalogue of the English Bible,* British & Foreign Bible Society, 1968.

Hill C., *The English Bible & the Seventeenth-Century Revolution,* Penguin Press, 1993.

Hills E.F., *The King James Version Defended,* Christian Research Press, 1996.

Letis T.P., *The Majority Text,* Institute for Renaissance and Reformation Biblical Studies, 1987.

——— *The Protestant Dogmaticians and the Late Princeton School on the Status of the Sacred Apographa,* unpublished Lecture given at New College, The Mound, Edinburgh.

Levi P., *The English Bible,*Churchman Publishing, 1985.

Lewis J.P., *The English Bible from KJV to NIV,* Baker Book House, 1992.

Loane M.L., *Masters of the English Reformation,* Church Book Room Press,1954.

Lupton L., *History of the Geneva Bible,* Volumes I to 25, The Olive Tree Press, 1966 - 1994.

MacLean W., *The Providential Preservation of the Greek Text of The New Testament,* Westminster Standard, 1983.

Macleane D., *Lancelot Andrewes and the Reaction,* George Allen & Sons, 1910.

McClure A., *Translators Revived,* Maranatha Publications.

McGrath A., *In the Beginning: The Story of the King James Bible,* Hodder & Stoughton, 2001.

Mozley J.F., *Coverdale and his Bibles,* Lutterworth Press, 1953.

Nicolson A., *God's Secretaries,* Harper Perennial, 2005.

Norton D., *A Textual History of the King James Bible,* CUP 2004.

Paine G.S., *The Men Behind the King James Version,* Baker Book House, 1977.

Paisley I.R.K., *My Plea For the Old Sword*, Ambassador Press, 1997.

Ridley J., *The Tudor Age,* Constable, 1988.

Robertson E.H., *Makers of the English Bible,* Lutterworth, 1990.

John Rylands LIbrary, *The History of the Transmission of the Bible,* 1935.

Scrivener F.H.A., *A Plain Introduction to the Criticism of the New Testament,* Cambridge, 1861.

——— *The Authorized Edition of the English Bible (1611),* CUP, 1884.

Stevenson W.H., *King James Bible: A Selection,* Longman 1994.

Thompson D.A., *The Controversy Concerning the Last Twelve Verses of the Gospel According to Mark*, Bible Christian Unity Fellowship.

Trevelyan G.M., *England Under the Stuarts,* Folio Society, 1996.
Vance L.M., *Archaic Words and the Authorized Version,* Vance Publications, 1999.
Welsby P.A., *Lancelot Andrewes 1555-1626,* SPCK, 1964.
Westcott B.F., *History of the English Bible,* Macmillan, 1872.
Willoughby H., *The First Authorized English Bible & Cranmer Preface,* University of Chicago, 1942.
Wylie J.A., *The History of Protestantism,* Cassell Petter & Galpin.

Notes

Preface

1. Preface to the Authorised Version.
2. Quoted by Gustavius Pain, *The Men Behind the KJV,* Baker Book House, 1959, p.viii.
3. A Nicholson, *God's Secretaries*, Harper Perennial, 2003, p.238ff.

Introduction

1. Lupton, *'Not Unto Us': History of the Geneva Bible,* vol. xxv., p.93.
2. Ward Allen , *Translating for King James*, Penguin Press 1970, p.4.
3. Preface to the Authorised Version.
4. Ibid.
5. Ibid.

Chapter 1. The History of the English Bible

1. Forshall and Madden's *edition of the Wycliffe versions of the Bible,* p.vi, note A.
2. Ibid.
3. *'Trialogus,'* Lib. iii., cap.xxxi, pp.239-240.
4. '*de Veritate Sacrae Scripturae,*' c.15.
5. Pennington A.R. *John Wiclif: His Life, Times, and Teaching,* SPCK, 1884, p.153.
6. Op.cit.
7. *The History of the Transmission of the Bible*, John Rylands Library, 1935, p.16.
8. Quoted by Pennington, p.174.
9. *Trialogus*, lib. iii., c.15, p.181.
10. Lupton, *Tyndale the Martyr*, Vol. XIX, p.63.
11. Tyndale's Doctrinal Treatises, Vol.I (Parker Society), p.xix.
12. *Works of Tyndale,* Exposition Vol.II (Parker Society, 1849), p.291.
13. Quoted by Marcus Loane in *Masters of the English Reformation,* CBR Press 1954, p.49.
14. Fuller D.O., *Valiant For The Truth,* Oliphants Ltd, 1962, p.136.
15. John Foxe, Vol. V, p.117.

16. Op.cit.
17. Op.cit.
18. Works, Vol. I, p.395.
19. Ibid., p.394.
20. Ibid., p.396.
21. Works, Vol. I, p.396.
22. Demaus R., *William Tyndale*, Religious Tract Society,1886, p.134.
23. Loane, p.59.
24. Lupton, *Towards King James,* Vol. XXII, p.13.
25. *The History of the Transmission of the Bible*, John Rylands Library, 1935, p.34-35.
26. L. Lupton, *op.cit.*
27. Works, Vol.II, p.307,333.
28. Ibid., pp.321,337.
29. Loane, p.78.
30. Ibid., p.82.
31. Foxe, Vol. V. p127.
32. Foxe.
33. Lupton, p.26.
34. The Bible: *Geneva Version*, 1560, Preface.
35. Op.cit.

Chapter 2. Queen James the First

1. Black J B, *The Reign of Elizabeth,* Clarendon Press, 1958, p.493.
2. Op.cit.
3. Ibid., p.495.
4. Williams N, *The Life and Times of Elizabeth the First,* Weidenfold & Nicolson, 1972, p.186.
5. Lord Herris, *Historical Memoirs of the Reign of Mary, Queen of Scots,* p.80.
6. Bevan B., *King James VI of Scotland & I of England,* Rubicon Press, 1976, p.4f.
7. Ibid., p.6.
8. Ibid., p.31.
9. Bevan, p.58.
10. Ibid., p.27.
11. Ibid., p.47.
12. Ibid. pp.71-72.
13. Ibid., p.176.
14. Ibid., p.187.
15. Sir Anthony Weldon, *Historical and Biographical Tracts,* p.53.
16. Bevan, p.117.

17. Ibid. p.81.
18. Ibid., p.51.
19. Ibid., p.160.
20. Ibid., p.57.
21. Ibid., p.68.
22. Ibid., p.75.
23. Antonia Fraser, *King James the First,* Weidenfeld & Nicolson, p.97.
24. Bevan, p.154.
25. Op.cit.
26. Antonia Fraser, p.117.
27. 1611 A.V. "The Epistle's Dedicatorie to King James 1."

Chapter 3. Puritan Hopes and Recusant Dreams

1. Bruce, John, ed., *Correspondence of James VI with Sir Robert Cecil and others in England,* Camden Society, 1861, pp.33-36. Quoted by Fraser, Antonia, *The Gunpowder Plot,* p.38.
2. Edwards, quoted by Frasier, Antonia, *The Gunpowder Plot,* p.89.

Chapter 4. Royal Charades

1. Barlow, *Summe and Substance of the Conference,* quoted in full by Thomas Fuller *The Church History of Britain,* Vol. III, 1837, pp.172-193.
2. Though all these Deans were summoned by letters, and present in the Presence-chamber; yet only five (namely, of the Chapel, Westminster, Paul's, Chester, and Salisbury) on the first day were called in.
3. A gown in grogram, a coarse cloth part wool, part silk, often worn by merchants. As opposed to the 'Romish rags' worn by the ritualistic bishops.
4. It seems the Bishop of London, jealous that he was reflected on, called the Doctor "schismatic".
5. Namely, in the Dominical Gospels.
6. In December, 1601.
7. Richard Vaughan.

Chapter 5. All The King's Men

1. Lupton, L., *England's Word,* Vol. XXIV, p.11.
2. Ibid., p.14.
3. Ibid., p.15.
4. Ibid., p.29.
5. Quoted by Gustavius Paine, *The Men Behind the KJV,* p.33.
6. Ibid., p.36.

7. Ibid., p.41.
8. A. Nicholson, *God's Secretaries,* p.193f.
9. Lupton, L., Vol. XXIV, p.48 .
10. Paine, p.27.
11. Op.cit., p.59.
12. The author has several early editions of the King James Version, and in his copy of the first quarto edition of 1612-13, there is, thankfully, no Apocrypha!
13. Nicholson, p.206.
14. Lupton, *England's Word,* p 91.
15. Ibid., p 92.
16. McClure A., *Translators Revived,* p.197f.
17. Lupton. L., *Not Unto Us,* Vol. XXV, p.74.
18. Penguin Press, 1970.
19. Paine, p.67f.
20. Lupton, Vol. XXIV, p.71.
21. Paine, p.24.
22. Twelve years later, the day before Twelfth Night, King James made young Prince Charles, Duke of York. For Twelfth Night there was Ben Johnson's *Masque of Blackness.* The Queen was six months pregnant, but again she and her ladies, with blackened faces and arms, appeared in the play with their hair down and wore rich gauzy draperies which shocked the guests. And later that year, the first production of Shakespeare's *Macbeth* was performed. On February 8 there was a play, *The Fair Maid of Bristol,* performed at Whitehall before the King.
23. McClure, p.127.
24. Ibid., p.131f.
25. McClure, p.132.
26. Ibid., p.133.
27. Ibid., p.136.
28. Ibid., p.136.
29. Ibid., p.137.
30. Op.cit.
31. Paine, p.48.
32. Op.cit.
33. McClure, p.139.
34. Allen W., *Translating for King James,* p.91.
35. Lupton, Vol. XXV, p.35.
36. Op.cit.
37. Paine, p.75f.
38. www.apuritansmind.com
39. Paine, p.107.

40. Paine, p.106.
41. Quoted by Dr I.R.K. Paisley, *My Plea for the Old Sword*, p.38.
42. Nicholson A., *The Men Who Wrote the Best Selling Book of All Time*, Daily Telegraph, 1 June 2002.

Chapter 6. Gunpowder Treason

1. Fraser, *The Gunpowder Plot,* p.74.
2. Wylie, *The History of Protestantism*, vol. III., p.526.
3. Bennet, *Memorials of the Reformation*, p.130; quoted by Wylie, p.529.
4. Quoted by Antonia Fraser, Ibid., p.150.

Chapter 7. Le Roy S'avisera

1. A. Nicholson, *God's Secretaries,* Harper Perennial, 2003, p.78.
2. Edward Hills, The King James Version Defended, p.220.
3. Stevenson W.H., *King James's Bible: A Selection,* Longman, 1994, p.34.
4. Lupton, p.79.
5. Dedication to the Authorised Version.
6. Ibid.
7. Lupton, p.106.

Chapter 8. The King's Printers

1. Herbert 282, 283, 284.
2. Herbert 288.
3. Herbert 297.
4. Herbert 289, 301.
5. Herbert 348.
6. Herbert 351.
7. Herbert, Historical Catalogue of Printed Bibles, p.132.
8. Lupton, Vol. XXV, p.87.
9. Herbert 309.
10. Herbert 444.
11. Herbert 942/3.
12. Herbert 310.
13. Herbert 424.
14. Herbert 520.
15. Herbert 1142.
16. Herbert 1194.

Chapter 9. The King's Jewel

1. J. H. Skilton, ed., *The Law and the Prophets: Old Testament Studies in Honor of Oswald T. Allis,* Nutley, NJ, USA: Presbyterian and Reformed, 1974, p.107.
2. Trinitarian Bible Society Article No. 63, Plain Reasons for keeping to the Authorised Version.
3. Farrar F.W., *The Bible: Its Meaning and Supremacy,* Longmans, Green & Co, 1901, p.251.
4. Farrar, Ibid., p.259.
5. John R. de Witt, Of Many Versions, *BOT Magazine* Number 81, June 1970 pp.20-21.
6. Bruce F.F., *The English Bible*, 1961, p.168.
7. William Lyon Phelps, *Human Nature in the Bible* (New York: Charles Scribner's Sons, 1922, www.sacred-texts.com/chr/hnb/intro.htm), p.x.
8. *The Christian's Penny Magazine and Friend of the People* (London, England: John Snow, 1860), vol.xv, p.54.
9. Heston, Charlton: *In the Arena: An Autobiography*, Harper Collins, pp.554-555.
10. Paine, G.S., *The Men Behind the King James Version,* Baker Book House, 1977, pp.182-183.
11. Churchill, Winston, *A History of the English-Speaking Peoples, Vol. I,* Cassells, 1974.
12. Knoll, Mark A., *The American Bible Tradition: The King James Version used to be our common text,* quoted in The Wall Street Journal, Friday, July 7, 2006.
13. Farrar, Ibid., p.304-305.
14. Preface to the A.V.
15. JC Philpot, April, 1857 quoted by David Otis Fuller, *True or False*, p.23.
16. *The Law and the Prophets*, Allis O.T., p.107.
17. Hills, p.229.
18. Owen, Vol. XVI., p.370.

Appendix 1

1. Coverdale, *Remains,* Parker Society, 1846, p.261ff.

Appendix 2

1. Foxe, John, *Book of Martyrs,* p. 375ff.

Appendix 3

1. Chandlos, J., *In God's Name*, Bobbs-Merrill, 1971, p.93ff.

2. Thomas Harding, Thomas Stapleton, Thomas Dorman and Nicholas Sanders: members of a group of English Roman Catholic controversialists, who left England after the accession of Elizabeth, and conducted polemical warfare against Bishop Jewel.
3. Like Dionysius, Tyrant of Syracuse, 4th century B.C., notorious for cruelty.

Appendix 4

1. Chandlos, J., *In God's Name*, Bobbs-Merrill, 1971, p.111ff.
2. Roman Catholic contrivers with Essex.
3. Jean Bodin, *Republica Libri Sex* (Paris, 1586), lib.I, cap.viii (De jure majestratis).
4. No divinity or demon of animal form called 'Nabis' exists in the records of classical Egyptian antiquity. But the name appears, with variant spelling, on Gnostic semi-precious stones, of later, Graeco-Toman times, often in connection with the word 'Chnoubis', and probably charged with magical significance. Such amulets were syncristic and cosmopolite, and circulated throughout the empire. The word 'nabis' is sometimes found on stones in company with the figures of hybrid monsters (e.g. part serpent, part lion), which may have caused Barlow's misunderstanding.

Appendix 5

1. Andrewes L., *XCVI Sermons,* 1641, p. 889ff.

Appendix 6

1. *Translating for King James: Notes made by a translator of King James Bible*, edited by Ward Allen and Published by The Penguin Press, 1970.
2. Ibid., p.47.
3. Ibid.
4. Ibid., p.113.

Appendix 7

1. Hills E., *The King James Version Defended,* p.221ff.
2. Owen J, , *Works vol. XVI*, T&T Clark, 1862, p.300.

Acknowledgements

	Page	
King James the First of England	Cover	By kind permission of the National Gallery of Scotland
Title Pages of the King James Bible, 1611	5	Scanned from Facsimile
Burntisland Parish Church	6	D. Allen
Israel at the Red Sea, from the Geneva Bible	58	Geneva Bible
John Wyclif, the Dorset Portrait	65	© National Portrait Gallery, London
Lutterworth Parish Church	66	Scanned from 19th biography of Wyclif, Lewis Sergeant
Page from Wyclif s New Testament	67	BFBS MSS 155
Portrait of that godly man, William Tyndale	68	By kind permission of the Governing Body, Hertford College, Oxford
Little Sodbury Manor	69	Internet
Martyrdom of William Tyndale	69	Foxe's *Acts & Monuments*
Title Page of Tyndale's 1532 New Testament	70	
Tyndale's Handwriting	71	Scanned from Demaus, p.536.
Page from Tyndale's 1526 New Testament	72	BFBS DM(H)2
Title Page of Tyndale's 1526 New Testament	73	
Miles Coverdale: drawn & engraved by J. Brain	74	Scanned from D. Allen's copy of Coverdale's Bible, 1835*
Title Page of Coverdale's Bible, 1535	75	D. Allen's copy
Title Page of Matthew's Bible	76	
Portrait of Queen Elizabeth I	105	© National Portrait Gallery, London
Sir William Cecil	106	By courtesy of the Marquess of Salisbury
Queen Elizabeth Rallying Her Troops at Tilbury	107	Scanned from Wylie, Vol. Ill, p. 145
Portrait of King James I, 1621	108	© National Portrait Gallery, London
Anne of Denmark	109	The Royal Collection ©2010. Her Majesty Queen Elizabeth II
Interior of Queen Mary's Room at Edinburgh Castle	110 & 111	By kind permission of the National Gallery of Scotland
Exterior of Queen Mary's Room, Edinburgh Castle	111	By kind permission of the National Gallery of Scotland
Henry and Charles Stuart	112	The Royal Collection ©2010. Her Majesty Queen Elizabeth II
Mary Queen of Scots 'with' Her Son	113	By kind permission of the Duke of Atholl, Blair Castle.
Execution of Mary Queen of Scots	114	By kind permission of the National Gallery of Scotland
George Buchanan	115	Scanned from Wylie, Vol.111 p.522
Esme Stuart	116	By kind permission of the National Gallery of Scotland

Tentmaker Publications

(Including titles published under Berith Publications)

List of Publications

BIOGRAPHIES

England

Title	Author	Price
Amazing Conversions: John Ashworth and his strange tales	John Ashworth	£13.95
Biographical Sketches of Preachers of the Primitive Methodists	George Herod	£17.95
Bunhill Fields (2 vols in 1)	Alfred Light	£19.95
George Whitefield: A Definitive Biography (2 vols)	E A Johnston	£49.95
John Wesley in the Reformation Tradition	Roland Burrows	£17.95
Journal of William Clowes, The	William Clowes	£13.95
Journals of Rev Charles Wesley, The (2 vols)	Charles Wesley	£38.95
Life & Times of John Wesley, The (3 vols)	Luke Tyerman	£64.95
Life & Times of Samuel Wesley, The	Luke Tyerman	£18.95
Life and Labours of Hugh Bourne, The (2 vols)	John Walford	£36.95
Lives of the Early Methodist Preachers, The (3 vols)	Thomas Jackson	£47.95
Oxford Methodists, The	Luke Tyerman	£17.95
Wesley's Designated Successor: John Fletcher of Madeley	Luke Tyerman	£19.95
Writings of Thomas Russell, The	Thomas Russell	£12.50

Wales

Title	Author	Price
Life & Times of Selina, Countess of Huntingdon, The (2 vols)	Aaron C H Seymore	£47.50
Life of Griffith Jones of Llanddowror, The (p/b)	David Jones	£6.95
Life of Howell Harris—The Welsh Reformer	Hugh J Hughes	£15.95
Some of the Great Preachers of Wales	Owen Jones	£19.95
Sweet Singers of Wales, The (bkt)	Elvett Lewis	£2.95

Scotland

Title	Author	Price
Life of John Kennedy DD, The	Alexander Auld	£13.95
Memoir of William Chalmers Burns, The	Islay Burns	£20.95

Ireland

Title	Author	Price
Irish Worthies	Thomas Hamilton	£12.50

USA

Title	Author	Price
My Life and Times	John Bailey Adger	£24.95

Missionary

Title	Author	Price
Faith working by love - Life of Fidelia Fiske	D T Fiske	£13.95

HISTORY

England

Title	Author	Price
Bible Christians, The	F W Bourne	£19.95
History of Dissenters from the Revolution (1688) to 1838 (3 vols)	Bogue & Bennett	£47.95

History of the Early Puritans .... J B Marsden £18.95
History of the Later Puritans .... J B Marsden £18.95
History of the Puritans (3 vols) .... Daniel Neal £64.95
Mow Cop Revival 1807, The (bkt) .... Dr David Allen £3.95
Origin & History of Primitive Methodism, The
(2 vols.) .... H B Kendall £49.95
Two Thousand Confessors of 1662, The .... Thomas Coleman £11.95

Wales

Echoes from the Welsh Hills .... David Davies £15.95
John Vaughan, or More Echoes from the
Welsh Hills .... David Davies £15.95
Favoured with Frequent Revivals
(Wales 1762-1862) † (spiral) .... D Geraint Jones £3.99

Scotland

Revivals in Highlands and Islands (p/b) .... Alexander Macrae £5.95
Echoes from Scotland's Heritage of Grace † .... Hugh Ferrier £12.95

Ireland

Days of Revival: History of Methodism in Ireland
(3 vols) .... C H Crookshank £48.95
History of the 1859 Ulster Revival, A (7 vols) Compiled by
Whitefield College of the Bible £139.95
Ireland Awaking (bkt) .... E Stuart Watt £3.50
Progress of the Reformation in Ireland, The .... Earl of Roden £10.95
St Patrick Writes (bkt) .... St Patrick £1.50

Europe

Israel of the Alps (The Waldenses) .... Muston/Hazlitt £15.95
Rise of the Huguenots of France, The (2 vols) .... Henry M Baird £44.95

USA

History of the Presbyterian Church in America, A .... Richard Webster £23.95

Denominational

Baptist History .... J M Cramp £19.95
History of the Plymouth Brethren, The .... William B Neatby £13.95

Missionary

Church of Scotland South Arabia Mission, The .... James Ritchie £19.95

History of the Geneva Bible (Lewis Lupton)

Vol 1 The Quarrel — Frankfort to Geneva. Cox v Knox .... o/p
Vol 2 Reform — Geneva Service Book, Calvin, Beza & Co. .... o/p
Vol 3 Truth — 1557 New Testament. W. Whittingham .... o/p
Vol 4 Travail — 1557 Psalms for prison. Rediscovered .... o/p
Vol 5 Vision — Geneva Bible 1560. Detailed account £15.00
Vol 6 Hope — Puritans persecuted. L. Tomson revised NT, Beza. £15.00
Vol 7 Joy — Bible circulation 1560-1600. Chris. Barker £15.00
Vol 8 Faith — Henry Lok Genevan poet, agent .... o/p
Vol 9 Love — Duchess of Suffolk in exile. Brave lady £15.00
Vol 10 Courage — Ld. Willoughby. Protestant hero £15.00
Vol 11 Endurance — 1st printed English Bible 1535.
Two volumes on Coverdale £15.00

Vol 12 Heaven — 2 long exiles, Bp. of Exeter, puritan. £15.00
Vol 13 Index to volumes 1-12 incl. summary of Welsh Bibles £15.00
Vol 14 Paint & Print — Zwingli 1500-1530. Bullinger. Two vols. .... o/p
Vol 15 Paint, Print & Exile — ...continued £15.00
Vol 16 Wyclif's Wicket — John Wyclif & the Bible .... o/p
Vol 17 Trodden Thyme — The Lollards, 1490-1520 .... o/p
Vol 18 Tyndale Translator — Birth, Oxford, exile. 2 Vols.
Detailed life, in Antwerp to end .... o/p
Vol 19 Tyndale Martyr — ...continued £15.00
Vol 20 Bethlehem to Lindisfarne — Jerome to Celtic £15.00
Vol 21 Chivalry — Gothic Scriptures, Medieval to Pre-Raphaelites £15.00
Vol 22 Towards King James — Earlier Bibles. Bishop's Bible. 4 vols.
On the AV. £15.00
Vol 23 Up to Hampton Court — ...continued £15.00
Vol 24 England's Word — ...continued £15.00
Vol 25 'Not unto us' — ...continued £15.00

COMMENTARIES

Classic Series

Critical and Exegetical Commentary on Exodus, A ..... James G Murphy £15.95
Gospel revealed to Job, The .... Charles Hulbert £19.95
Christ and His Church in the Book of Psalms .... Andrew Bonar £15.95
Commentary on the Book of Psalms, A (2 vols) † ...... De Burgh £28.95
Penitent, The (Psalm 51) .... James Morgan £11.95
Song of Solomon .... Robert Hawker £12.50
Jonah, His Life, Character, and Mission .... Patrick Fairbairn £13.95
Obadiah .... Edward Marbury £11.95
Habakkuk .... Edward Marbury £19.95
Lectures on the Prophecies of Zechariah .... Ralph Wardlaw £15.95
Commentary oin the Acts of the Apostles, A (2 vols) .. John Fawcett £39.95
Analytical Exposition of Romans, An .... John Brown £19.95
Lectures on Paul's Epistles to the Philippians .... John Hutchison £15.95
Lectures on Paul's Epistles to the Thessalonians .... John Lillie £18.95

Nichol Series

Contemplations on the Historical Passages of the OT & NT
.... Bishop Joseph Hall £24.95
Individual Psalms .... Pierson, Gouge
.... & Smith £24.95
Proverbs, Ecclesiastes & Canticles .... Muffet & Cotton £24.95
Isaiah 5 .... Nehemiah Rogers £11.95
Jonah, Obadiah & Haggai .... King & Rainolds £24.95
Malachi & Ruth .... Stock& Torshell,
.... Bernard & Fuller £24.95
Ephesians .... Paul Bayne £24.95
Philippians & Colossians .... Airey & Cartwright £24.95
Commentary on Philippians & Colossians .... Jean Daillé £19.95
Colossians .... Byfield £24.95

Commentary on 1 Peter (Leighton Vol 1) .... Robert Leighton £19.95
1 John .... Nathaniel Hardy £24.95

Miscellaneous

Christ in the Old Testament (4 vols) .... Robert Gordon £75.00
David, The King of Israel .... F W Krummacher £19.95
Revelation Spiritually Understood † .... Charles D Alexander .. £17.50

THEOLOGY

Sets

Lectures in Theology (4 vols) .... John Dick £79.95
Miscellaneous Works of Philip Doddridge (2 vols)
(large format) .... Philip Doddridge £69.95
Works of Ebenezer Erskine (3 vols) † .... Ebenezer Erskine £55.00
Works of Henry Smith (2 vols) .... Henry Smith £39.95
Works of James Hamilton (6 vols) .... James Hamilton £109.95
Works of Rev. Thomas Boston (12 vols) .... Thomas Boston £224.95
Works of Robert Leighton Vol 1 1 Peter
(large format) .... Robert Leighton £19.95
Works of Robert Leighton Vol 2 Miscellaneous works
(large format) .... Robert Leighton £19.95

Individual volumes

Assembly's Shorter Catechism Explained .... James Fisher, Ebenezer &
.... Ralph Erskine £17.95
Atonement & the Cross .... Octavius Winslow £11.95
Being Filled with the Spirit, A (Nichol Puritan reprint) ... John Goodwin £18.95
Bible Doctrine of Man, The .... Robert Laidlaw £14.95
Body of Divinity, A † .... James Ussher £25.95
Bunyan Characters in Pilgrim's Progress .... Alexander Whyte £18.95
Christ is All (5 vols in 1) .... Henry Law £22.95
Covenant of Grace, The .... Samuel Petto £13.95
Discourses Suited to the Administration of the
Lord's Supper .... John Brown £14.95
Expository Lectures .... John Kennedy DD .... o/p
Glimpses in the Inner Life of Christ .... William G Blaikie &
.... Robert Law £9.95
Homilies, The .... Church of England £18.95
Knowledge of God Objectively Considered, The .... Robert Breckinridge ... £20.95
Knowledge of God Subjectively Considered, The .... Robert Breckinridge ... £25.95
Lord's Prayer, The .... Octavius Winslow £11.95
Lord's Supper, The .... Thomas Cranmer £11.95
Manna † .... J C Philpot £15.95
Moses the Man of God (Volume 5 of Works) .... James Hamilton £19.95
Nearing Home - Comforts & Counsels for the Aged .... William Schenck £15.95
Preacher, The, (Volume 3 of Works) .... James Hamilton £19.95
Scripture Doctrine of the Church, The .... Douglas Bannerman .. £20.95
Sermons and Lectures (Volume 6 of Works) .... James Hamilton £19.95

Sermons in Times of Persecution in Scotland -
Covernanters ...... Covernanters £22.95
Sermons on the Incarnation † ...... C A Alexander £11.95
Spiritual Life, The ...... Octavius Winslow £11.95
Theology of the Old Testament ...... G F Oehler £17.95
Tree of Promise † ...... Alexander Stewart £15.95
Work & Conflict: The Divine Life in its Progress ...... John Kennedy £13.95

Modern Authors

Hymns of W Vernon Higham ...... Vernon Higham £11.95
Meditations at the Table (pb) ...... Jim Waring £4.95

ISSUES

Character and Claims of Freemasonry, The ...... Charles Finney £7.95
Charismatic Confusion † ...... William Goode £19.95
Freedom & Discipleship (bkt) ...... Jerram Barrs £2.95
From Spiritual Powers to Liberating Grace (pb) ...... Torbjorn Swartling £6.95
Gift of Tongues, The (bkt) ...... Phil Roberts £1.95
God's Credentials ...... Philip Blair £13.50
Letters on the Masonic Institution (pb) ...... John Quincy Adams £5.95
Serpent and the Cross, The ...... Alan Morrison £25.00
Support for the Sufferers (bkt) ...... Hazel Stapleton £1.50
Women in Ministry (bkt) ...... Phil Roberts £1.95

INDICES

The Finder: Reformed Index ...... Michael Keen £13.95
Bibliographical Encyclopaedia - Author index
(3 vols) ...... James Darling £79.95
Bibliographical Encyclopaedia - Scripture index
(2 vols) ...... James Darling £49.95

All books are casebound unless otherwise stated.
† indicates a title from another publisher produced by Tentmaker Publications.
Prices correct for December 2010.

Tentmaker Publications
121 Hartshill Road
Stoke-on-Trent
Staffs. ST4 7LU

www.tentmaker.org.uk (UK) www.tentmakerpublications.com (USA)